IMAGES
of America

CHAMBERS COUNTY

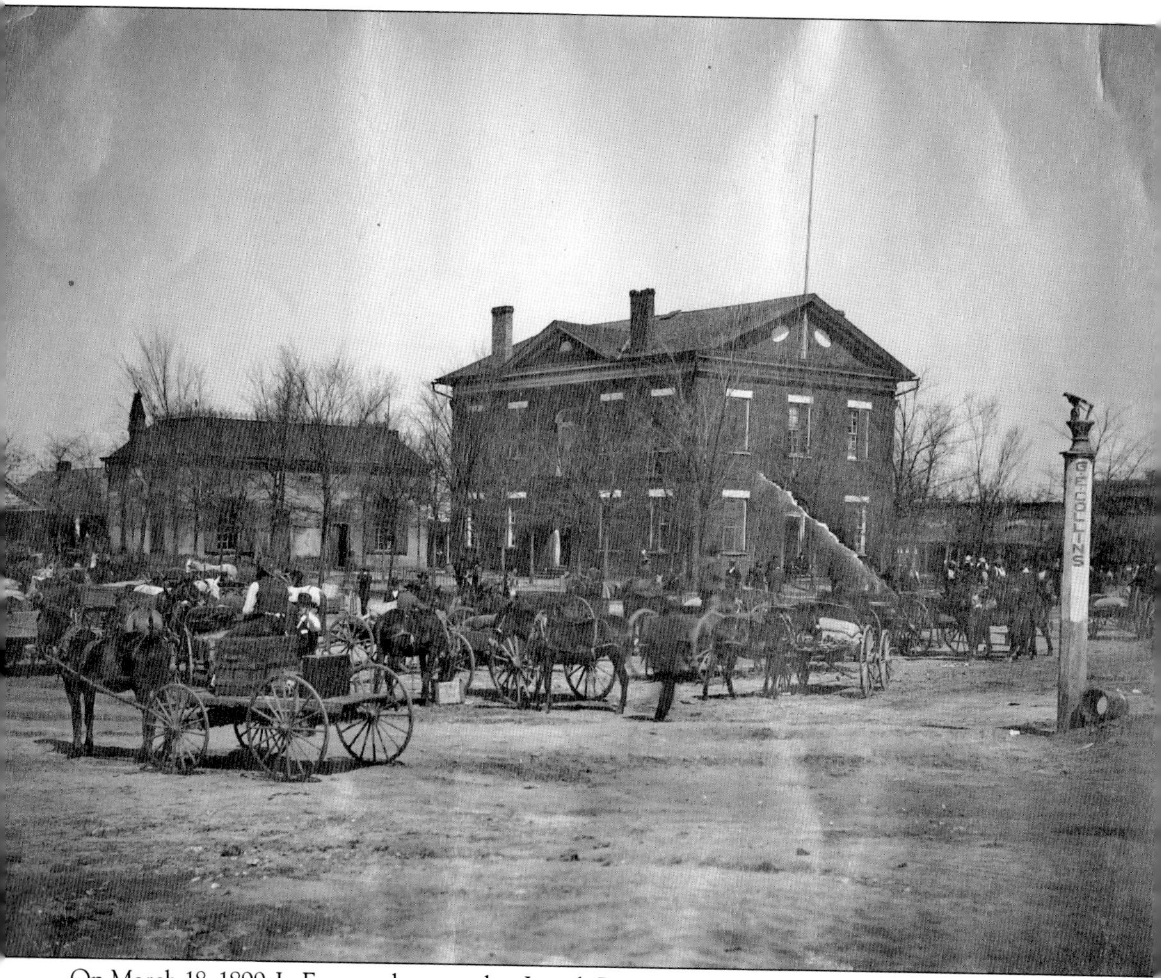

On March 18, 1899, LaFayette photographer Joseph Banning Lake, a native of Yalobusha County, Mississippi, made this photograph of the 1836 Chambers County courthouse from the southwest (Collins Drug Store) corner of the square. The probate judge's office is the two-room building in the northwest corner of the yard. Within a few days of this photograph, both buildings were razed. (Courtesy of CMA.)

On the Cover: The Reverend W. C. Bledsoe baptized young people in the waters of Ossannippa Creek in August 1908. Reverend Bledsoe served as pastor of seven Chambers County Baptist churches over 49 years. He was the clerk of the East Liberty Baptist Association for 50 years. For 47 years, he was the grand chaplain of the Grand Lodge of Free and Accepted Masons of Alabama. (Courtesy of CMA.)

IMAGES
of America

CHAMBERS COUNTY

Chattahoochee Valley Historical Society
and Chambers County Museum

ARCADIA
PUBLISHING

ISBN 978-0-7385-8640-3

Published by Arcadia Publishing
Charleston, South Carolina

Printed in the United States of America

Library of Congress Control Number: 2010924519

For all general information, please contact Arcadia Publishing:
Telephone 843-853-2070
Fax 843-853-0044
E-mail sales@arcadiapublishing.com
For customer service and orders:
Toll-Free 1-888-313-2665

Visit us on the Internet at www.arcadiapublishing.com

This book is dedicated to the generations of Chambers County citizens who have treasured and preserved our artifacts, documents, and images.

Contents

ACKNOWLEDGMENTS

The people of Chambers County, both past and present, are responsible for the creation of this book. During the first 150 years of the history of Chambers County, thousands of families sought public and private ways of preserving their valued stories of the past. The Chattahoochee Valley Historical Society and the Chambers County Museum appreciate the efforts of individuals and families to preserve local stories, images, and other treasures, so that each new generation may benefit from knowledge of the local history. We are indebted to the families who have surrendered their documents and images to the Cobb Memorial Archives and the Chambers County Museum for safekeeping and interpretation.

We must also acknowledge the willingness of the many individuals to share their privately preserved materials in support of the efforts to prepare this book. We wish to thank the steering committee from our collective membership, who volunteered their time and expertise to advertise this project, to scan and document privately held images, to review and scan locally archived images, and to prepare this book. More than a thousand images were inventoried. The steering committee members were Mary Helen Stitzel Benford, Lynda Langley Burton, Virginia Prather Weldon, Linda Hughes Holderfield, Don Clark, and Horace McLean Holderfield. Archivist Miriam Ann Kirkwood Syler, Marjorie Dixon Wheeling, Jeanne Whitehead, and Paula Gilmore Kirkpatrick were most patient and helpful in directing our searches in the collections of the Cobb Memorial Archives. Mary Hamilton, director of the Chambers County Library, provided technical and equipment support as well as working space. We appreciated the good assistance of Betty Barrett and Monica Barber at the LaFayette Pilot Public Library. We also wish to express our appreciation to Arcadia Publishing for its professional and thorough preparation, which guided our production of this book, and to Katie Shayda at Arcadia Publishing for her rapid responses to our questions and her expert assistance and guidance in this project. Many images in this volume appear courtesy of the Cobb Memorial Archives (CMA) and the Chambers County Museum (CCM).

Introduction

In 1832, the Alabama Legislature established the boundaries of Chambers County. This new political jurisdiction was situated in the frontier lands that recently had belonged to the Creek Nation. The county was almost 20 miles square. Its many creeks and branches drained into the Tallapoosa River to the west and the Chattahoochee River to the east, as the hills and high ridges of the Piedmont Uplands ended their continental march to the southwest and softened into an undulating topography at the coastal plain. The virgin soil was rich with humus from thousands of years of natural forest decay. As hunter-gatherers, the native inhabitants had enjoyed the bounty of the native animals and fruits, nuts, and seeds for thousands of years. For hundreds of years, Native Americans had appreciated the rich soil of the flood plains of the two great rivers and the many tributaries where they cultivated native and later European plants and fruit trees.

The first traders and farmers began moving onto this rich land before the native Americans were forced to sell and were taken west in 1836. Although the frontier was dangerous, families and speculators poured into the county through Georgia and Tennessee in the 1830s and 1840s. After the brief Indian War of 1836, settlers rapidly occupied the land and established almost self-sufficient homesteads where the rich earth abundantly produced a variety of cereal grains, peas, peanuts, tobacco, corn, squash, pumpkins, melons, and beans, as well as cotton.

The pioneer families entered and initially settled the county from east to west along old Native American paths. One path entered the northeastern corner of the county from shoals on the Chattahoochee to the early villages of Standing Rock and Hickory Flat and proceeded westward and south to the Upper Creek villages on the Tallapoosa. A second path emerged from Georgia north of West Point and crossed the county westward through Buffalo Wallow and Marcoot to reach the Tallapoosa.

The early years of life in the county were hard and rough, as characterized by satire and humor in the writings of Johnson Jones Hooper, a newspaper publisher in LaFayette, the county seat of Chambers. In the northern hilly sections of the county lived the largest population of yeoman farmers, who held a hundred acres or more but did not primarily depend upon slave labor for the production of cotton. The southern and southwestern regions of the county contained more level land and richer soil. In this region and in the flood plains of the two great rivers, many plantations with large slave populations were established. Decade by decade, cotton became the dominant cash crop of the county.

By 1860, Chambers County contained a varied population of squatters and landless white people, yeoman farm families, plantation owners, and slaves working the soil. But by 1860, the productivity of rich earth, which had been mother and sustainer to generations of native peoples, had begun to decline. The natural richness of the soil was slowly being destroyed by continuous cropping and erosion. Many families were already moving westward searching for new rich land in Mississippi, Louisiana, Arkansas, and Texas.

The material losses and political changes resulting from the Civil War redefined life in Chambers County. Hundreds of young and productive men were either dead or wounded. Families lost their land and knew hunger. The freedmen and freedwomen and landless white families were brought into a new pattern of labor, the tenancy system. Capital investment in labor and land had disappeared, and credit was most dear. The agrarian optimism of the frontier was gone forever and replaced by a hard-eyed commitment to survival in a new age characterized by a growing population, industrialization, a singular agricultural emphasis on cotton production, frequent depression cycles, declining land fertility, and limited sources for credit. The frontier dream of every farmer owning his own self-sufficient family farm had degenerated by 1939, when only 24 percent of the men who held the plow owned their own land, and 76 percent of the plowmen were wage hands, sharecroppers, or tenants.

The new social and agricultural production patterns evolving following the Civil War stabilized in the 1880s, as a new optimism inspired local leaders to expand textile industries and build railroads to stimulate a new prosperity for the county. The greatest new economic development for the county in the last half of the 19th century and the first half of the 20th century was the successful establishment of four textile mill villages and a textile town under the management of one corporation, the West Point Manufacturing Company. By the 1960s, this company had built in Chambers County the largest textile employment in the world under one mill facility roof, the Lanett Mill. Although the West Point Manufacturing Company was named for the Georgia town where its offices were situated, its production plants and its five villages were located in Alabama. This mill system, with its enlightened and paternalistic community development, absorbed excess rural labor produced by the ever-increasing farm population and the ever-declining opportunity for small farm prosperity.

Economic conditions improved before World War I as export demands increased for the agricultural products and textiles of the county. But disaster arrived with the boll weevil; cotton production declined and farms were lost to creditors. The work-seeking migration by both white and black families to the northern industrial cites established a pattern of outward migration that continued for decades.

Optimism in the future of farm life and agricultural production did reemerge in the 1920s and continued for the next 40 years as the Land Grant Extension movement promoted soil conservation and assisted farm land owners in the selection of new crops, new breeds of commercial livestock, the application of commercial fertilizers, and the mechanization of production. Dairying and beef production increased as non-mechanized cotton production declined. But the rural population continued to decline in the 1950s as a national system of commercial agricultural supply and demand developed that allowed thousands of acres of idle fields in the county to be planted into commercial pine plantations. As the forest product industry became increasingly important to the economic future of the county, the rural areas slowly lost their inhabitants and communities gradually vanished.

This book seeks to present a history of Chambers County and its people through the images that have survived in albums, old trunks, and other family storage places. The intent for this book of images is to inspire the reader to inquire more deeply into the rich and varied stories and experiences of the people of Chambers County. The panorama revealed in these pages is limited by the number and content of the photographs that families have preserved and shared for this publication.

One

People on the Land

The people who lived on the land in the first 150 years of Chambers County history may be described individually by ethnic background, social and economic classes, and by race, but all of these people based their hope for a prosperous future upon the fertility of the soils. Prior to 1860, yeomen built secure farmsteads and planters made fortunes. Following the Civil War and until World War II, natural soil fertility declined. With increasing amounts of commercial fertilizer, the land continued to support a planter group of large farms as well as a rising middle class of family farms. The photographs in this chapter show the changes, physical and aesthetic, in rural housing and clothing as the family farms responded successfully to the threats and opportunities of the times. The images also reveal interests and efforts in using new technology on the farm. The scenes in the photographs demonstrate a willingness of the farmers in the 20th century to desert King Cotton and diversify farm production. These surviving farms adopted new crops and a scientific approach to agriculture by allying with the new Agricultural Extension Service. Cash was always in short supply in the 19th and early 20th centuries. The agricultural system from 1865 to 1940 had an excess of cheap labor in the landless freed slaves and their descendants who were captured in the sharecropping system, and the white families who also became sharecroppers and tenants in increasing numbers after losing their farms due to indebtedness. Most families living as sharecroppers had too little income to pay for photographs. This large population is mostly invisible and cannot be understood through images in the same manner as the more prosperous rural families that were able to accommodate the difficult decades.

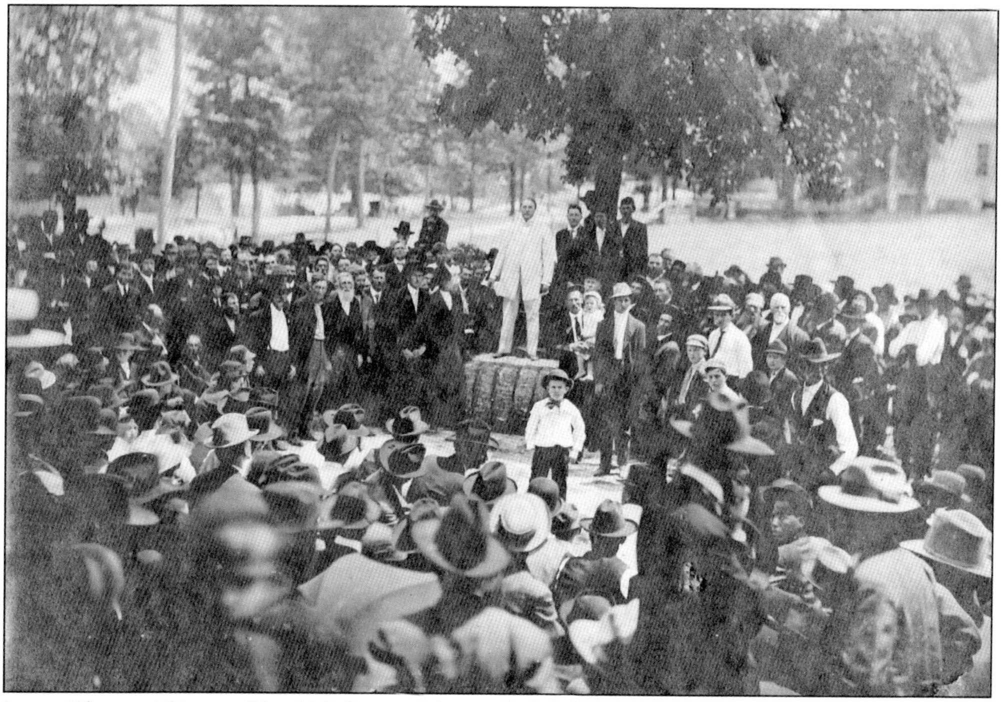

James Thomas "Cotton Tom" Heflin stands on a bale of cotton giving a political speech in 1910. He became conspicuous in the history of Alabama through his leadership in drafting the 1901 Alabama state constitution. He served as Alabama secretary of state, a member of the U.S. House of Representatives, and as a U.S. senator. (Courtesy of CMA.)

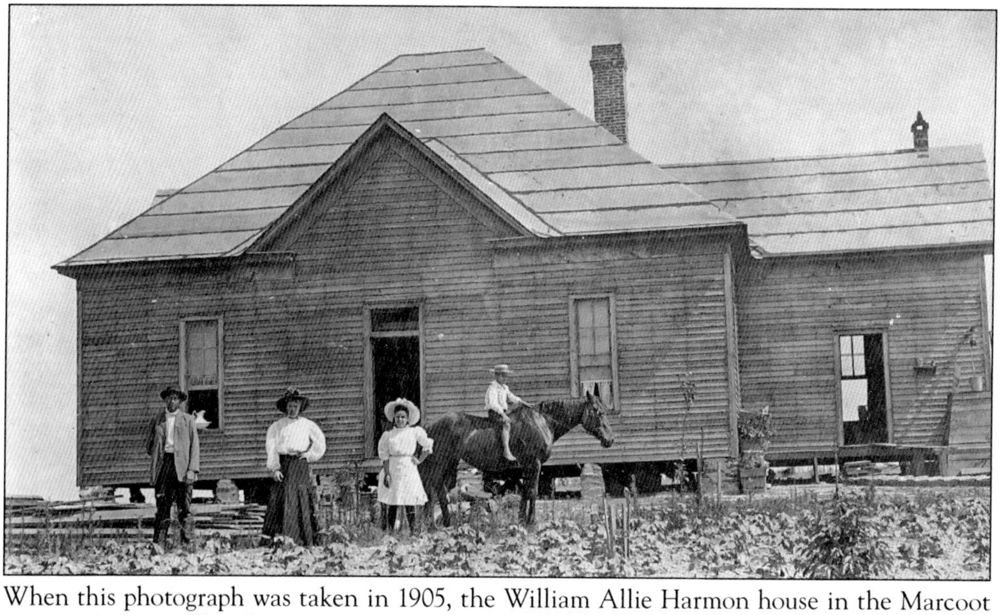

When this photograph was taken in 1905, the William Allie Harmon house in the Marcoot community was still under construction in a cotton field. Pictured from left to right are Herbert Jackson Harmon, Mollie Lett Harmon, and Clera and Morgan Harmon. Allie Harmon was a merchant in partnership with Seaborn Still and later moved to White Plains, selling this property to Willis Childers. (Courtesy of Nell Tomlinson Leverett.)

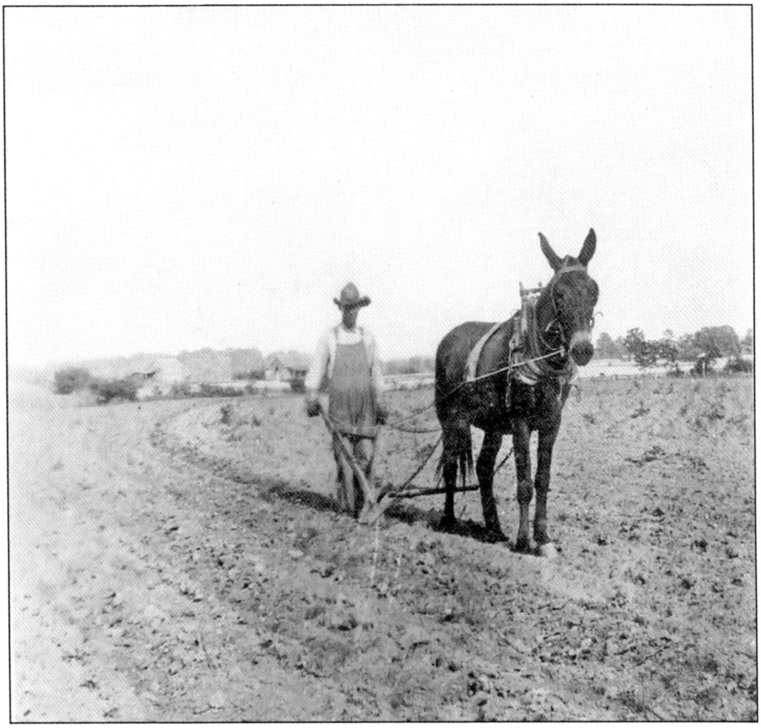

The solitary ploughman was a common sight during the era of the cotton culture. David Brittain Holderfield plows his field to plant cotton or corn in the spring of 1914. His 80-acre farm east of Stroud was located on the second highest ridge in Chambers County. He served as the mayor of Stroud in the 1920s. (Courtesy of Leita Holderfield Day.)

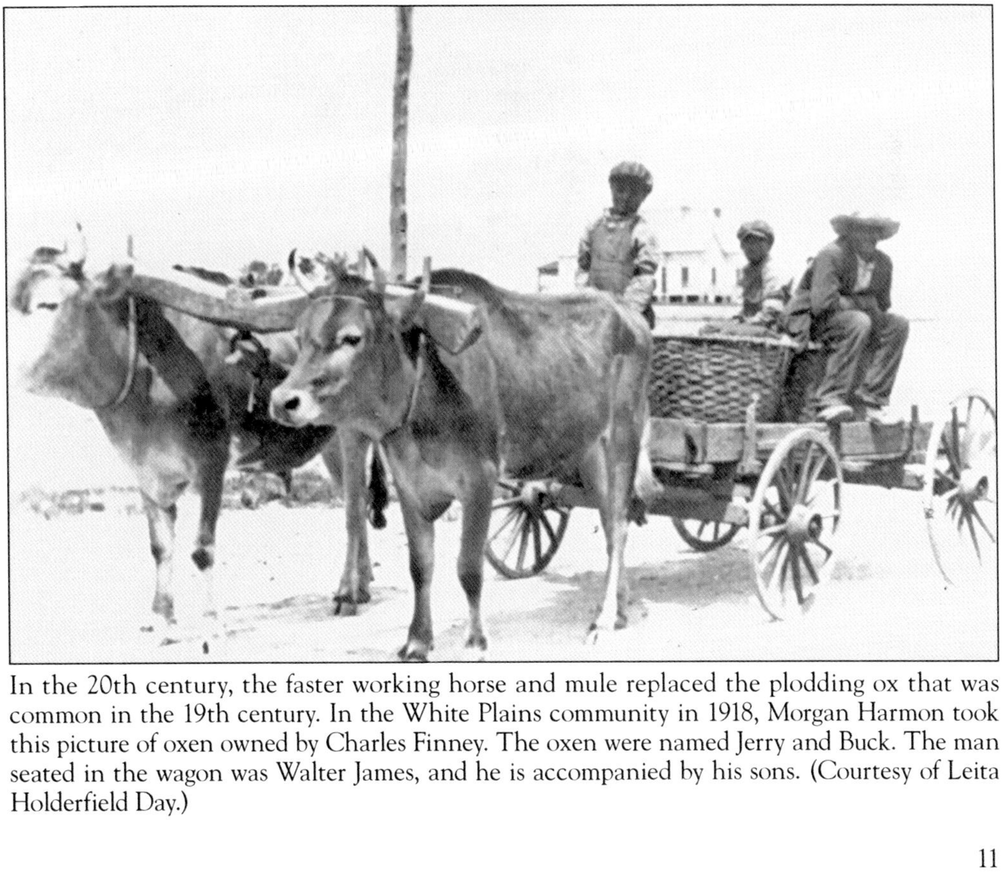

In the 20th century, the faster working horse and mule replaced the plodding ox that was common in the 19th century. In the White Plains community in 1918, Morgan Harmon took this picture of oxen owned by Charles Finney. The oxen were named Jerry and Buck. The man seated in the wagon was Walter James, and he is accompanied by his sons. (Courtesy of Leita Holderfield Day.)

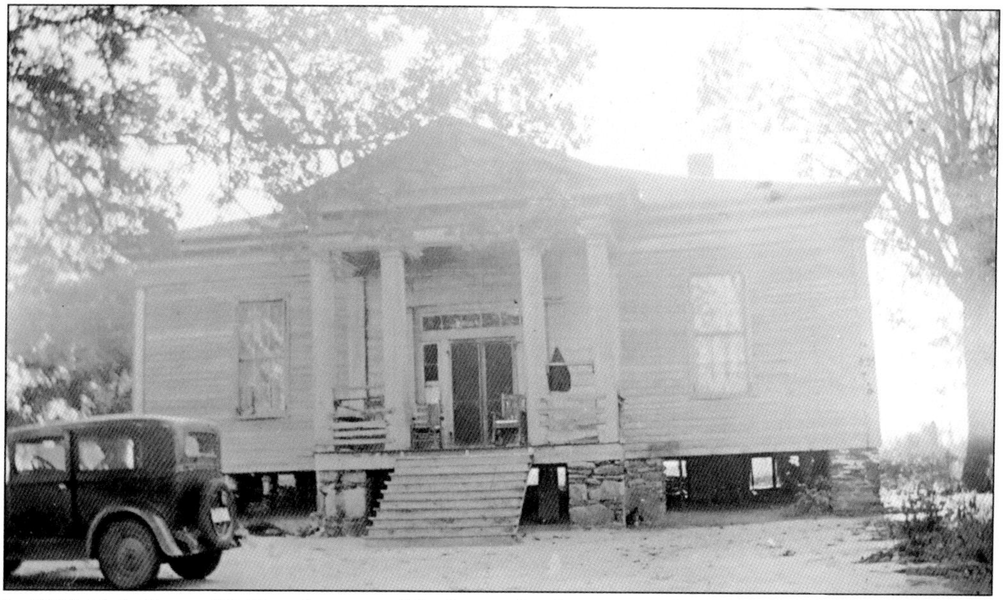

In 1860, Col. George W. Huguley, one of the largest landowners in the county, owned 75 slaves who cultivated his cotton fields. John Howard Parnell, brother of the famous Irish statesman Charles Stewart Parnell, purchased 1,482 acres in 1867 from Colonel Huguley and later this antebellum plantation house for the Parnell residence. The photograph of the decaying plantation house was taken about 1930. (Courtesy of Joyce Schuessler Clark.)

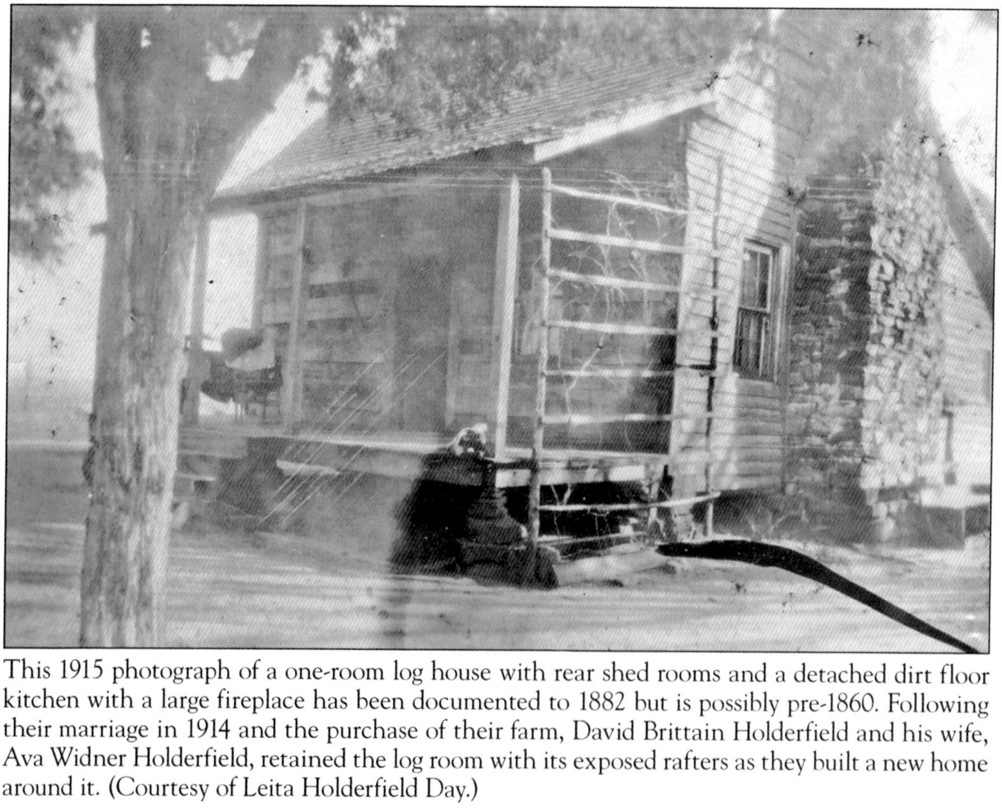

This 1915 photograph of a one-room log house with rear shed rooms and a detached dirt floor kitchen with a large fireplace has been documented to 1882 but is possibly pre-1860. Following their marriage in 1914 and the purchase of their farm, David Brittain Holderfield and his wife, Ava Widner Holderfield, retained the log room with its exposed rafters as they built a new home around it. (Courtesy of Leita Holderfield Day.)

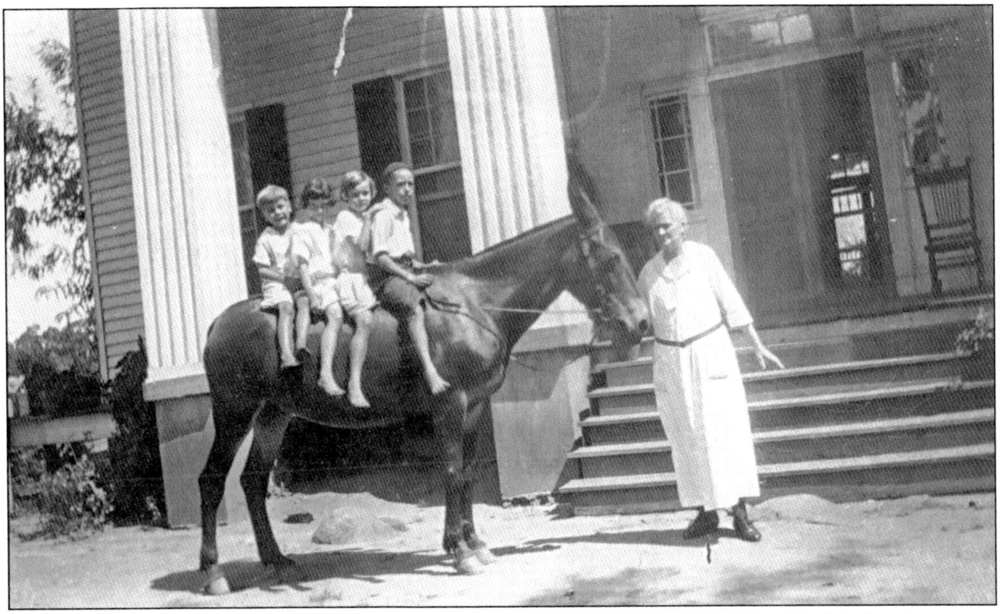

Located on the road from Oak Bowery to Cusseta, the prosperous Edward S. McCurdy cotton plantation contained almost 4,000 acres and 79 slaves in 1860. The largest cotton plantations in terms of acreages and slave work forces were located in the southern regions of the county. In the 1920s, Lula Jones Wyche, who is holding the horse, lived in the antebellum plantation house. (Courtesy of Don Clark.)

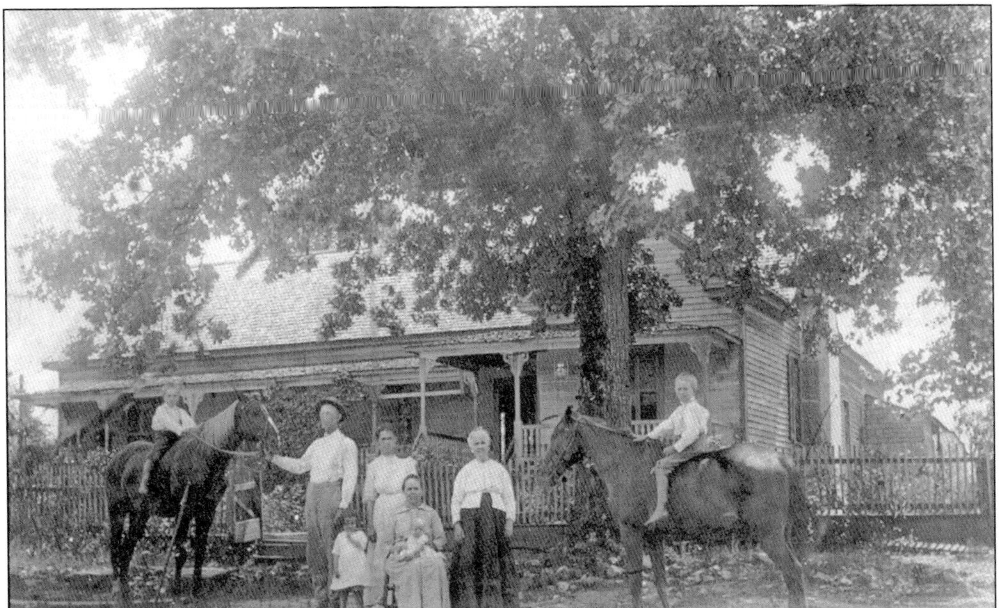

This 1913 photograph of the Seaborn A. Jarrell Sr. farm family from the Marcoot community displays two horses and a well-established home. From left to right are Seaborn A. Jarrrell Jr. (on Prince), Seaborn A. Jarrell Sr., Mary Ernest, Ada C., Georgia B. Humphrey Jarrell holding Lela, Mary Elizabeth Whatley Humphrey, and George H. (on horse). This family farm was purchased in 1884 for $5,200. (Courtesy of Wayne Greathouse.)

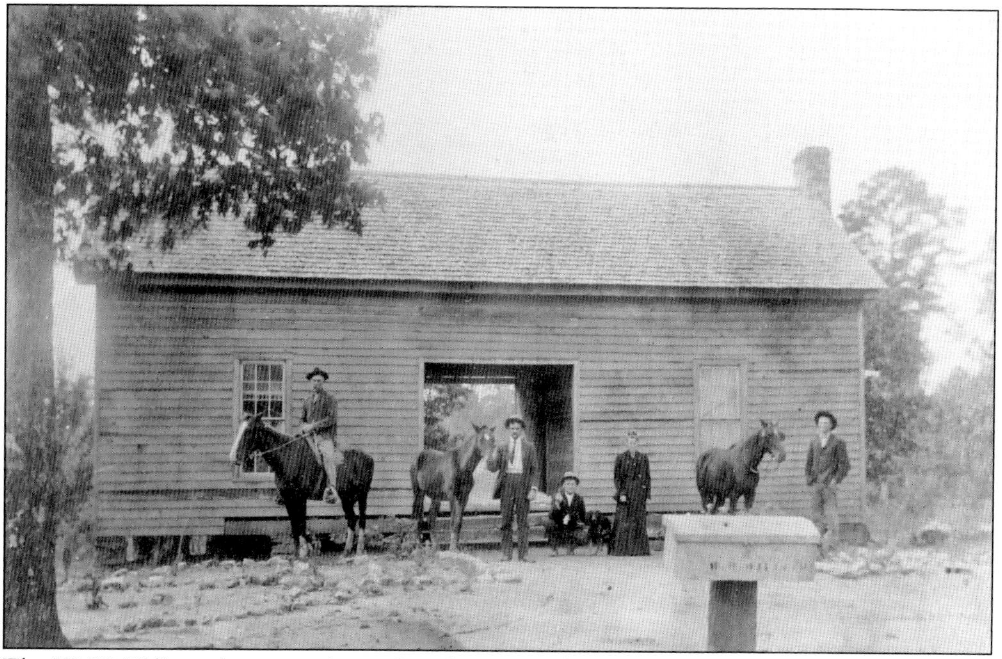

The W. W. Williams home was located in the Hopewell Community in the southeastern corner of the county. The 1910 photograph shows men with their horses and a 19th-century styled dogtrot house with a pile of recently picked cotton in the passageway between the front rooms. As resources were available, farm families would add porches and additional rooms to their initial room configuration. (Courtesy of Ronald David Williams Jr.)

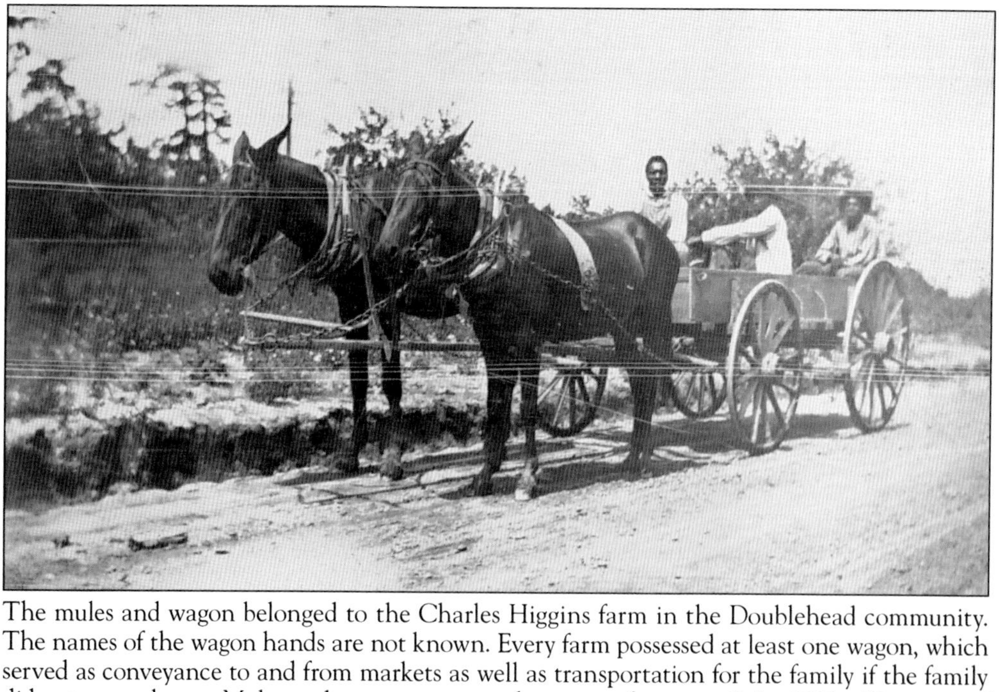

The mules and wagon belonged to the Charles Higgins farm in the Doublehead community. The names of the wagon hands are not known. Every farm possessed at least one wagon, which served as conveyance to and from markets as well as transportation for the family if the family did not own a buggy. Mules and wagons were used on many farms until the 1950s. (Courtesy of Ann Higgins Rist.)

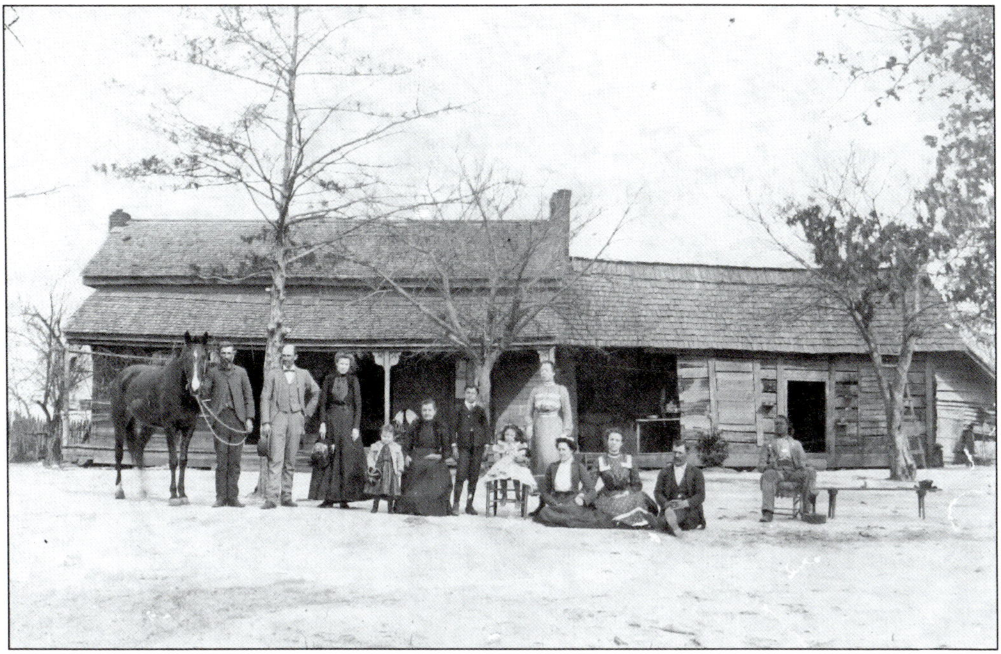

Elias Harmon (far left), who served as color bearer in Company G, 37th Alabama Infantry Regiment, CSA, stands with family members (from left to right) William Allie, Mollie Lett, Morgan, Nancy Jackson, Herbert J., Clera, Gillie Belle, Susie, Clara Perdue, Dr. Andrew Harmon, and an unidentified man. The house, located on the Chapman Trail, is a 19th-century farmhouse with a log kitchen and a large cooking fireplace. (Courtesy of Alma Harmon Clark.)

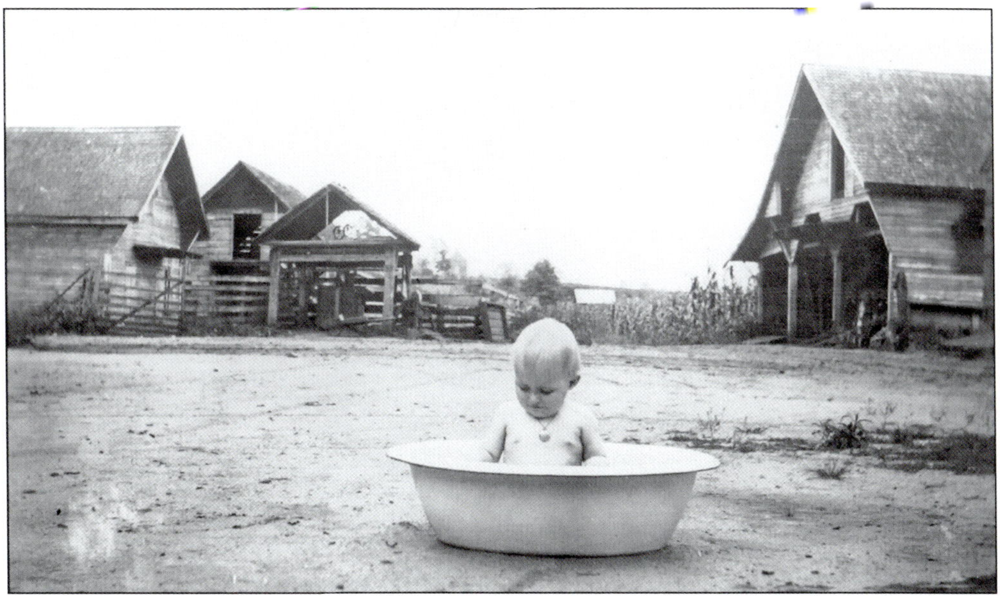

The John Thomas Lee Sr. farmyard barns and sheds survive as background in this picture of his granddaughter, Frances Lee, taken in 1919. On the right is the three-bay wagon and buggy barn. On the left are the corncrib, the mule barn, and the well for the livestock. A wheelbarrow and grinding wheel are under the well shed. (Courtesy of Kathy Burnett Sellers.)

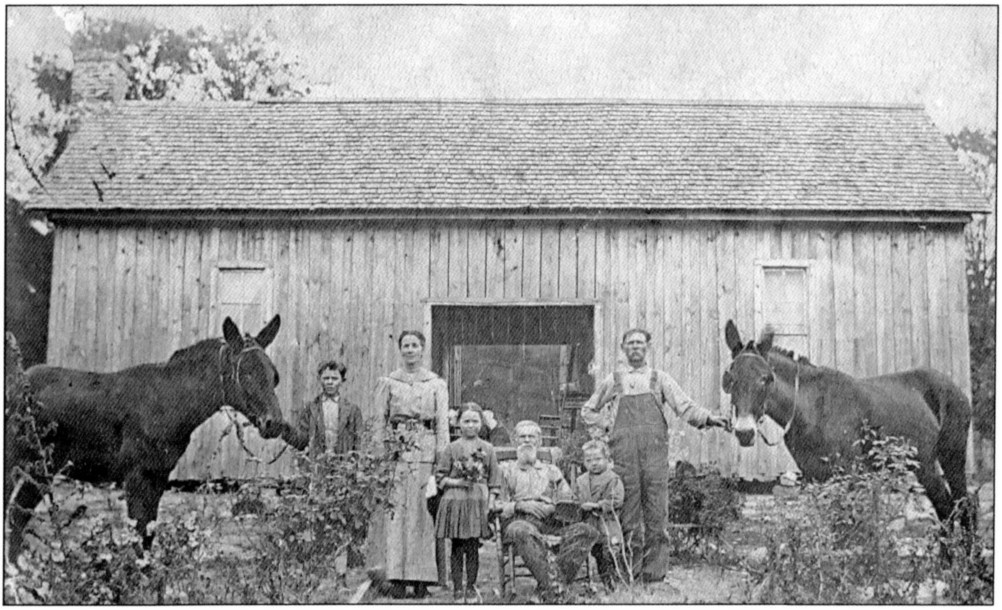

The 1913 photograph of the Joseph Benjamin Granger family near Abanda shows a typical dogtrot house without a porch and demonstrates the pride of farm families in their livestock. The two mules were named Kate and Walker. The Granger family members, pictured from left to right, are W. D., Ida Ellen, Alma, I. W. Miles (grandfather), Dock, and Joseph Benjamin Granger. (Courtesy of Glenda Granger Hall.)

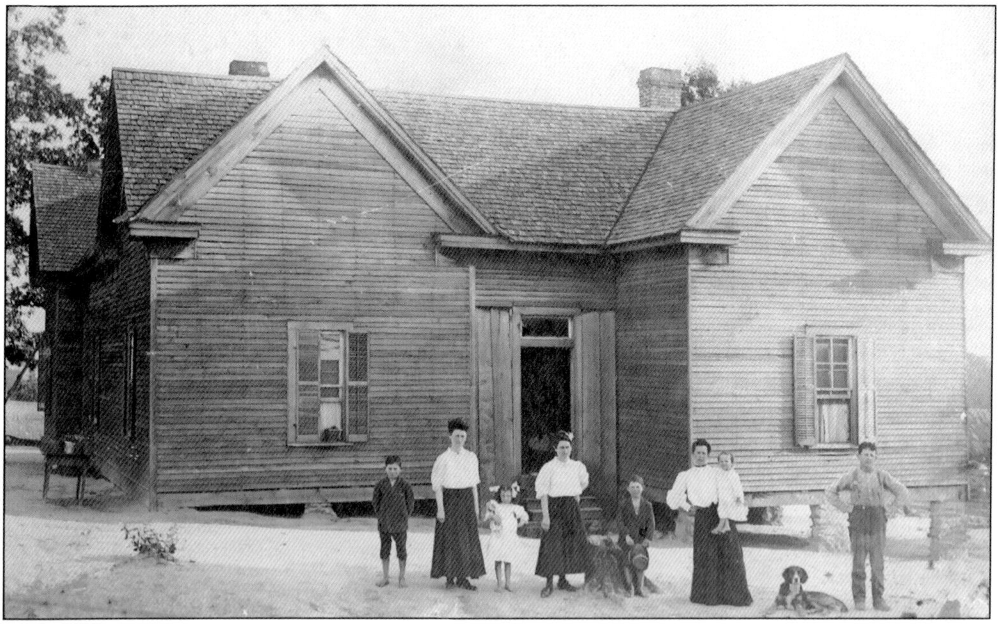

Dr. Josiah Ashby Ison, a physician who practiced in the northwestern part of the county, died at the age of 76 in 1937. His farm and family home were located at Trammell's Cross Roads, where the photograph was taken in 1907. Dr. Ison was not at home when this picture was taken. From left to right are Guy, Ester, Mattie, Pearl, Thomas, Mary Langley Ison holding Joseph, and unidentified. (Courtesy of Mary Alsobrook.)

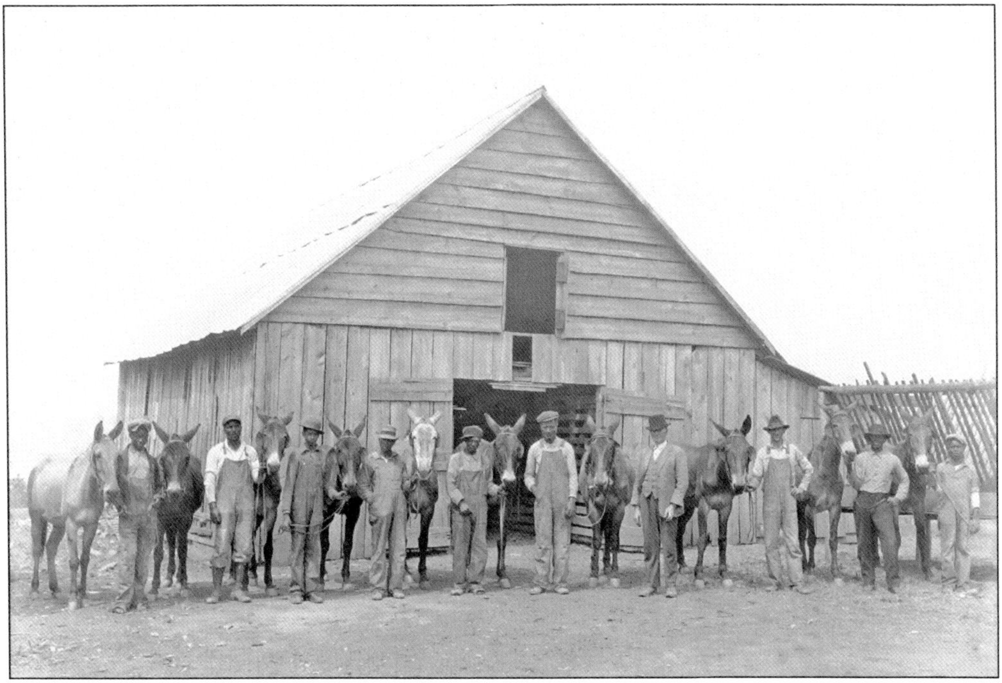

Many cotton plantations hired wage hands for plowing and farm work. Charles E. Burton was the overseer for Dr. W. D. Gaines' large farm in the western part of Chambers County when this picture was taken in 1910. Charles Burton is wearing a suit and the wage hands are standing by their mules, preparing to lead or ride them to the fields. (Courtesy of Lynda Langley Burton.)

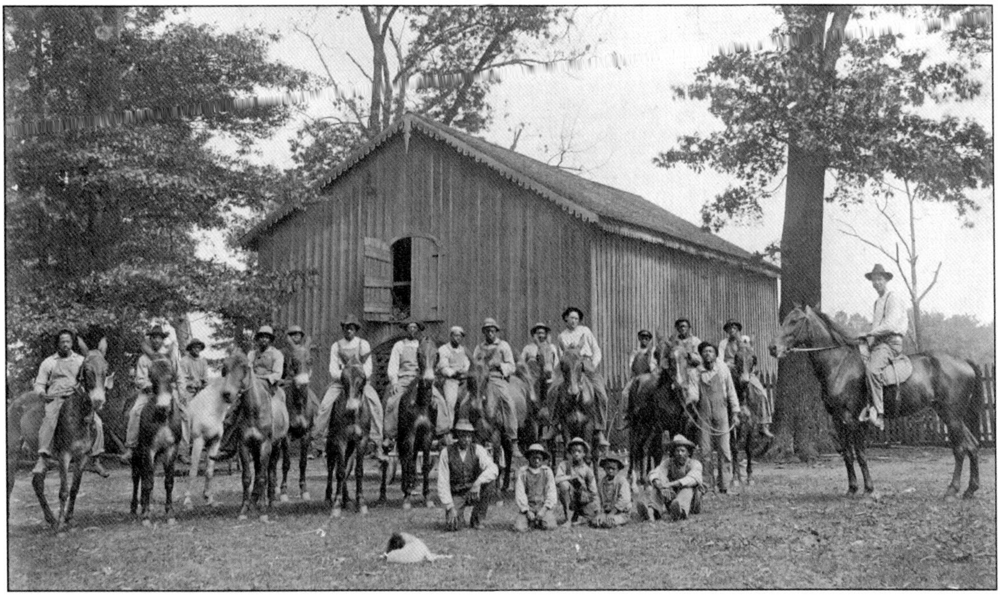

Before Dr. Leckinski Ware Spratling retired to Roamer's Roost in 1921, Marshall Davis, the overseer for the plantation, lived with his family in the Spratling house. In this 1915 photograph, Marshall Davis is mounted on the saddled horse and 14 wage hands are mounted, ready to ride to the fields. The board and batten barn has an unusually fine roof trim. (Courtesy of Miriam Ann Kirkwood Syler.)

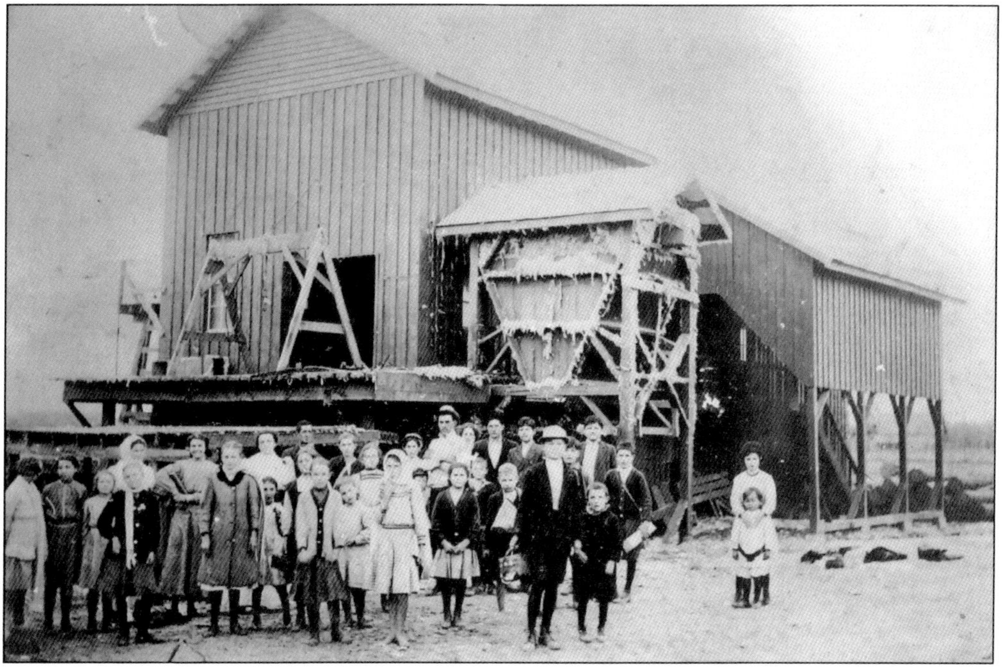

By 1900, cotton gins were found at many crossroads in the county. This 1912 photograph of the Sherman cotton gin at Penton shows a group of schoolchildren in front of a busy lint-shrouded gin house. On the deck above the children stands the 6-foot-high sawhorse from which each cotton bale would be manually weighed with a large steelyard scale. (Courtesy of Cenus Phillips Heptinstall Collection.)

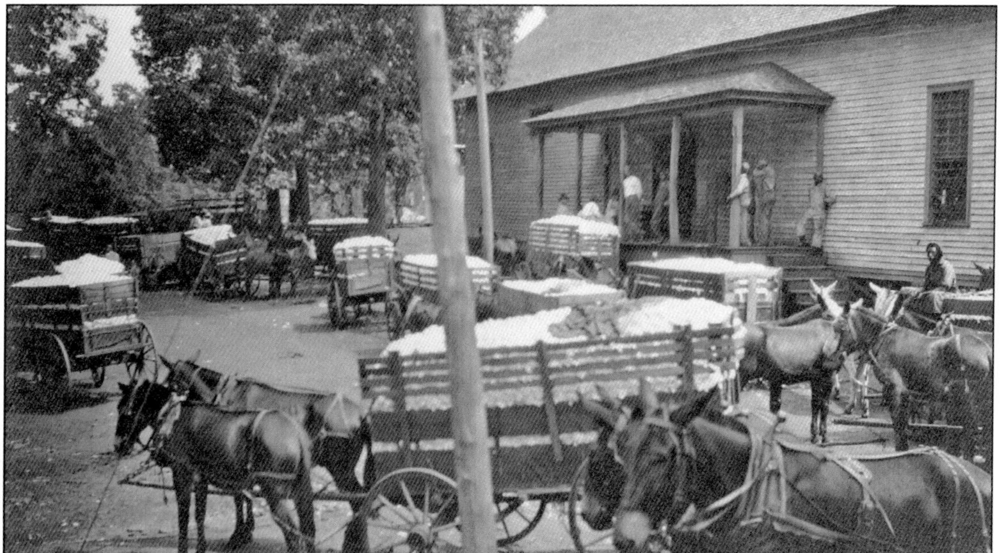

One cotton gin, which served the highly productive cotton plantations in a southernmost region of the county, was located just across the Lee County line at Gold Hill. In this image from 1910, the mules and their wagons of recently picked cotton are lining up to go into the gin shed across the county road from the J. E. Ellington store and commissary. (Courtesy of Miriam Ann Kirkwood Syler.)

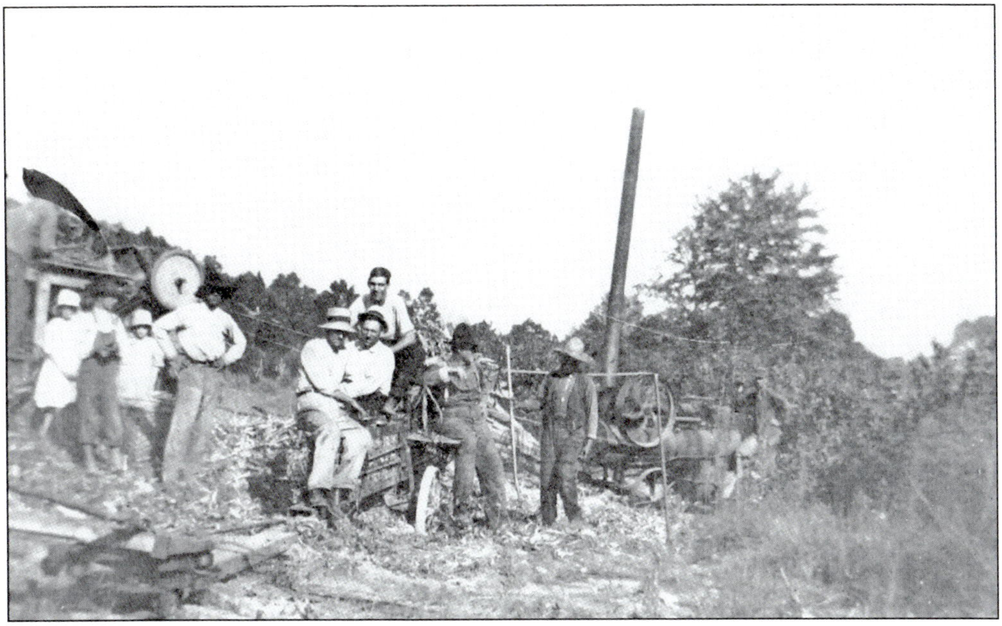

Before 1900, Simon Peter Smith, a blacksmith near Welch, acquired a steam engine and various tools powered by the engine. The photograph illustrates three pieces of equipment that he would move from farm to farm, performing contract work. The steam engine is on the left, the men are sitting on a stationary baler, and a seed sheller is mounted on the wagon on the right. (Courtesy of Marjorie Newell.)

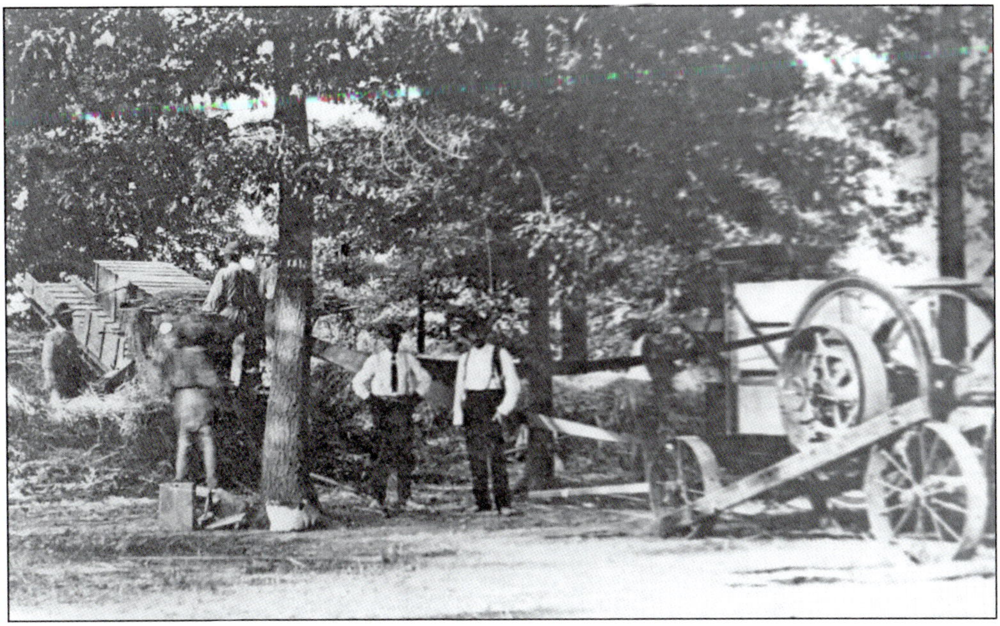

In the Waverly community about 1912, Gilbert Maulsby, a representative of the International Harvester Company, is supervising the setup of a large hit-and-miss engine to power a threshing machine. He is demonstrating this machinery to local farmers and planters. This expensive equipment would have been purchased by owners of large plantations. (Courtesy of Mary Helen Benford.)

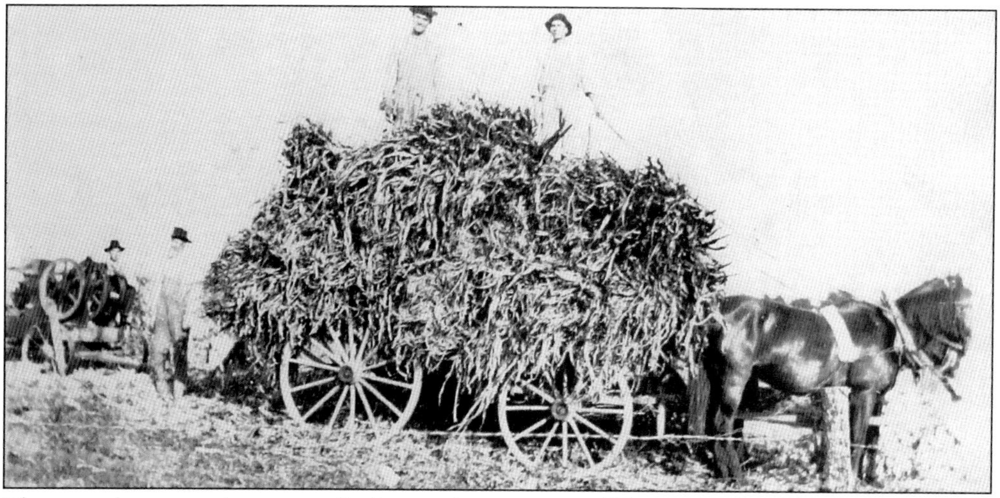

The green leaves on the corn stalks late in the season would be stripped and bundled and left to dry as fodder for the livestock. Wagons would go into the fields later to bring the dry feed into the barns. The photograph from 1910 shows a two-horse wagonload of fodder on the farm at Stroud of William Henry Smith, standing on the right. (Courtesy of Horace McLean Holderfield.)

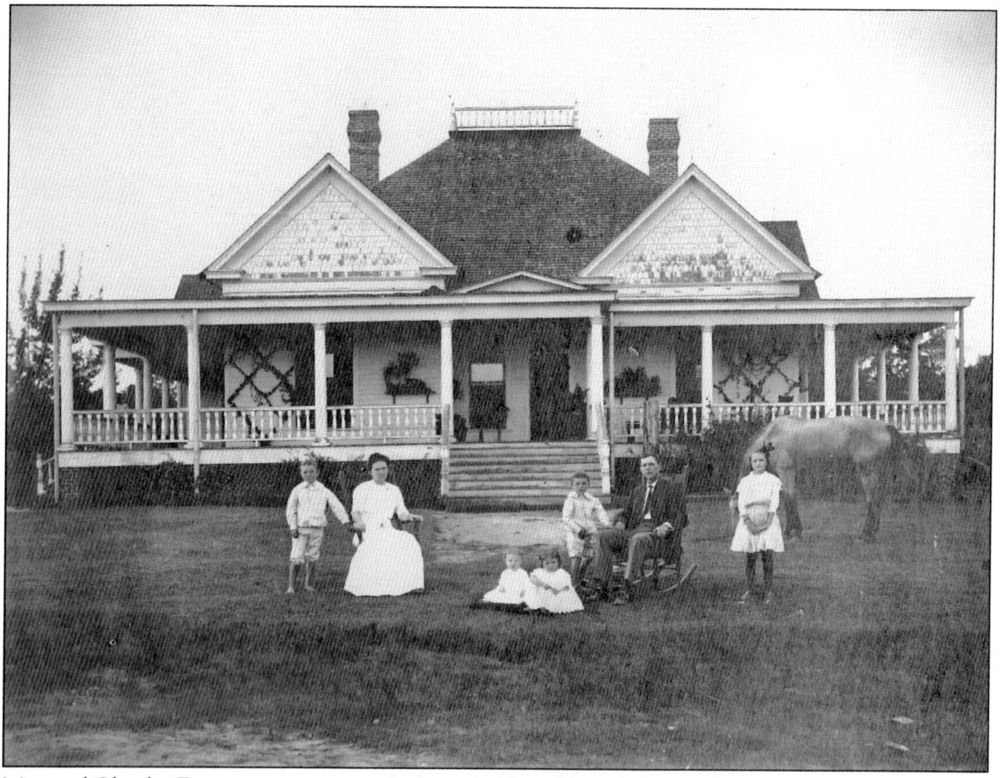

May and Charles Finney are sitting with their children (from left to right) Harold, Lewis, Rebecca, Jack, and Catherine. The family is posing in front of the Finney home on their prosperous farm in White Plains about 1912 with a horse named Dan. This house is located on the highest elevation in the county. (Courtesy of Lynda Langley Burton.)

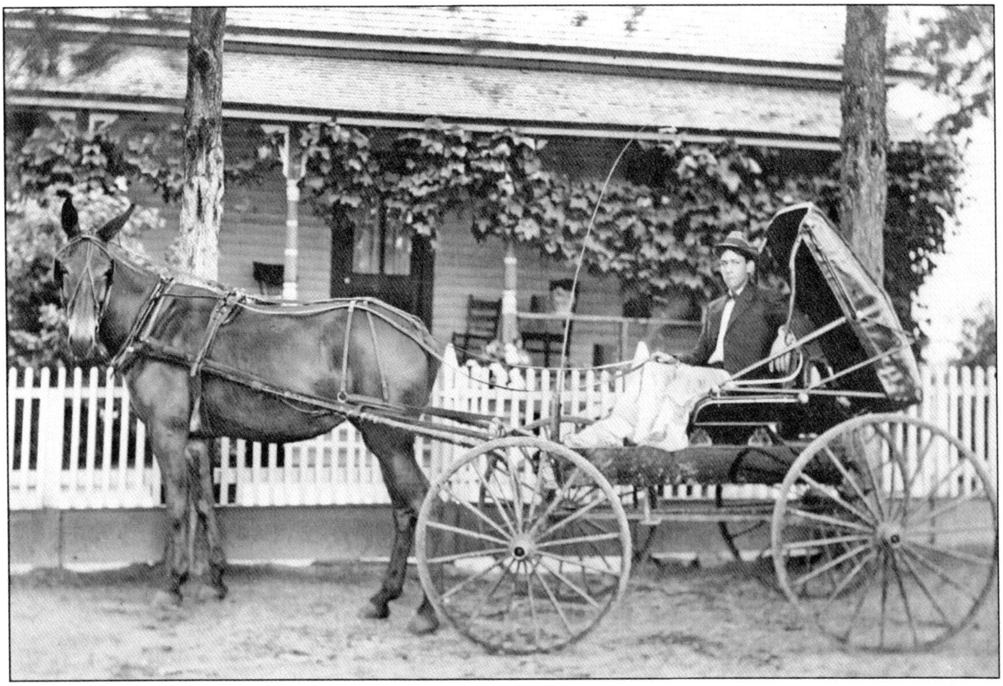

In 1910, James Leonard Andrews sits in his courting buggy in front of the Zachary Taylor Andrews home in the Ridge Grove community. The ownership of a horse-drawn buggy with a folding top by a young man was a sign of high status to the young women, who would be anxious to go for a buggy ride. (Courtesy of Kay Frost.)

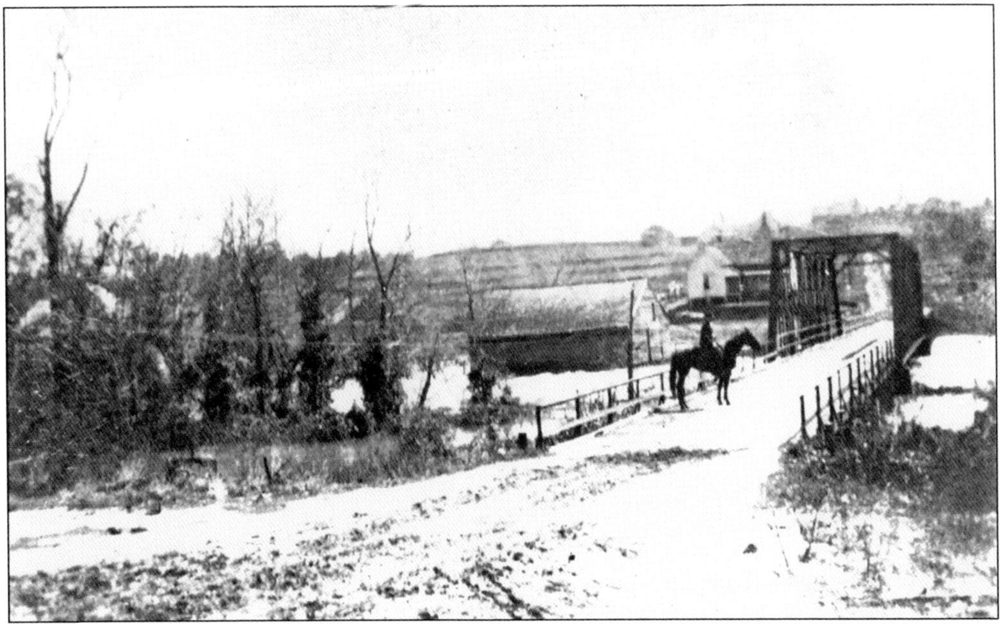

In many communities in the county, 50 percent or more of the land would be under cultivation and subject to severe erosion and runoff following storms. The photograph from the first decade of the 20th century shows the Milltown Bridge over the Chickasanoxie Creek in flood stage. The view is from north to south. (Courtesy of Frank Gaines.)

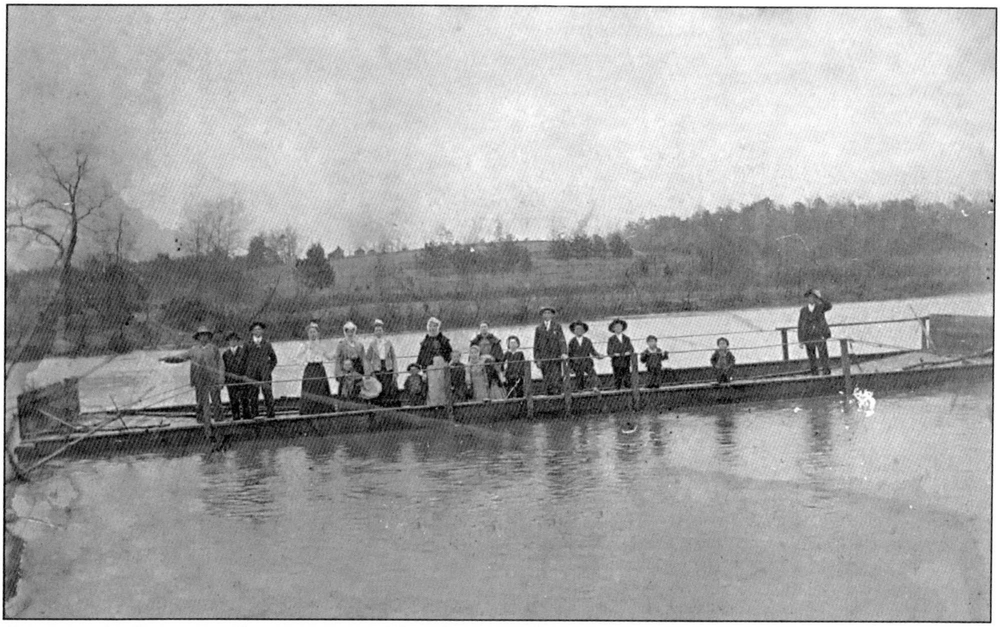

Since no bridge existed, citizens could only cross the Tallapoosa River by ferries. In this 1904 photograph of Fant's Ferry (originally Talbot's Ferry), from left to right are William Laney, Lucious Fant, Joseph E. Fant, Kittora Fant Allen, Jane Laney, Laney child, Lizzie Smith Fant, a Fant boy, Exia Fant, a Fant girl, Alta Fant, Alma Bishop Fant, Homer Fant, "Ode" Barker, four unidentified people, and "Lon" Fant (ferryman). (Courtesy of Don Clark.)

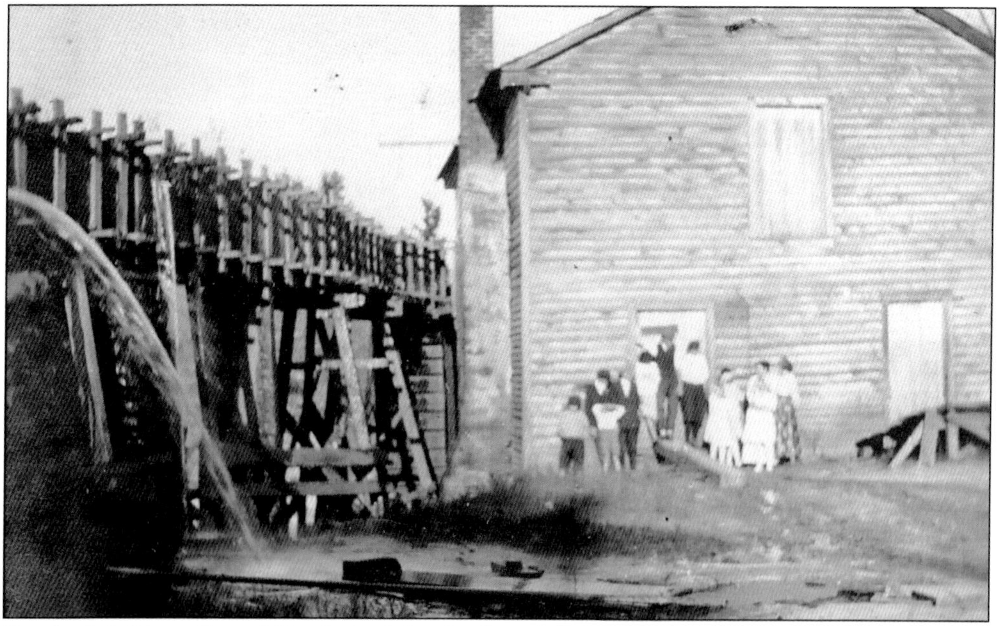

Cumbee's Mill on Stroud Creek, built by the Rev. John Cumbee in the 1870s, produced flour and meal for the next 70 years and provided a location for July Fourth picnics, political rallies, community fish fries, and family gatherings. The race (wooden trough) carrying the water from the dam to the wheel dates the photograph to about 1905. (Courtesy of Carol Cumbee Holderfield Shelnutt.)

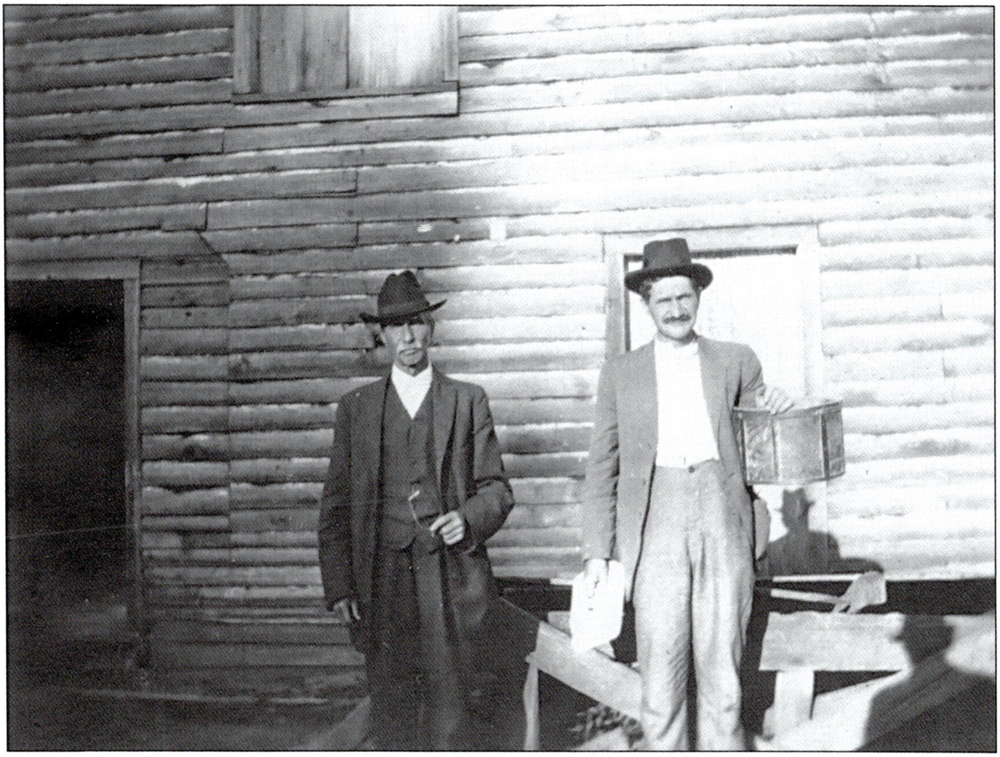

The Cumbee farm was established on Stroud Creek in 1876 by Rev. John Cumbee, a Baptist minister who moved his farming and business interests to this location from Fredonia. In this 1923 photograph, sons John Reuben (left) and William stand in front of their gristmill. John Reuben principally managed the Cumbee farm and William operated the gristmill. (Courtesy of Carol Cumbee Holderfield Shelnutt.)

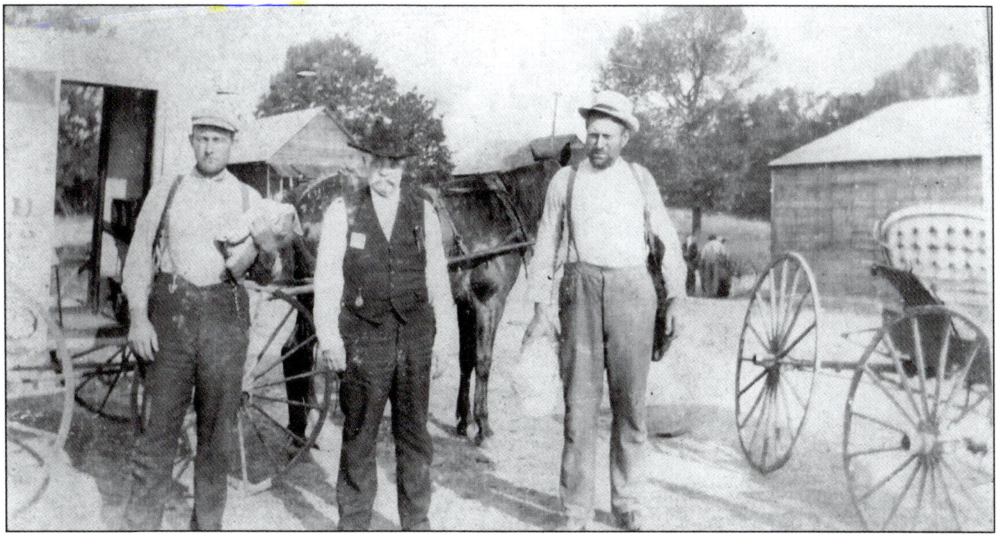

Rural Free Delivery (RFD) was 17 years old when this photograph was taken in 1907 at the Stroud post office. Postmaster Willis S. Johnson stands in the center with mail carrier William Henry Smith on the right and an unknown carrier on the left. Each carrier has a leather pouch with mail. On the left is the box-shaped mail carrier's buggy. (Courtesy of Janie Awbrey Shelnutt.)

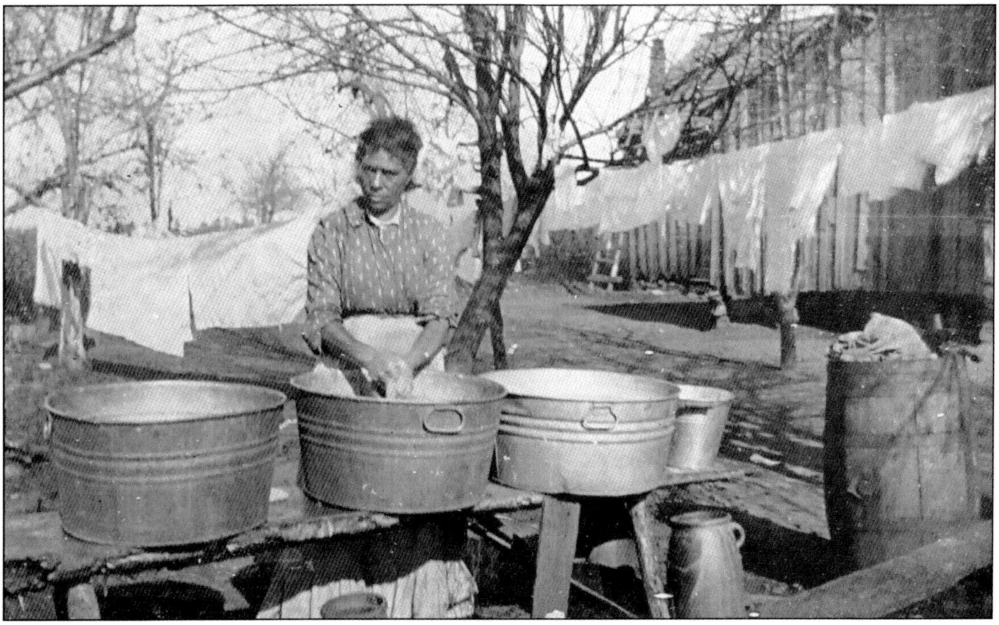

The unidentified washwoman in this early 1900s photograph in the Stroud area has clothes on the line and in the washtubs. The kettles heating the water are not seen, but the stoneware jugs containing the homemade soft soap are visible under her workbench. The appearance of the home in the background was typical for the condition of tenant houses. (Courtesy of Janie Awbrey Shelnutt.)

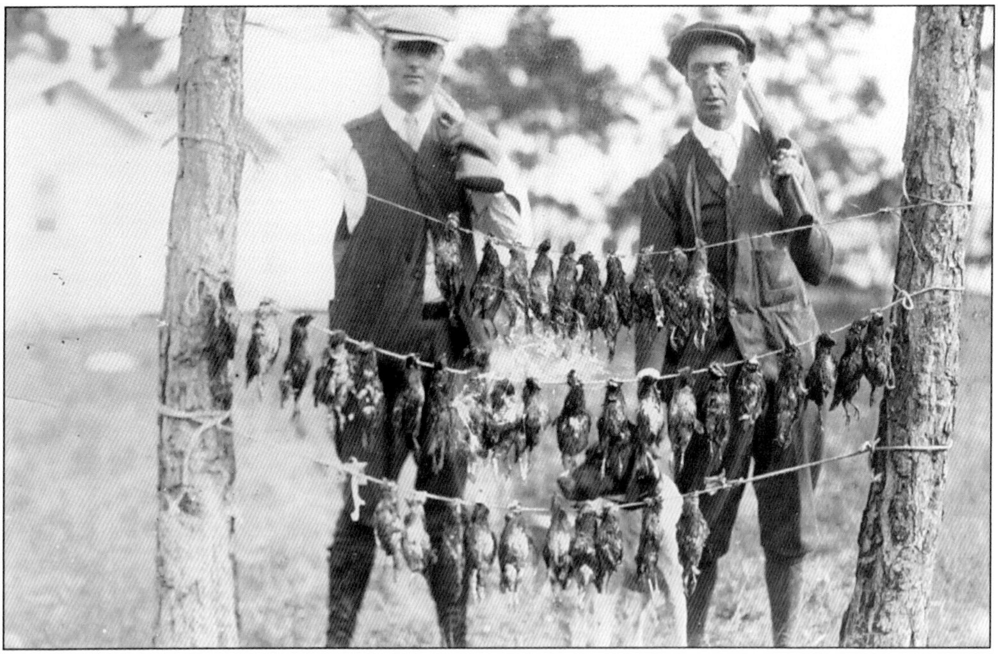

The photograph taken about 1920 shows Marion Bluford Gross, who lost the full use of his right arm as a child, and T. F. Arnold, with dog Rex, after completing a successful bird hunt. The family farm where Gross was reared was near Hickory Flat. Gross taught school at Hickory Flat and Stroud before moving to Florida. (Courtesy of Tom Carden.)

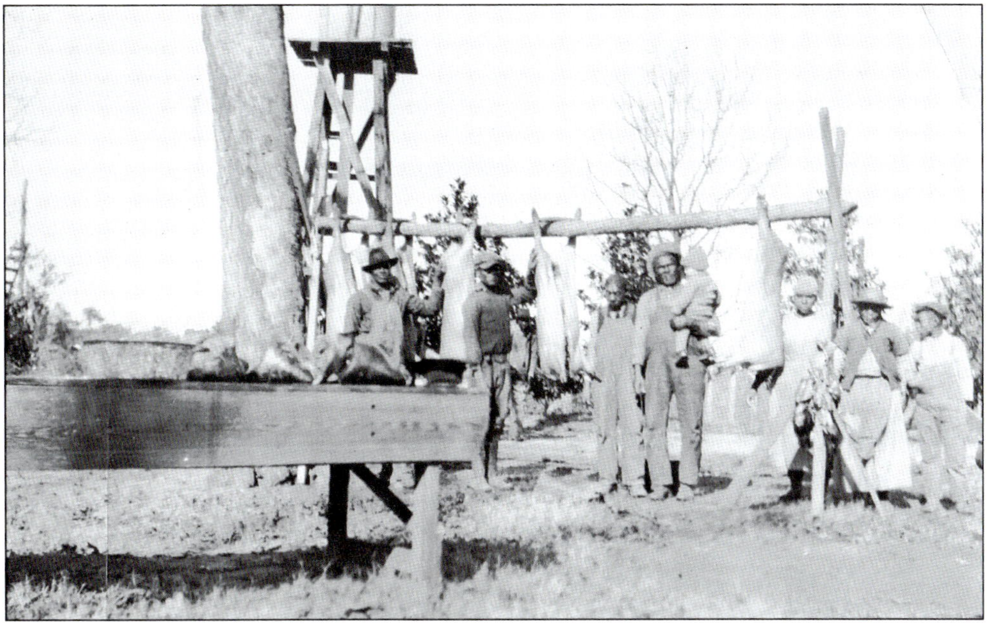

Before refrigeration, the farmer anticipated the cold days of winter when the hogs could be slaughtered and the meat salted and smoked for later consumption. The wage hand, Big Sam, holds Kenneth Spratling "Husky" Kirkwood in the photograph of a hog killing about 1924 on the Spratling plantation, Roamer's Roost. A Delco electric system pumped water periodically into the water tank visible in the background. (Courtesy of Kenneth Spratling Kirkwood.)

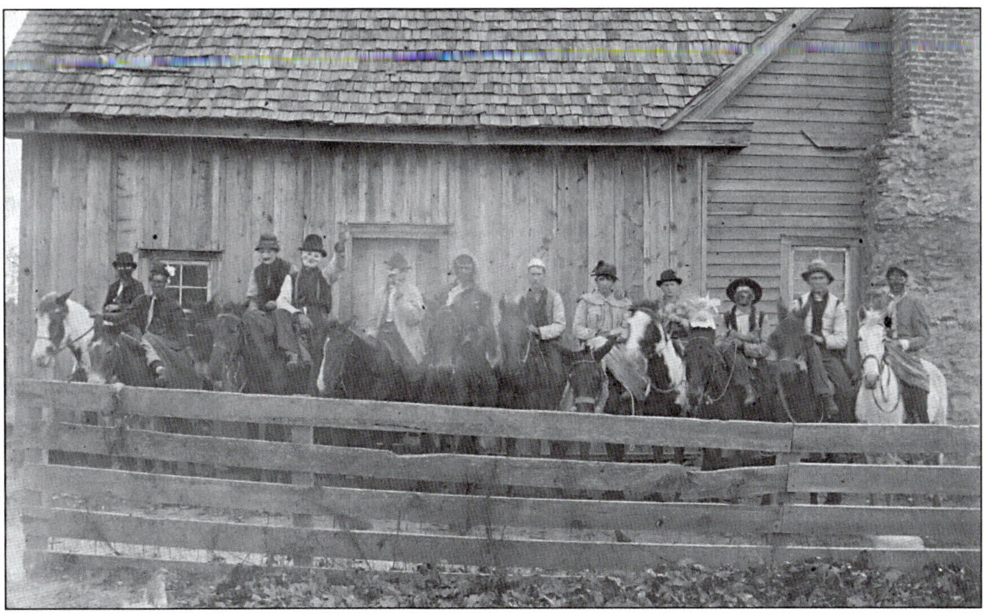

In the 19th century, mounted young men called the "fantastic riders" roamed rural communities making noise with guns, pots, and pans on Christmas day and demanding cake, other sweets, and sometimes drink. These boys would be dressed in outlandish garb, sometimes wearing women's clothing and "dough faces." The location of this photograph from the 1890s is in north Chambers County but the house is unknown. (Courtesy of Horace McLean Holderfield.)

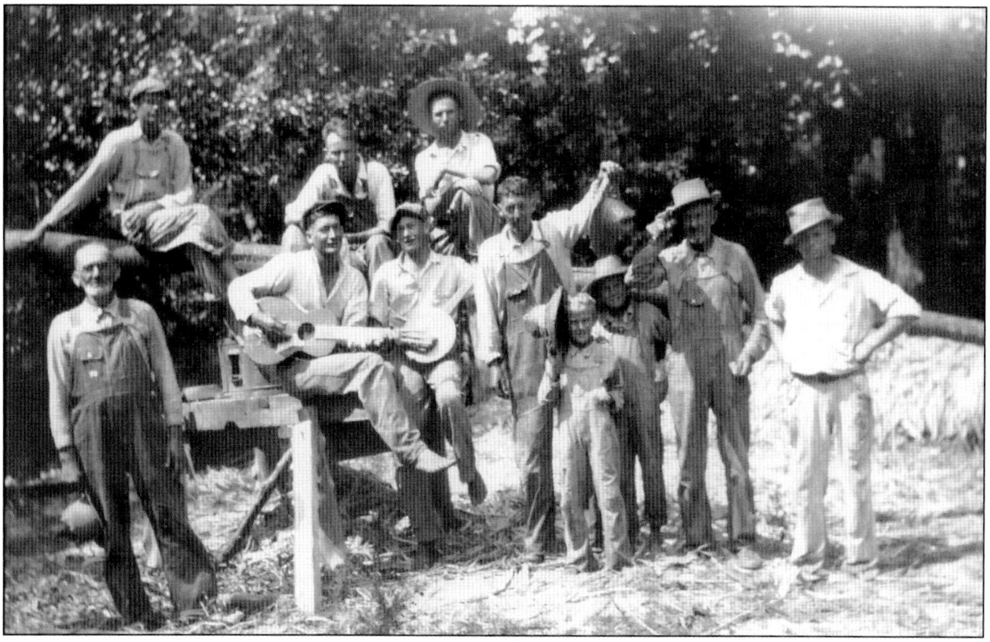

The Sanders and Moss families in the Tiller Crossroads area made syrup in the 1930s. The cane mill is behind the young men on the left, and the crushed cane stalks, called pummy, litter the ground. Locally made syrup and locally made music were important aspects of rural life. From left to right are (first row) J. A. Sanders, Woodrow Moss, John Moss, Tom Moss, two Miles boys, Grandpa Miles, and Melvin Sanders; (second row) Joe Moss, Ora Johnson, and Woodfin Sanders. (Courtesy of Jason Sanders.)

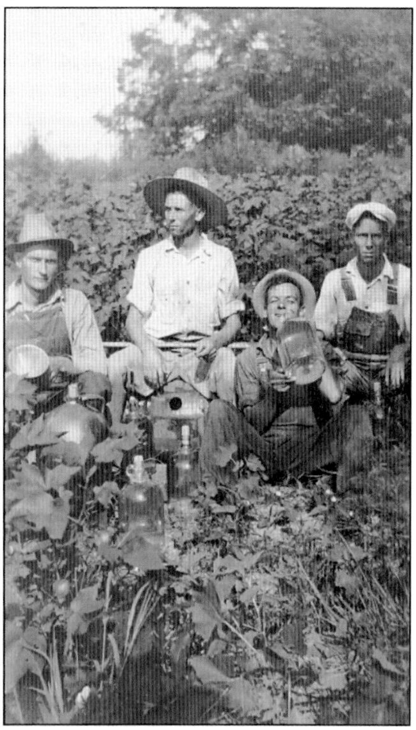

These brave and foolhardy young men were displaying a not-uncommon product of rural areas in the first 150 years of Chambers County history. They were authentic moonshiners on the western side of the county. From left to right in the 1936 photograph are Joe Moss, Woodfin Sanders, Dink Sims, and Ora Johnson. (Courtesy of Jason Sanders.)

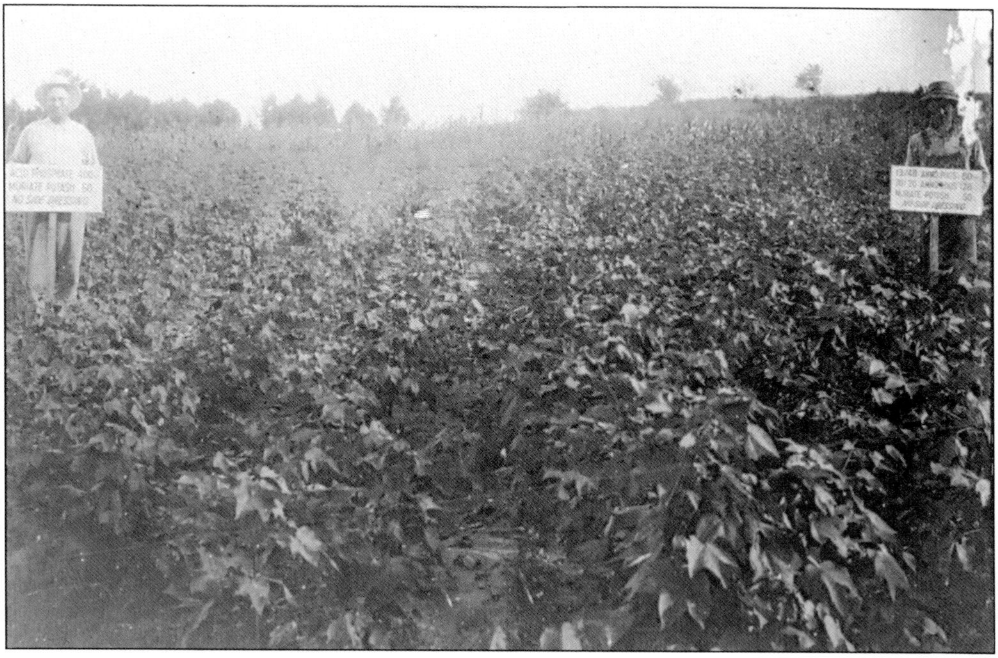

The Alabama Polytechnic Institute, presently Auburn University, and its county extension agents had a significant impact on improving the productivity of crops and livestock. The Chambers County Extension Office conducted a fertilizer trial in 1932 on William Henry Smith's farm at Stroud. William Henry Smith (left) and his son William Frank Smith hold signs listing different applications of fertilizer on cotton test plots. (Courtesy of Horace McLean Holderfield.)

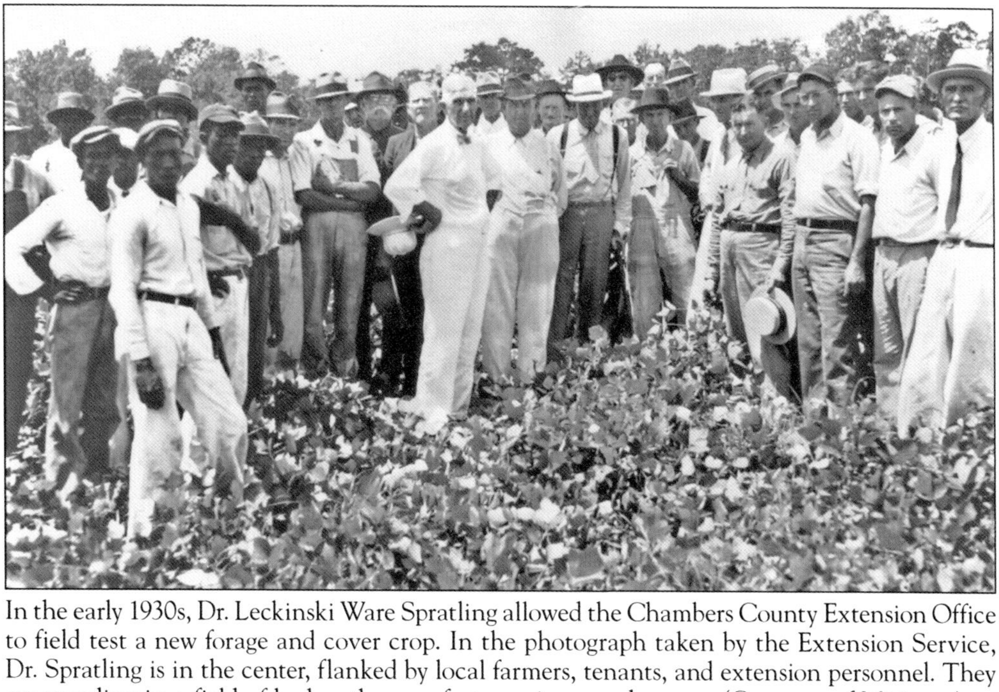

In the early 1930s, Dr. Leckinski Ware Spratling allowed the Chambers County Extension Office to field test a new forage and cover crop. In the photograph taken by the Extension Service, Dr. Spratling is in the center, flanked by local farmers, tenants, and extension personnel. They are standing in a field of kudzu, the new fast-growing wonder crop. (Courtesy of Miriam Ann Kirkwood Syler.)

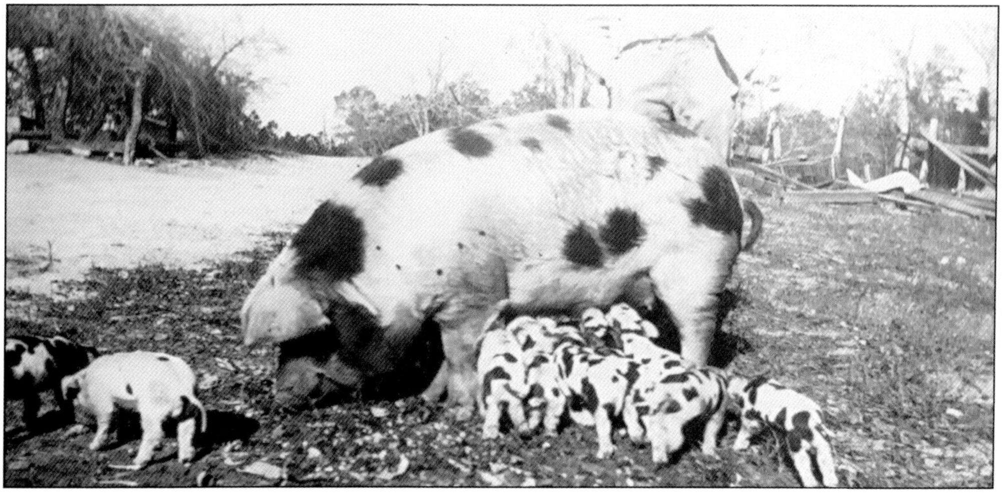

Pork was the most important meat for the rural southern family before refrigeration. Almost every farm had multiple hogs and pigs. This sow had her picture taken with her piglets in the 1920s on the Mack Lee Hamlin farm at Doublehead. The breed of the hog could be an Old Spot or Gloucester Spot, breeds that now have heritage status. (Courtesy of Mary Helen Benford.)

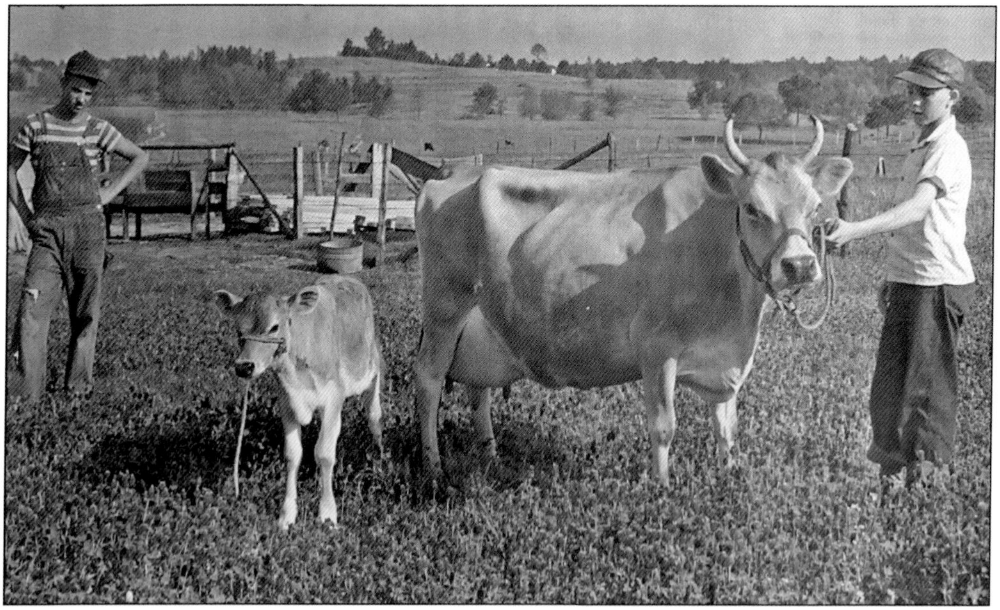

The Jersey breed of milk cow was popular from the 19th century until the 1950s in Chambers County. The small, gentle, tan cow produced milk high in butterfat. Benjamin Burton, holding the rope, showed the cow and calf in 4-H Club competitions. His brother James looked on from the left and gave instructions. (Courtesy of Lynda Langley Burton.)

After World War II, farmers continued to diversify their crops and livestock production. In the early 1950s, Clarence Prather Slay and Lillian Daniel Slay, now well-known farmers in the White Plains community, owned a flock of laying hens. They retailed eggs from their farm in the Red Level community. (Courtesy of Mount Olive Community Club Scrapbook.)

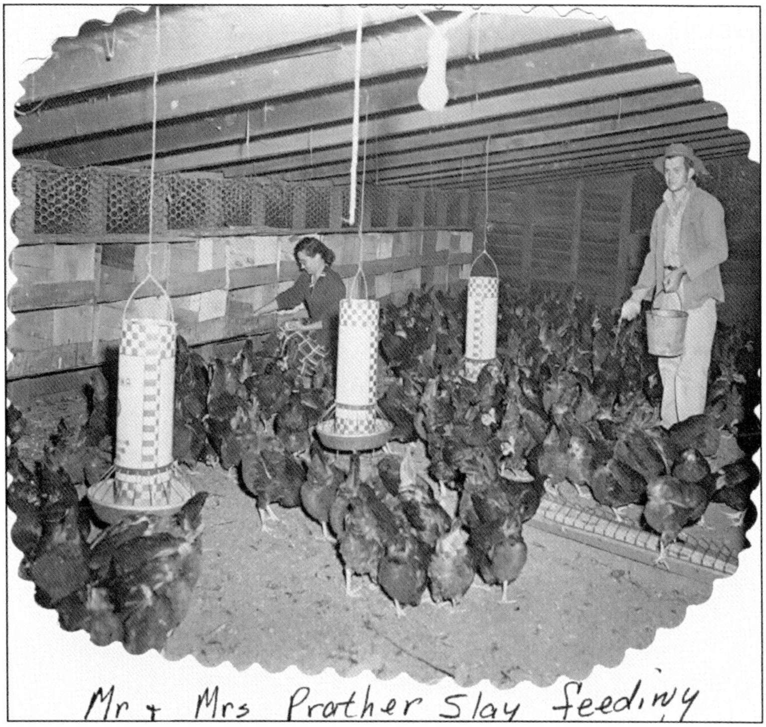

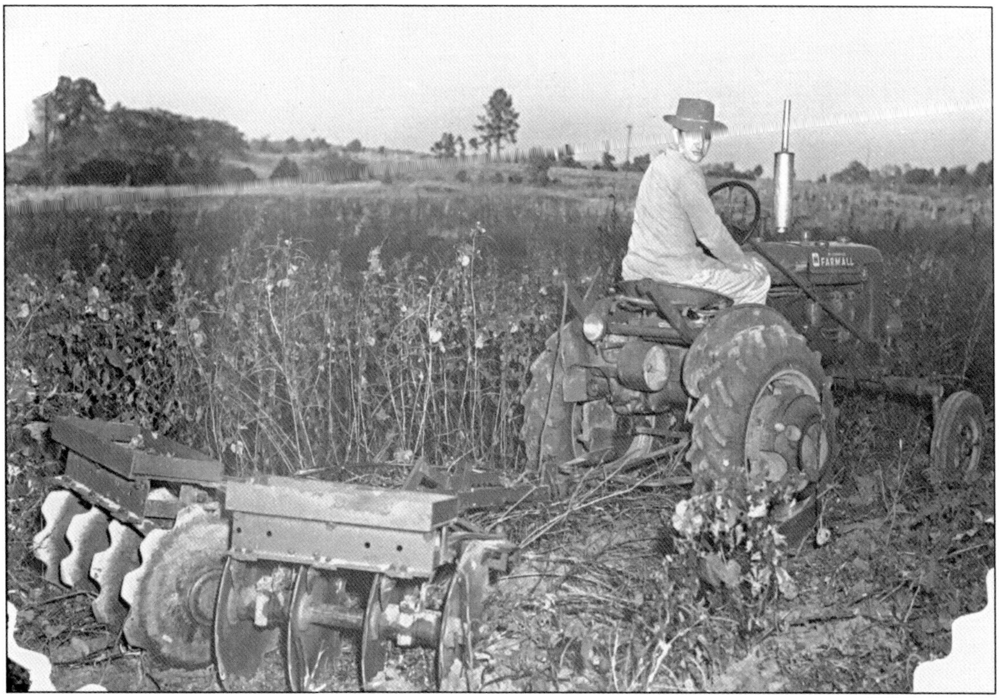

In the late 1940s, tractors were replacing draft animals on farms. The Farmall A was a popular row-crop and starter tractor for many farmers. Pictured here about 1950, Robert Walter Slay is using his new tractor with a bush and bog disc harrow to cut down and turn under the old crop in the fall of the year. (Courtesy of Mount Olive Community Club Scrapbook.)

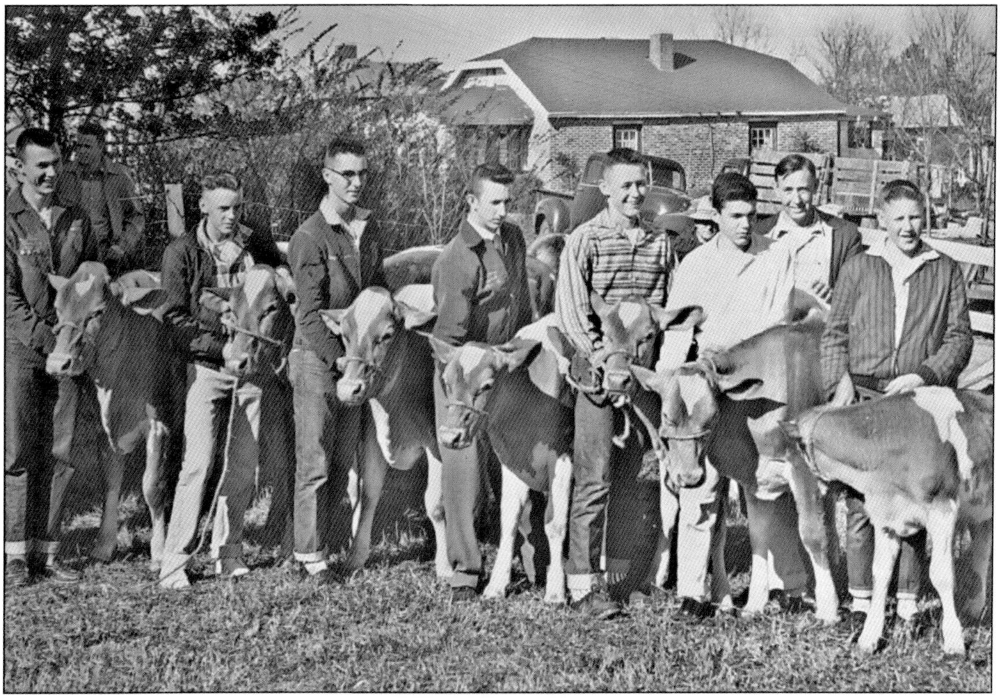

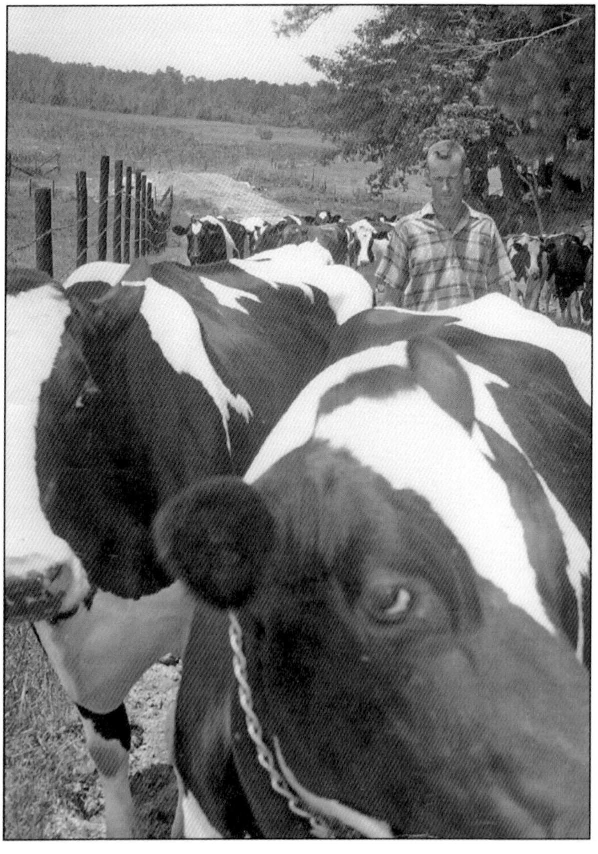

In the late 1950s, the West Point Manufacturing Company provided funds for the Chambers County Future Farmers of America Chapter to purchase six Guernsey heifers and a young bull from Edisto Farms in Edisto, South Carolina. With their Guernseys are, from left to right, Robert Sims, Harold Kendrick, Wayne Stephens, Henry Lovelace, Thomas Burton, Joseph Lambert, Edison Burton (Thomas's father), and Thomas Rodney Sims. (Courtesy of William Earl Thomas.)

Dairying grew in importance from the late 1930s through the 1950s. James Lewis Robinson III was a beef, hay, and dairy farmer whose Cumbee forefathers had prospered from the cultivation of cotton. The Robinson Dairy at Cumbee's Mill chose the Holstein breed for the production of Grade A milk. In the photograph, Jim is bringing the cows to the milking parlor. (Courtesy of James Lewis Robinson IV.)

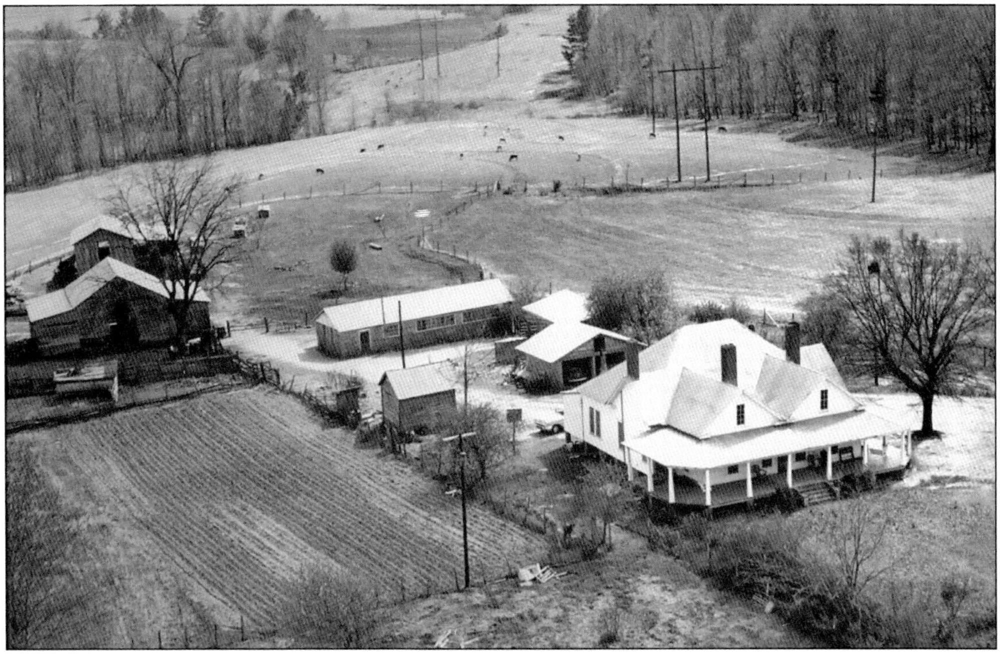

The aerial photograph provides a view of the John Morgan Spence farm about 1954. This is an excellent example of a cotton farm that made the transition to a thriving dairy farm. The dairy is the long building located behind the Spence home. The garden is located to the left of the house, and the pastures with their cattle are seen in the rear. (Courtesy of Jean Spence Nunn.)

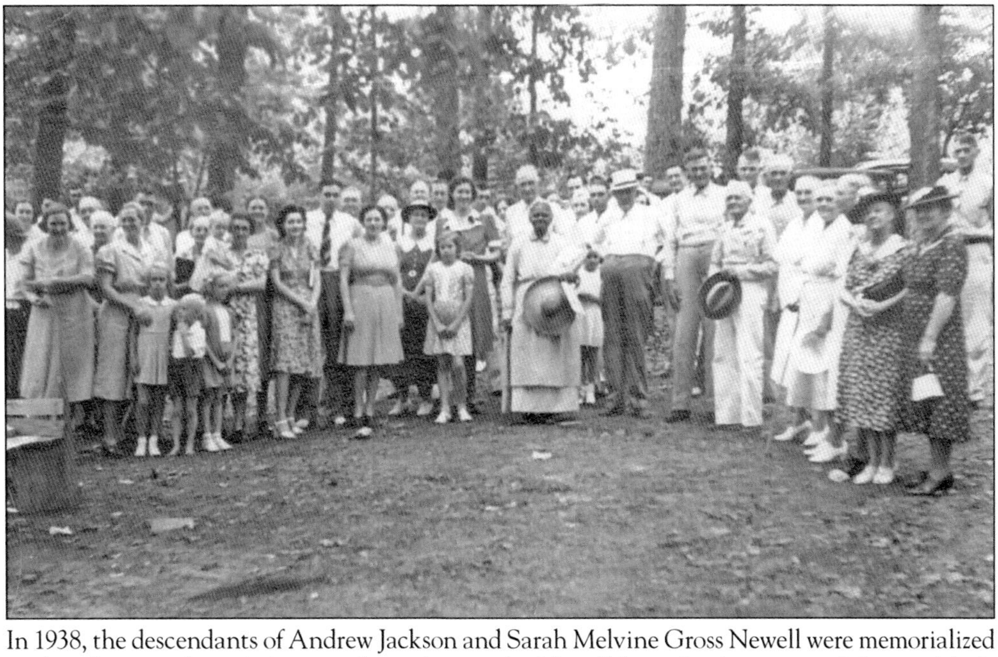

In 1938, the descendants of Andrew Jackson and Sarah Melvine Gross Newell were memorialized in this photograph at their annual reunion on the Newell farm. In the center of the semicircle is a beloved small, elderly black woman, Melvine "Vine" Newell Post. Her mother was the only slave owned by the Newell family when Vine was born in the Newell log home in 1863. (Courtesy of Margorie Newell.)

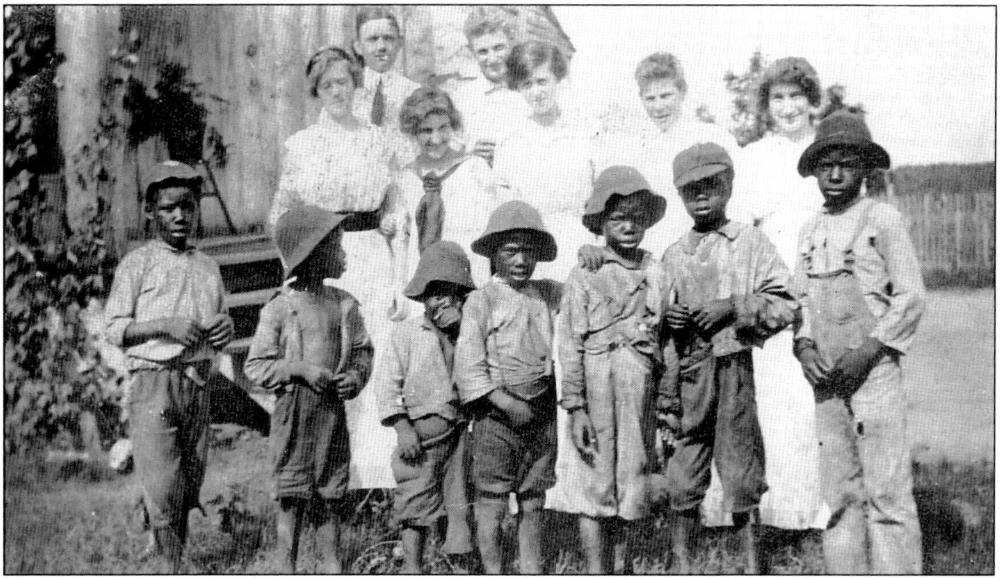

This photograph, taken around 1915, shows a group of children on the Ferrell-Nolan-Fletcher Plantation on State Line Road north of West Point. The plantation house was situated in Alabama, but most of the property, originally 1,200 acres, was located eastward in Georgia. The white children may be Nolan children and relatives, and the African American children would have belonged to tenant families living on the plantation. (Courtesy of CMA.)

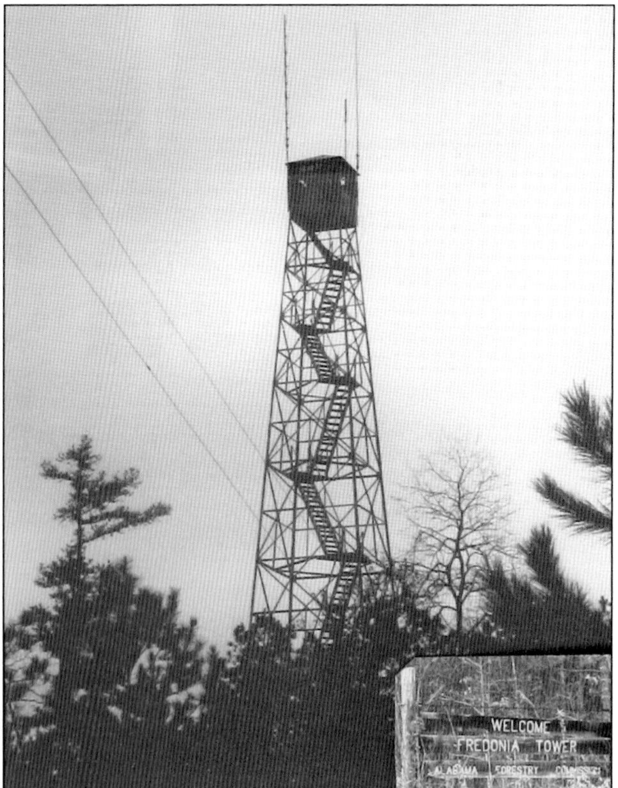

The Fredonia fire tower, erected on the site of the 1850s Southern Military Academy, served its region from the 1940s to the 1980s. This manned tower demonstrated the importance of forest products to landowners as the cotton culture declined. Much farmland never experienced cultivation by tractors but was converted to forests as mule and plow cropping declined in the 1940s and 1950s. (Courtesy of Forrest Abney.)

Two

Communities, Villages, and Towns

Only two incorporated areas in Chambers County sustained growth in population and economic diversity in the first 150 years of the history of the county. These were the textile town of Lanett and LaFayette, the commercial agricultural center and county seat. The villages of Cusseta, Oak Bowery, Fredonia, Stroud, and Five Points received town charters but did not sustain growth. Cusseta, Oak Bowery, and Fredonia experienced bursts of prosperity and population growth in the antebellum period but stabilized as agricultural communities in the late 19th century. The Five Points and Stroud charters resulted from local optimism surrounding the completion in the 1880s of a Central of Georgia Railroad line, which was built south to north on the central ridge from Opelika in Lee County to Roanoke in Randolph County. Following an initial period of house, store, and school construction, Five Points and Stroud experienced decline by the 1940s. Stroud lost its charter, and Five Points lost its train station. Both villages continued to exist with their farm supply stores and post offices at their crossroads.

Before 1900, at least 70 community locations were identified as post offices at one time or another. Many of these designations would persist throughout the 19th century in the rural crossroads communities where one or two farm supply stores, a gristmill, sawmill, and cotton gin might be located. Most of these designations and their little communities would simply disappear over time as land ownership consolidated and populations declined when rural families moved to locations that offered opportunity for a better life. Many of the community names, such as Bloomingdale, Finley, Mount Jefferson, and Wickerville, are almost lost to memory and may be identified only through archival materials. Some small communities, such as Five Points and Milltown, did survive with their clubs, schools, churches, and general stores through the mid-20th century.

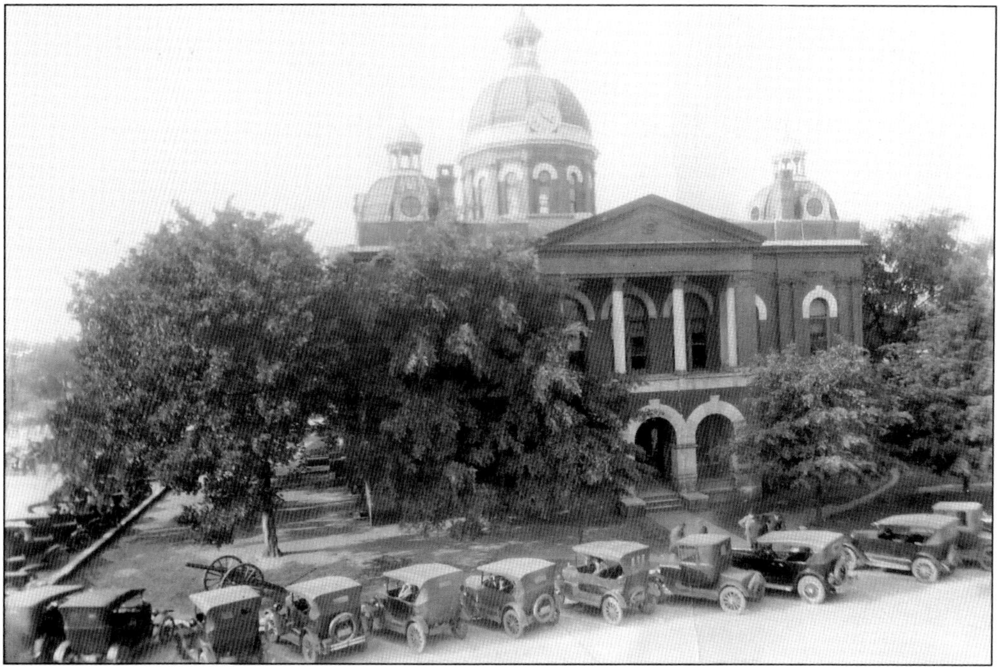

In 1899, under the leadership of probate judge A. J. Driver, citizens of Chambers County built a new courthouse at a cost of $30,000. This view of the south entrance looking north was photographed from atop Collins Drug Store. A cannon once used for coastal defense at Key West, Florida, guarded the southwest corner of the lawn and was donated for scrap during World War II. (Courtesy of Bill Bowling.)

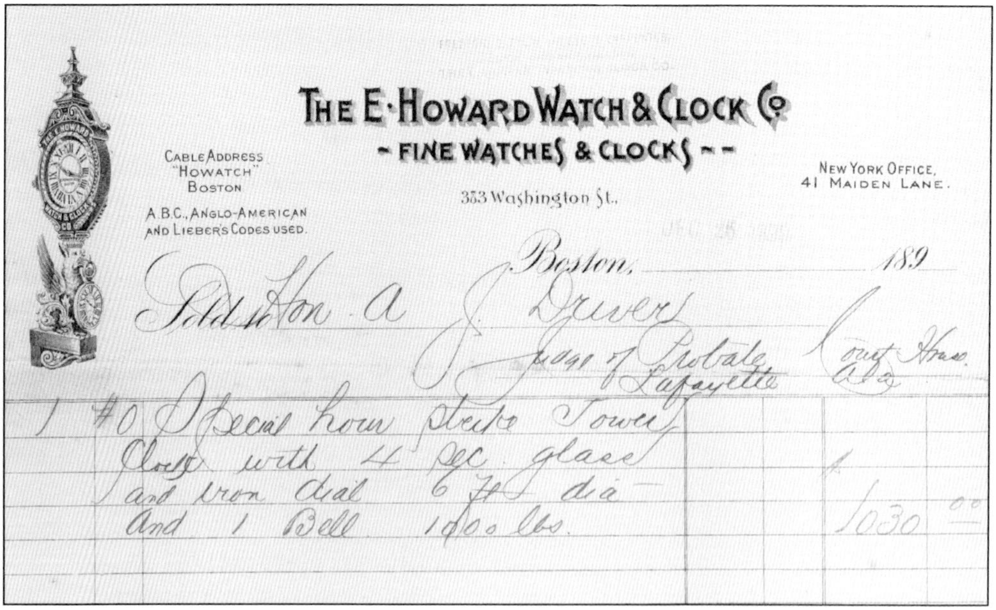

THE E·HOWARD WATCH & CLOCK Co

- FINE WATCHES & CLOCKS - -

Cable Address "Howatch" Boston

A.B.C., Anglo-American and Lieber's Codes used.

333 Washington St.,

New York Office, 41 Maiden Lane.

Boston, 189

Sold to Hon. A. J. Driver, Judge of Probate, Lafayette, Court House, Ala.

1 #0 Special hour strike Tower Clock with 4 sec. glass and Iron dial 6 Feet dia. And 1 Bell 1000 lbs. $1030 00

The origin of the clock in the 1899 Chambers County Courthouse has been the subject of much debate and speculation over the years. Many people believed it to be from the previous courthouse. However, this 1899 receipt from the E. Howard Watch and Clock Company in the amount of $1,030 proves the clock was purchased for the new courthouse. (Courtesy of CCM.)

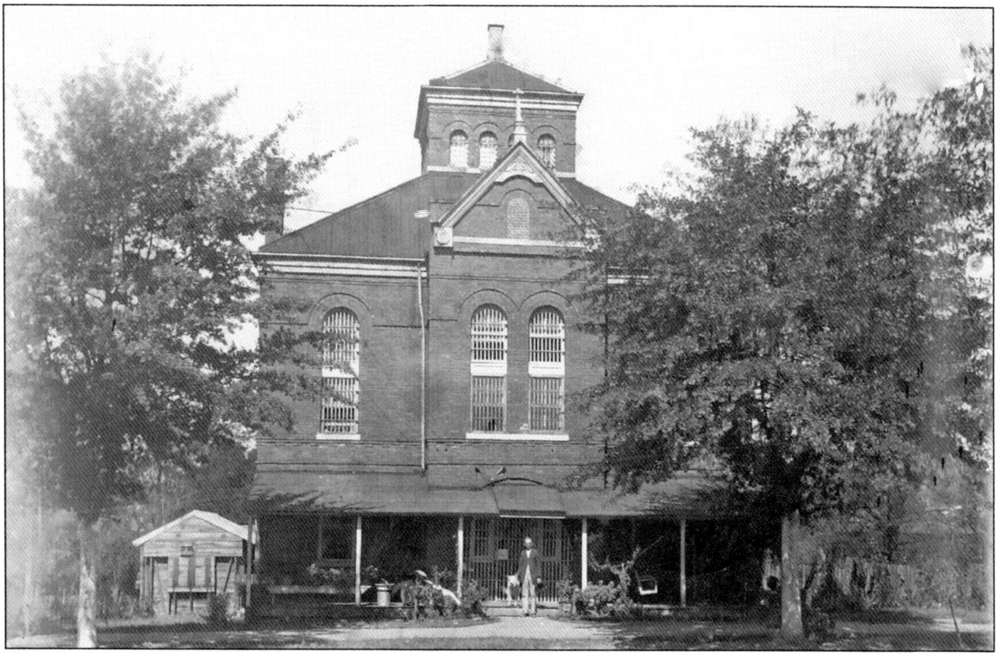

This foreboding structure was the 19th century place of incarceration for lawbreakers in Chambers County and was known as the "calaboose." The jail keeper and his family lived on the first floor, preparing meals, washing, and performing other housekeeping duties for the prisoners on the floors above. The building was demolished in 1955. (Courtesy of Vicki Brown Sanders.)

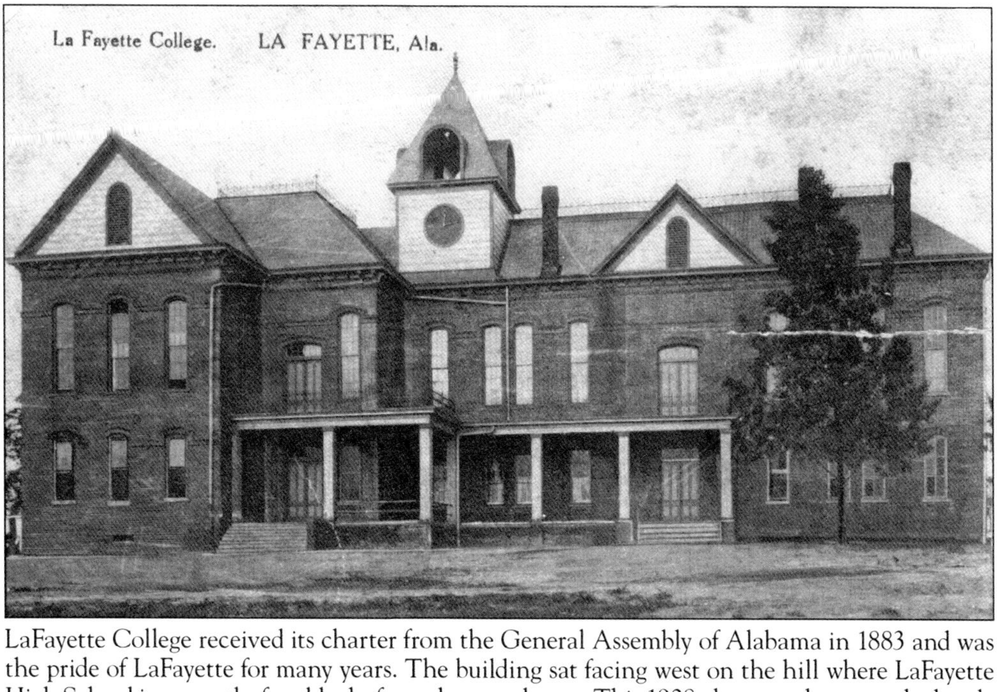

LaFayette College received its charter from the General Assembly of Alabama in 1883 and was the pride of LaFayette for many years. The building sat facing west on the hill where LaFayette High School is presently, four blocks from the courthouse. This 1908 photograph was made shortly after a major addition was completed. A large percentage of the alumni entered the teaching profession. (Courtesy of the Leonard Blanton Collection.)

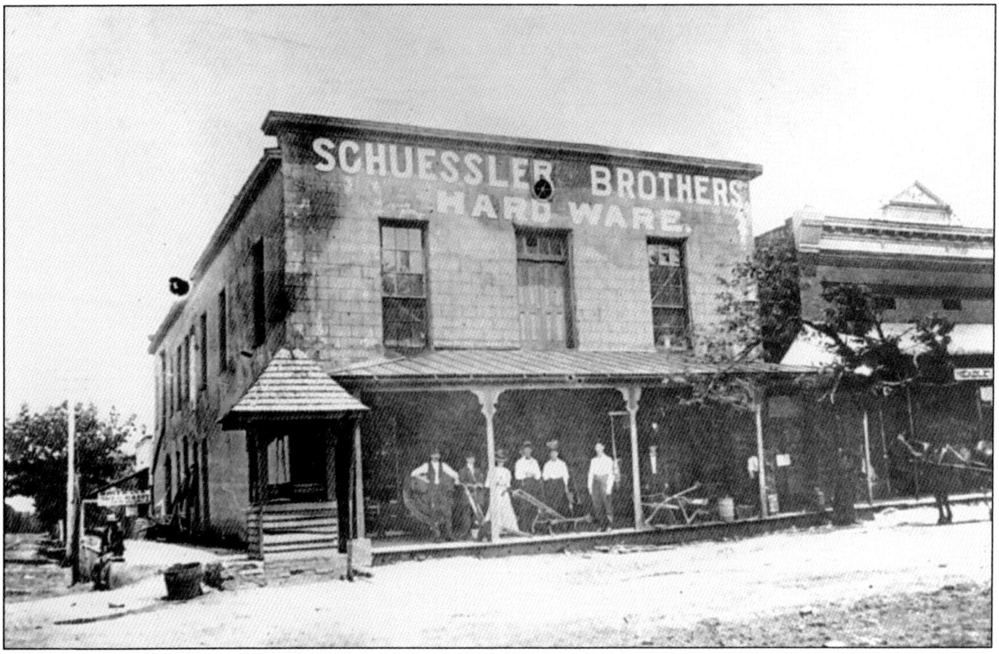

Schuessler Brother Hardware was located on the northwest corner of the square in LaFayette. Lewis Schuessler, a German immigrant, came to Chambers County and was very successful in his business ventures. This building was later replaced by the Martin Theatre. One of several public wells around town can also be seen in this photograph. (Courtesy of CCM.)

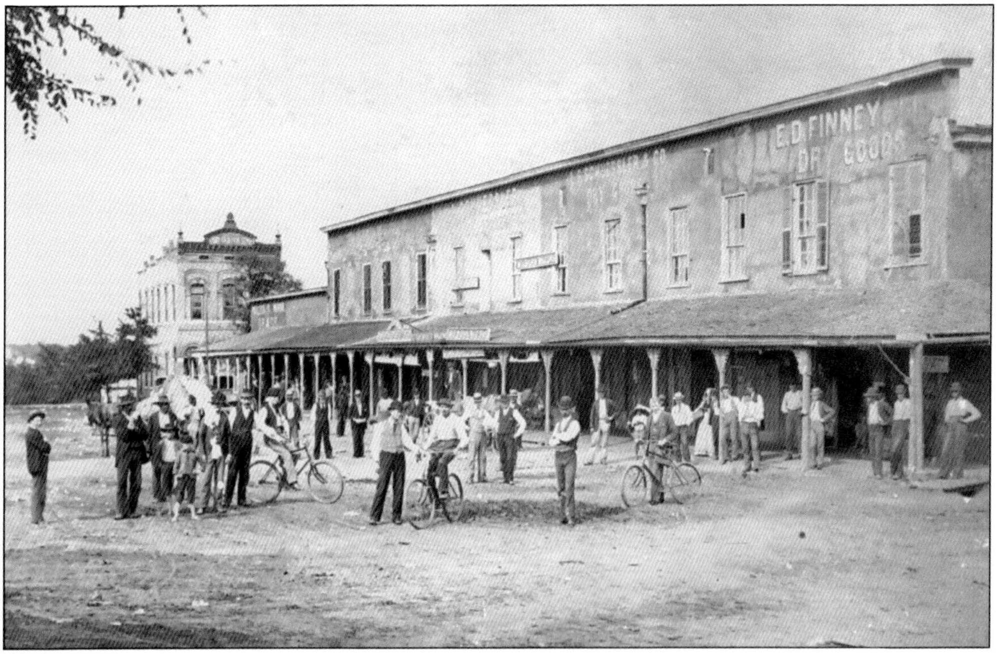

This early 1890s view of the east side of the square in LaFayette shows the two-story Bank of LaFayette building in the distance. Walter B. Wood's Drug Store is the building on the corner. The remaining two-story brick buildings were destroyed by a fire some years later. (Courtesy of CCM.)

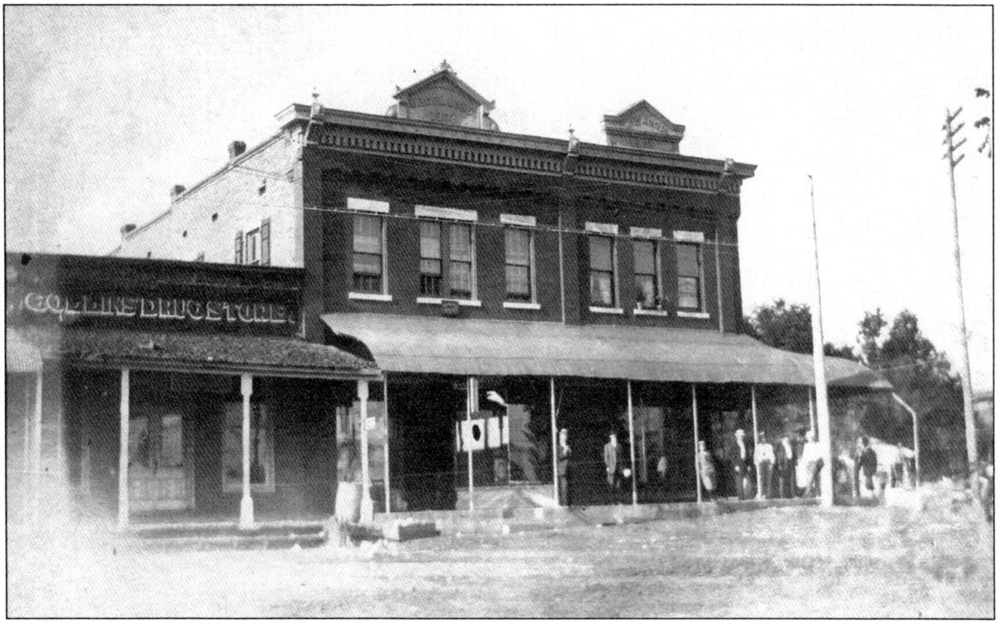

G. E. Collins established Collins Drug Store in 1888. This *c.* 1910 photograph shows the business in a small building next door to the two-story structure built by Collins and Walter B. Wood in 1908. Offices on the second floor were used by various attorneys and doctors. In 1929, Collins expanded and occupied the entire first floor. A landmark in LaFayette, the drug store closed in 1996. (Courtesy of Bill Bowling.)

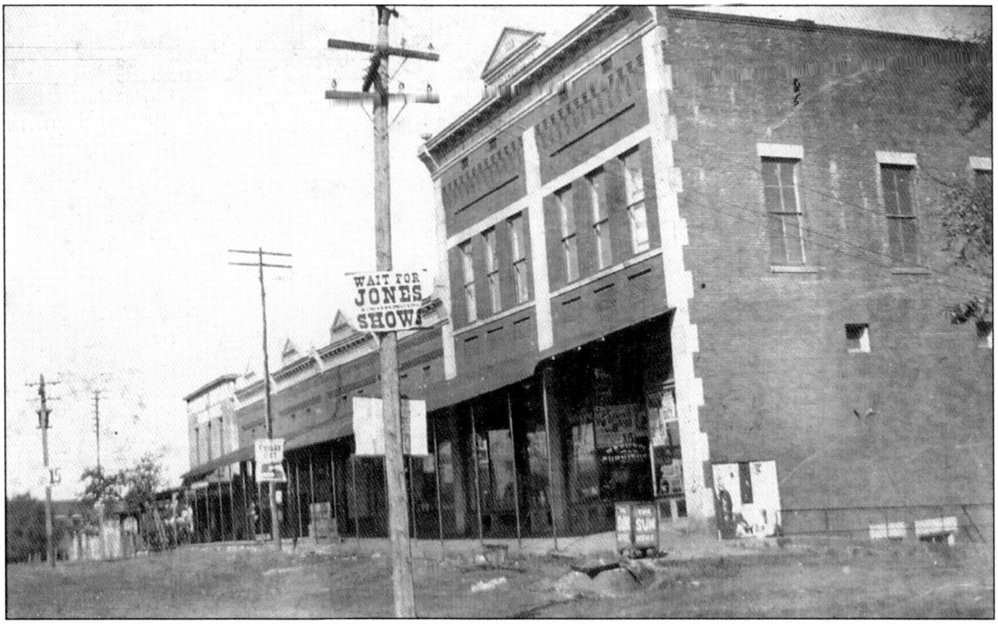

Wood's Opera House was built in 1902 on Bacheldor's Corner by Walter B. Wood and J. C. Griffin. The second-floor opera hall boasted electric lights, exquisite stage scenery, and other modern equipment and furnishings. Hollingsworth Dry Goods occupied the retail space of the lower floor. This cultural achievement was said to "give LaFayette an ascendancy over her sister cities." During the 1940s, it was destroyed by fire. (Courtesy of Bill Bowling.)

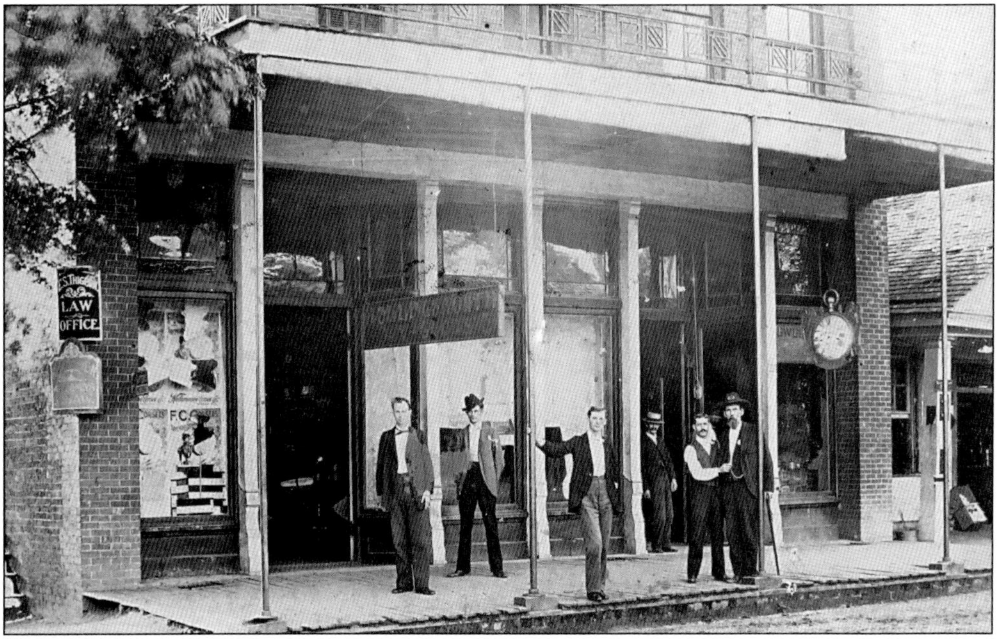

This 1890s photograph shows sheriff Reuben F. Gilder at far right with a group of unidentified men in front of the Hightower Building in LaFayette. Signs identify the law offices of J. Thomas Heflin and E. S. Thigpen on the second floor. Hollingsworth Dry Goods and McConnaghy Jewelers are identified on the street level. (Courtesy of Bill Bowling.)

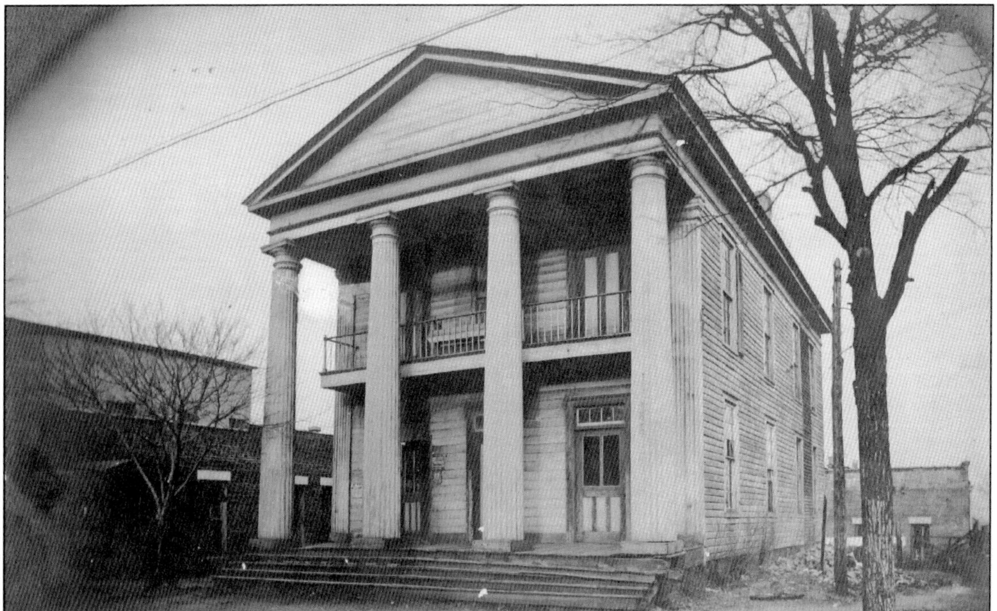

This handsome Greek Revival building was completed around 1855, with the Masonic lodge in LaFayette occupying the second floor. Ground floor offices were used by various individuals and also Western Union Telegraph. The broad front steps were a popular place for citizens to stop and chat. In 1926, the building was replaced by the present brick structure. (Courtesy of Bill Bowling.)

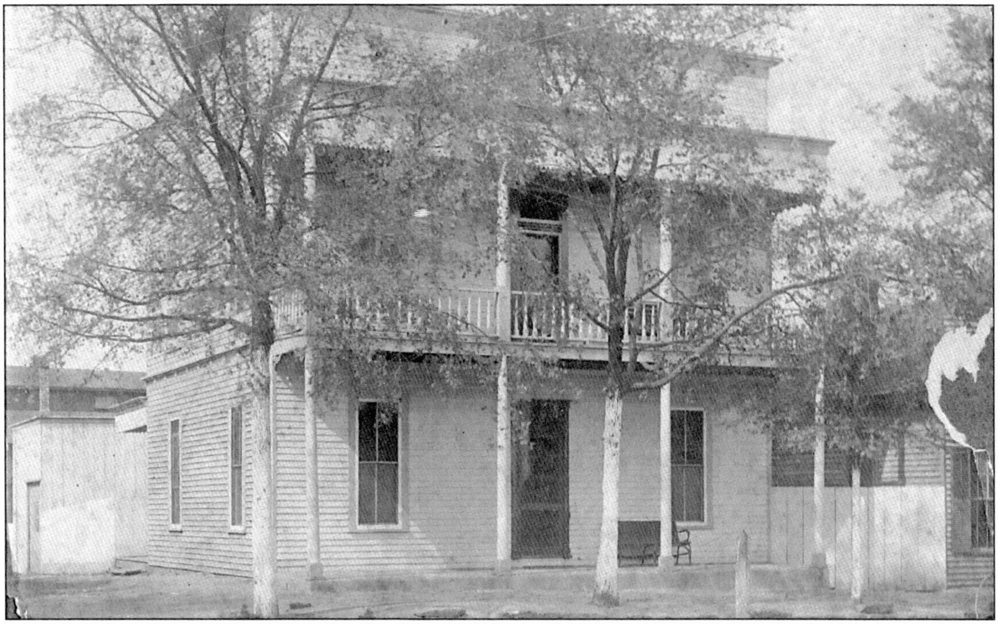

The Gaines-Wheeler Sanitarium in LaFayette was opened by Dr. William D. Gaines, who for a short period was in partnership with Dr. Nicholas A. Wheeler Sr. Dr. Wheeler later opened Wheeler Clinic and Hospital. Dr. Gaines spent a large part of his later career working in Atmore, Alabama. A 1903 map of LaFayette shows this building being used as a photographer's gallery. (Courtesy of Carolyn Edge Wheeler.)

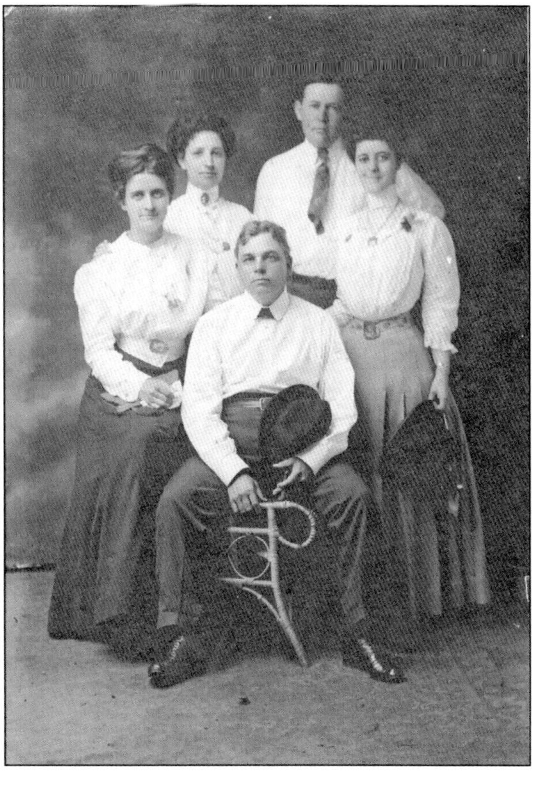

Pictured standing from left to right in this early 1900s photograph are Jessie West, Maggie Pearson, Dr. Nicholas A. Wheeler Sr., and Leila Rogers (later Mrs. Wheeler). Seated is probate judge John W. A. Vardaman. The three ladies were nurses at the Gaines-Wheeler Sanitarium in LaFayette. (Courtesy of Carolyn Edge Wheeler.)

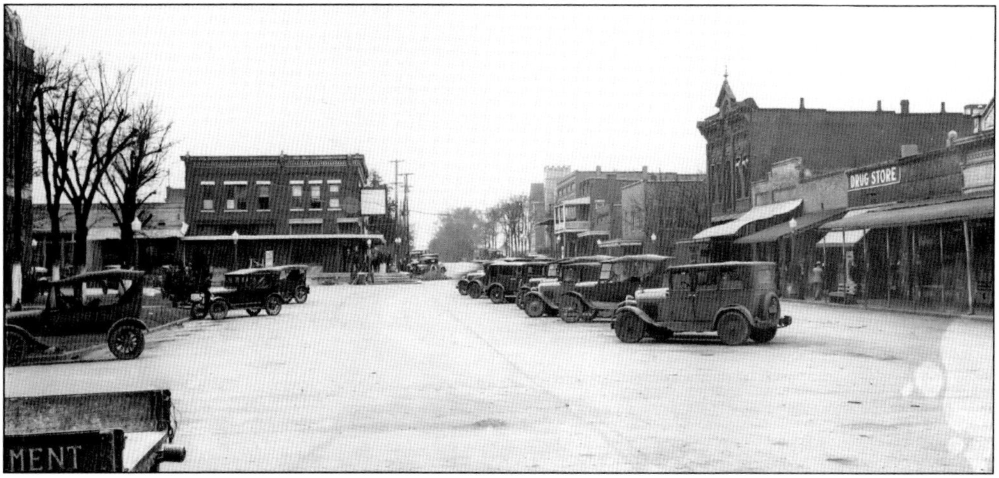

This 1930s LaFayette photograph was taken from the west corner on the north side of Courthouse Square, looking south on what is now U. S. Highway 431. Directly opposite on the left is Collins Drug Store. The tall structure to the right is the Hightower Building. (Courtesy of the Leonard Blanton Collection.)

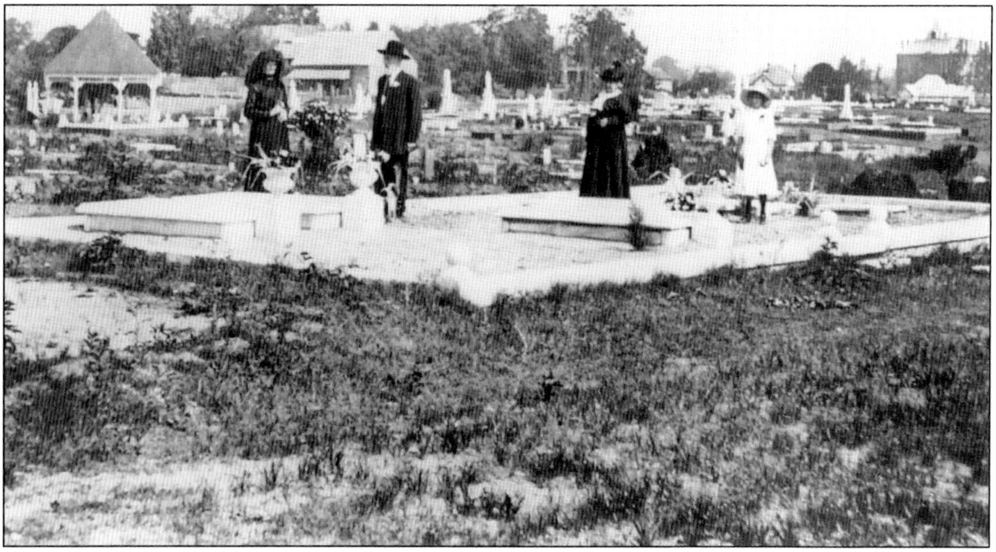

Members of the William Allen family are shown at the family plot in LaFayette Cemetery in the early 1900s. At left is Harriet Allen Bowling, who appears to be dressed in mourning clothes. The gazebo in the background at left was built for Confederate Memorial Day programs. At far right is LaFayette College with the old Blanton home directly in front of it. (Courtesy of Allen Jones.)

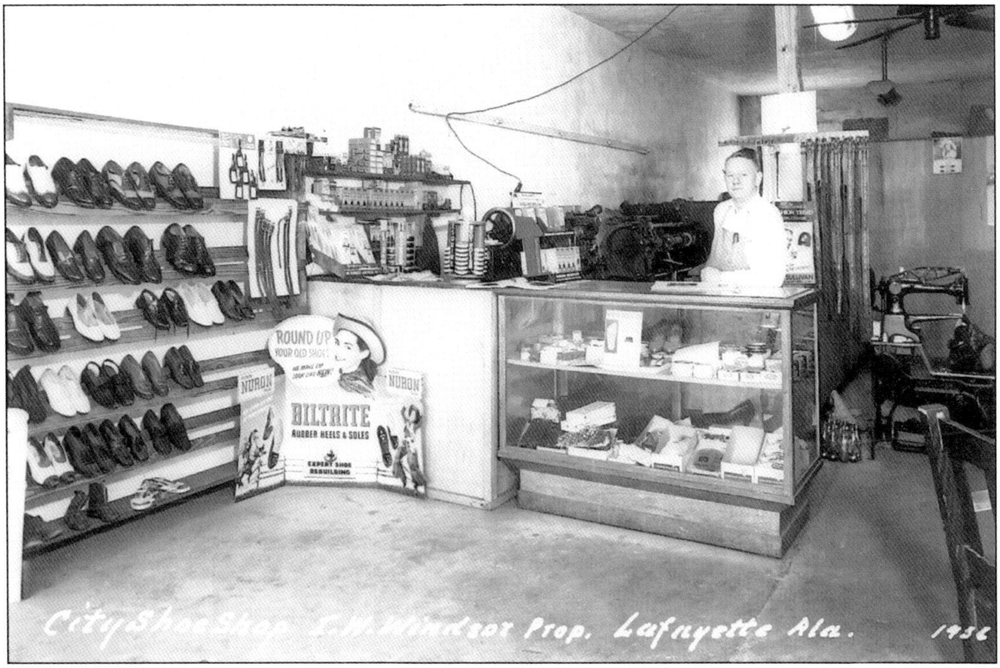

This 1956 photograph shows I. W. "Red" Windsor, the proprietor of City Shoe Shop in LaFayette. The repair of shoes and other leather goods was in demand, as the town also had two other such establishments—Gresham's and Roy Smith's shoe shops. The smell of leather and Windsor's good nature always greeted his customers as they entered the shop. (Courtesy of CMA.)

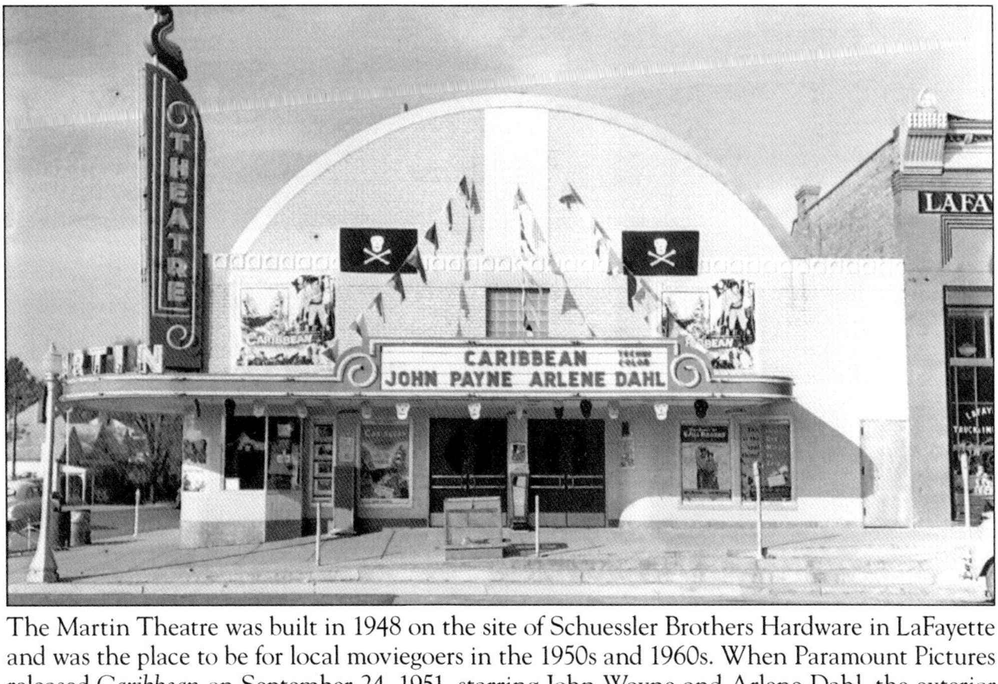

The Martin Theatre was built in 1948 on the site of Schuessler Brothers Hardware in LaFayette and was the place to be for local moviegoers in the 1950s and 1960s. When Paramount Pictures released *Caribbean* on September 24, 1951, starring John Wayne and Arlene Dahl, the exterior of the theatre was decorated in a pirate theme to promote the movie. (Courtesy of C. A. Spence Jr. Collection.)

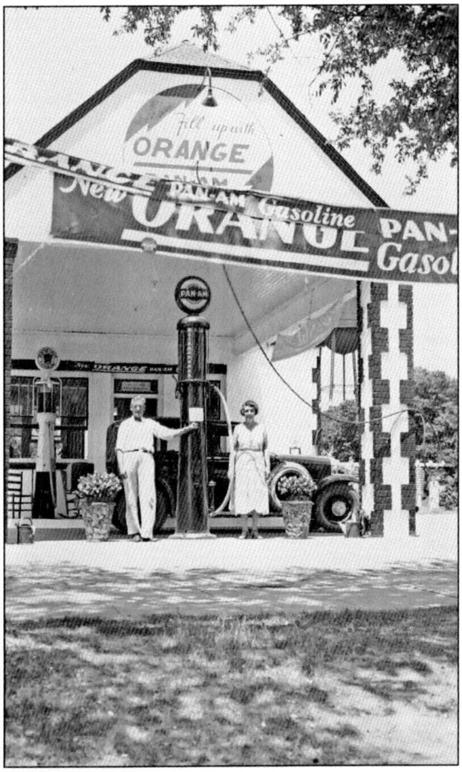

In the 1930s, W. B. and Mary Trent opened a gas station on the corner north of the Baptist church on LaFayette Street. Two earlier houses originally stood on this site, one owned by Henry Kellam, an early Chambers County sheriff, and another by the David G. Allen family. Jimmy Rogers later operated a restaurant in this building for many years. (Courtesy of Drusilla Lamb Abernathy.)

Until it was demolished in the early 1960s, the Bank of LaFayette building, constructed around 1885, stood on the front lawn of the present Farmers and Merchants Bank. The entire second floor was used as office space and meeting chambers for the Knights of Phythias, a fraternal organization. The bank closed in the early years of the Depression but reopened in the mid-1930s. (Courtesy of C. A. Spence Jr. Collection.)

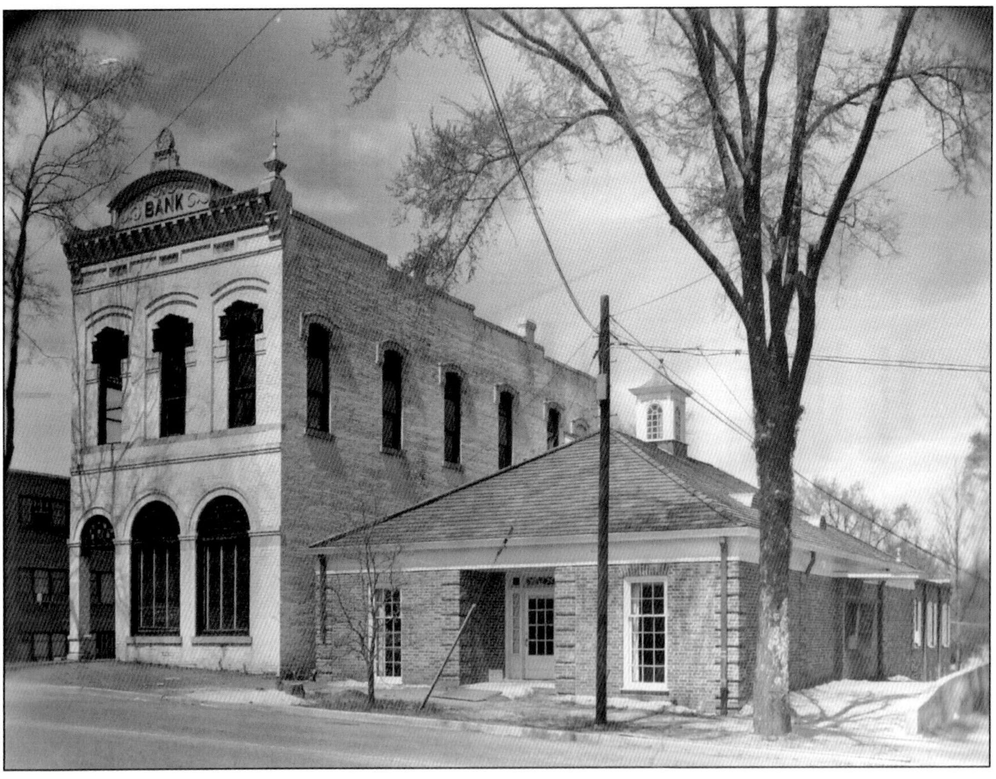

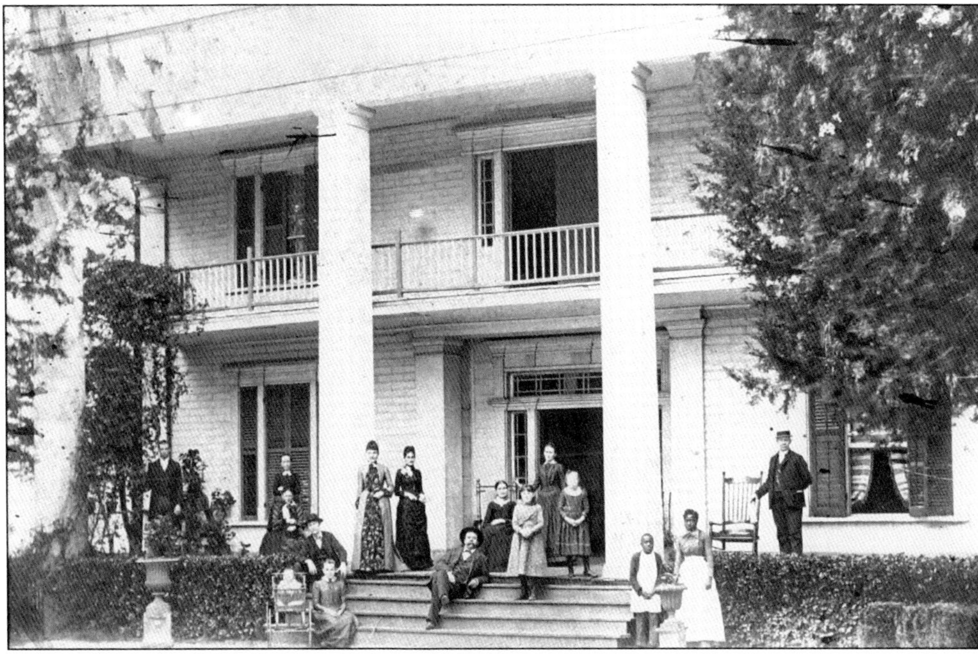

Sarah Andrews, the widow of Dr. Isham W. Andrews, is seated on the front veranda of her home with other family members. This 1850s house was located directly south of the Baptist church. During the Civil War, lookouts were stationed on the high flat roof to warn the town of any approaching enemy. (Courtesy of Marjorie Andrews.)

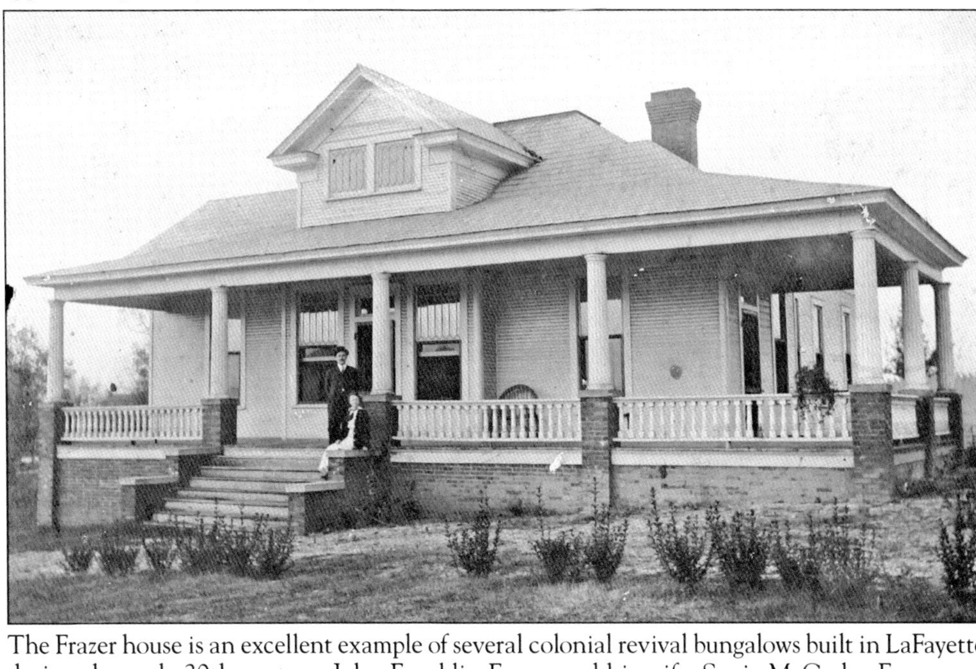

The Frazer house is an excellent example of several colonial revival bungalows built in LaFayette during the early 20th century. John Franklin Frazer and his wife, Senie McCarley Frazer, are shown shortly after their home was completed. Frazer was postmaster in LaFayette from 1913 to 1934. The Frazer and McCarley families were early settlers in the Buffalo community. (Courtesy of Reiley House.)

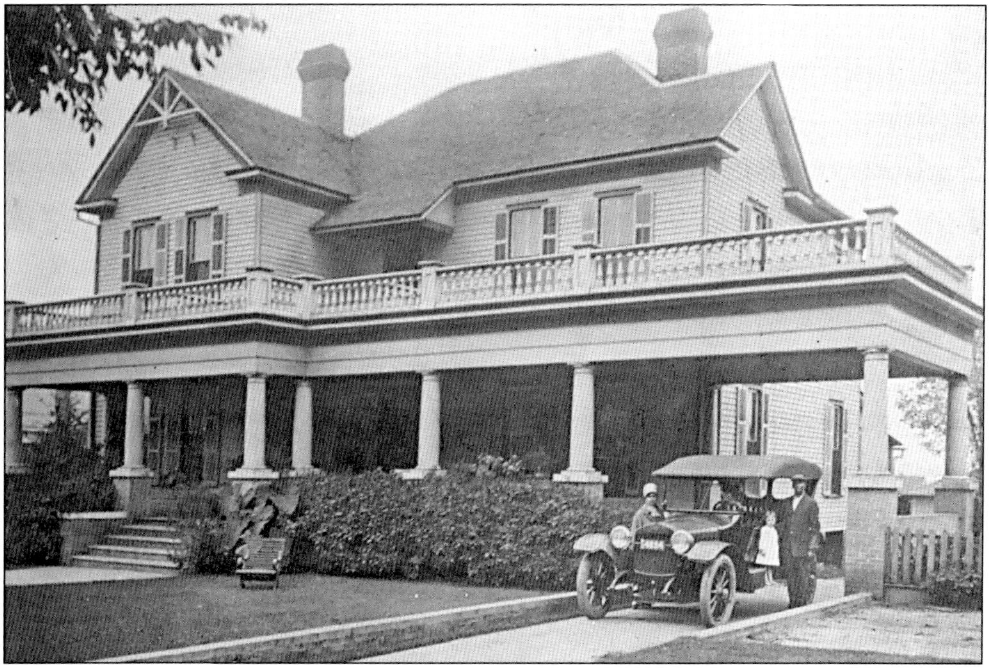

LaFayette physician Dr. William D. Gaines, wife Leila Tucker Gaines, and daughter Will are shown at their residence on Montgomery Street sometime after remodeling their antebellum house in 1913. The house featured a porte cochere or "carriage porch" that was a popular design feature at the time. In recent years, the old cook's house in the back was sacrificed for a swimming pool. (Courtesy of Carolyn Edge Wheeler.)

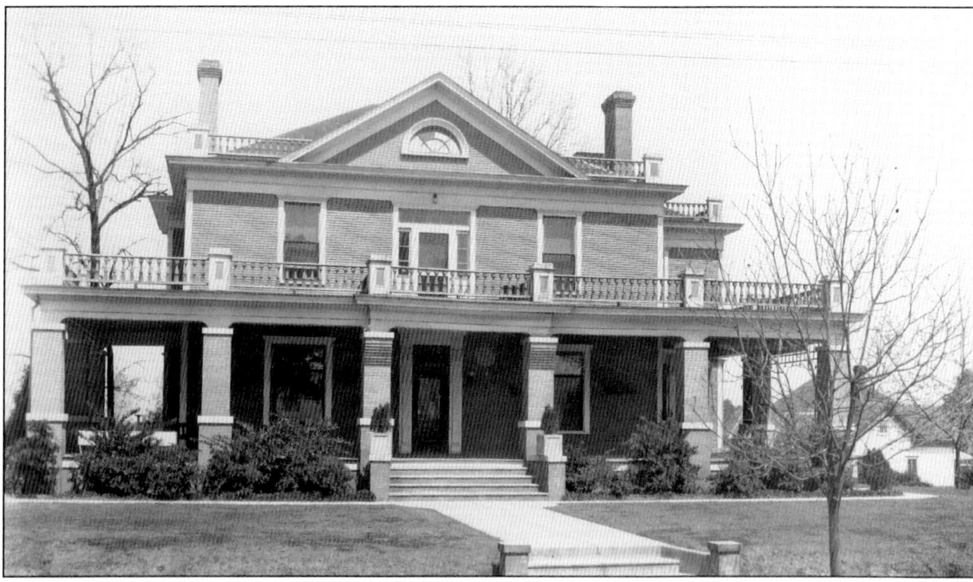

On Magnolia Street in LaFayette, Thomas E. Stanley removed pioneer Josiah Bacheldor's house from its prominent setting and replaced it in 1912. Only clear lumber free of knots was used in the construction. This house was one of the first town houses to have indoor plumbing. The families of Elder H. Roy Avery and Rev. Wayne Barrett have been the most recent owners. (Courtesy of Bill Bowling.)

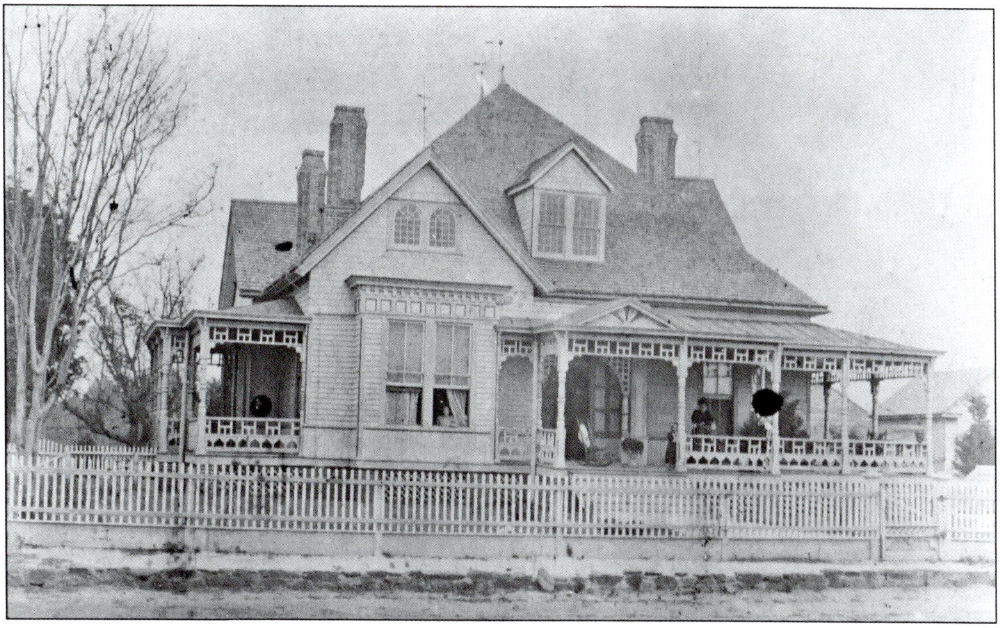

The Robinson house, built 1 mile east of LaFayette in the 1890s by judge J. J. Robinson Sr., was occupied by the J. J. Robinson Jr. family when this photograph was made. A fine example of high-style Victorian architecture, the house and lands were later sold to the Hunter family. Hunter Subdivision, north of Highway 50, was developed from this property. (Courtesy of Betty Chambers Carr.)

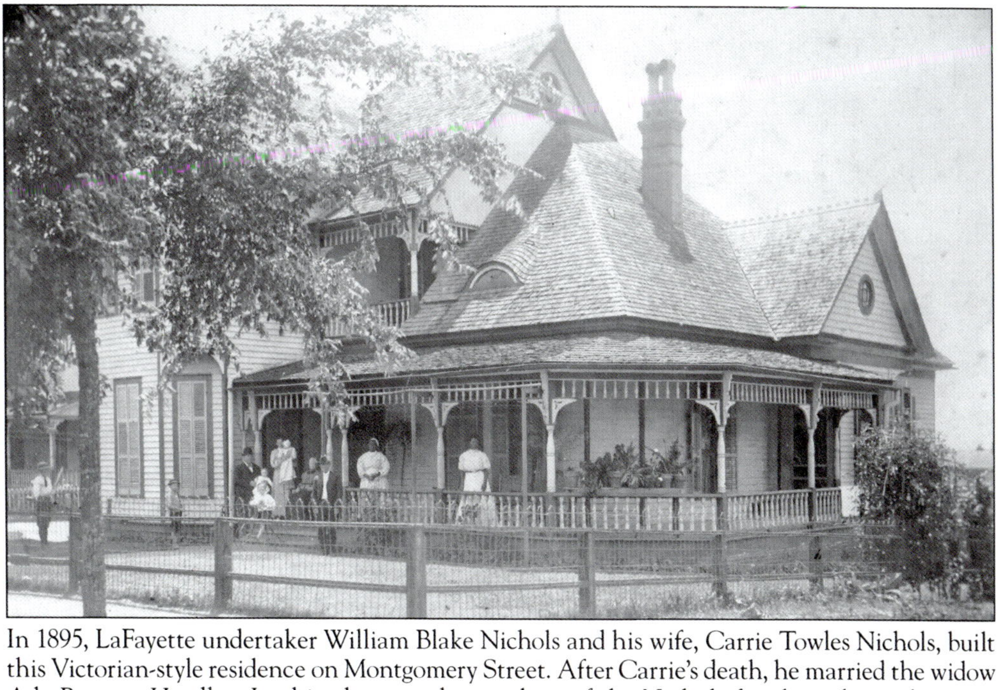

In 1895, LaFayette undertaker William Blake Nichols and his wife, Carrie Towles Nichols, built this Victorian-style residence on Montgomery Street. After Carrie's death, he married the widow Ada Pearson Headley. In this photograph, members of the Nichols family and two domestic helpers are posed on the veranda. In 1925, the house was bought by the Charles L. Torbert family. (Courtesy of Betty Chambers Carr.)

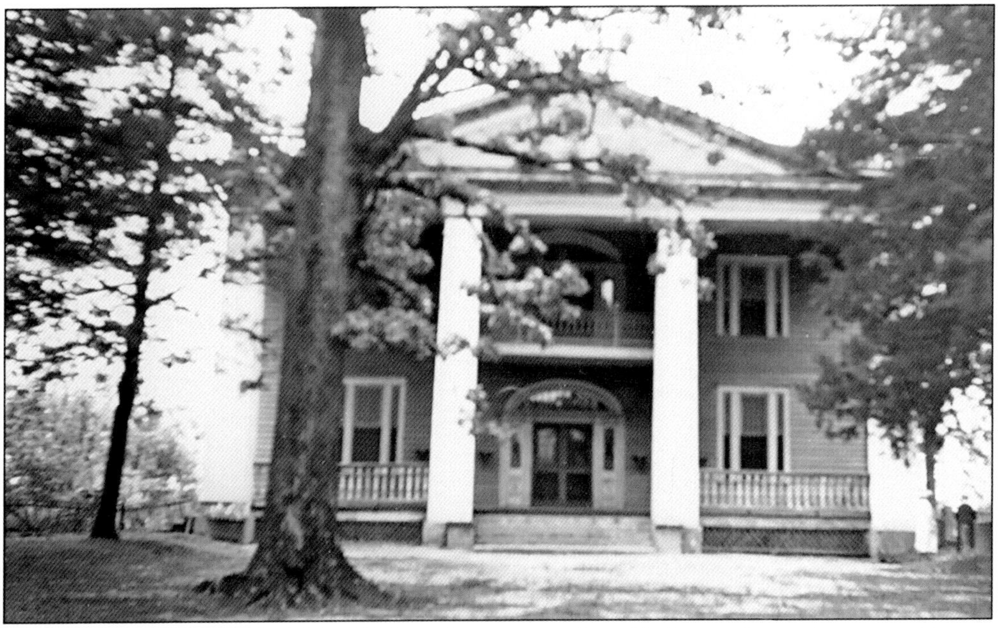

In 1840, a house built by Col. Waid Hill on the western edge of LaFayette burned. A second house of Greek Revival design was built, utilizing the four massive chimneys from the first house. In 1868, the house and lands were owned by Judge Jonathan Ware and were later inherited by his daughter Ella M. Ware Dowdell. Other owners have been the Ford, Grady, and Wallace families. (Courtesy of Bill Bowling.)

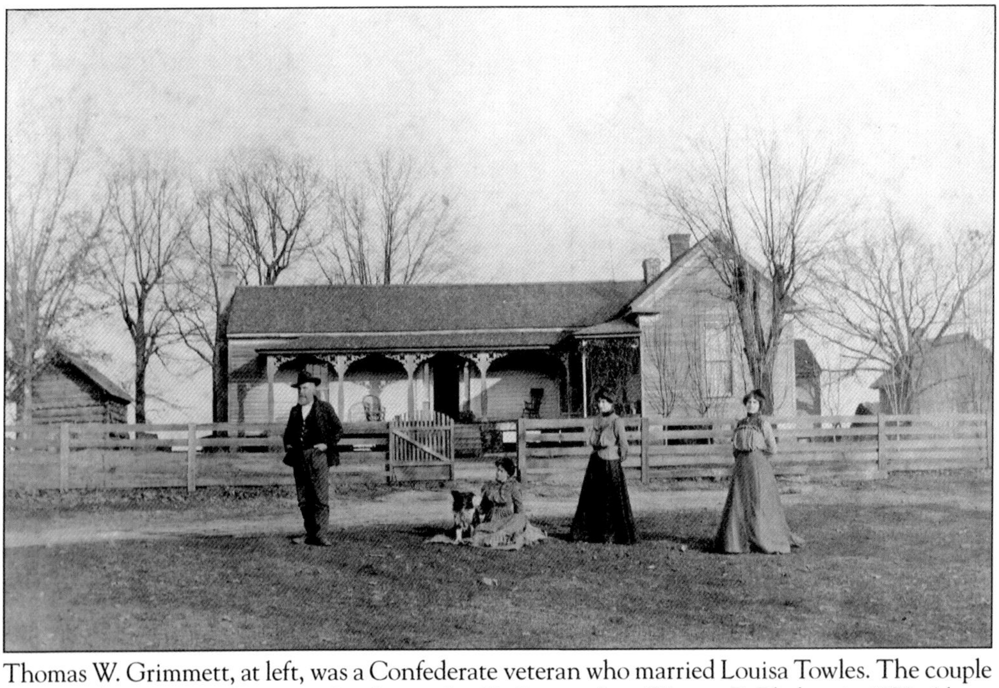

Thomas W. Grimmett, at left, was a Confederate veteran who married Louisa Towles. The couple purchased a 400-acre plantation 2 miles south of LaFayette from Warren B. Bledsoe in 1872. About 1890, a parlor room was built on the right and the Victorian trim was added. Later the Julian Cotter family lived here. The house burned around 1987. (Courtesy of Betty Chambers Carr.)

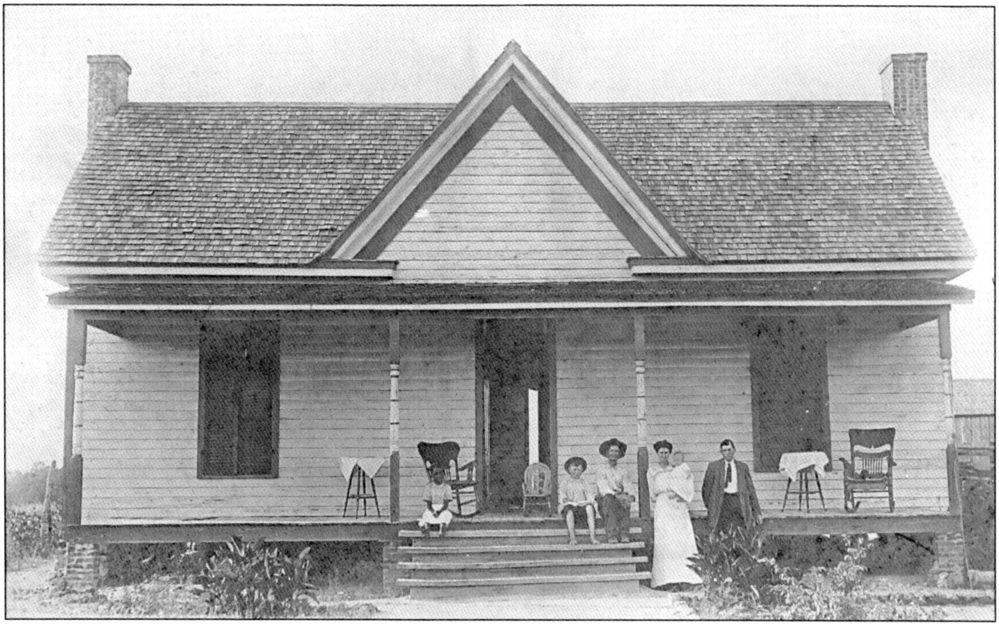

The David Allen Henderson home, located 2 miles south of LaFayette, was built in 1909. Adjoining acreage was given to the Hendersons as a wedding gift. From left to right are Effie Frederick (tenant's child), John Allen, John Wesley Henderson, Laura Lurlene Gammill Henderson holding Allene Henderson, and David Allen Henderson. Many similar houses were built by prosperous farmers in the early 20th century. (Courtesy of Allen Jones.)

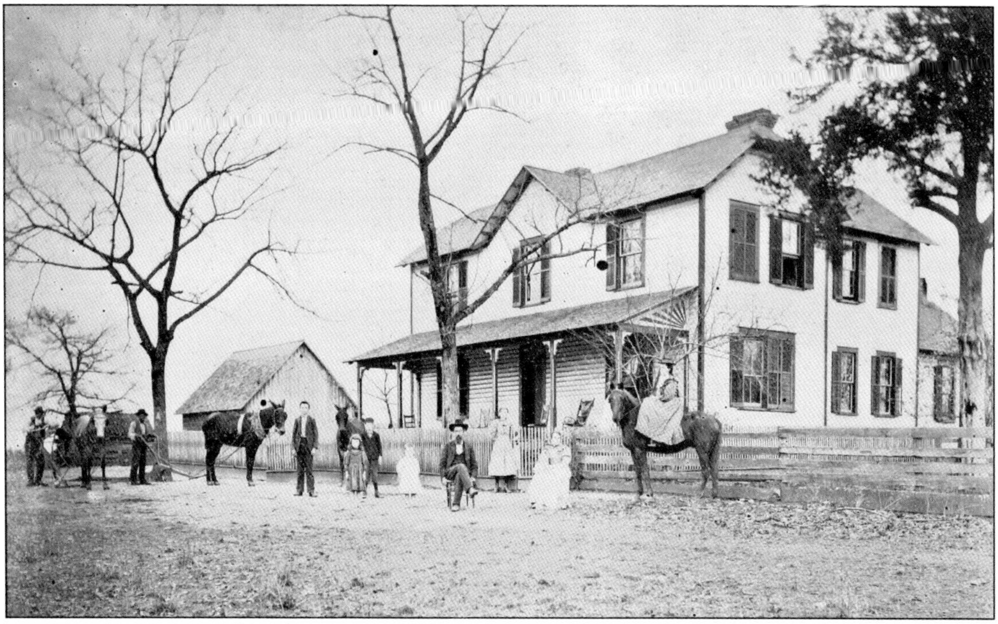

In 1898, the family of Mark Summerfield Andrews in the Sturkie community gathered for the American View Company's photographer to record their image. Andrews and his wife, Eliza F., are seated. Their eldest daughter, Mary Viola, who taught school at Sturkie, is on horseback. She later married Tom R. Ford. Wage hands and other Andrews children are also pictured. (Courtesy of Victoria L. Ford.)

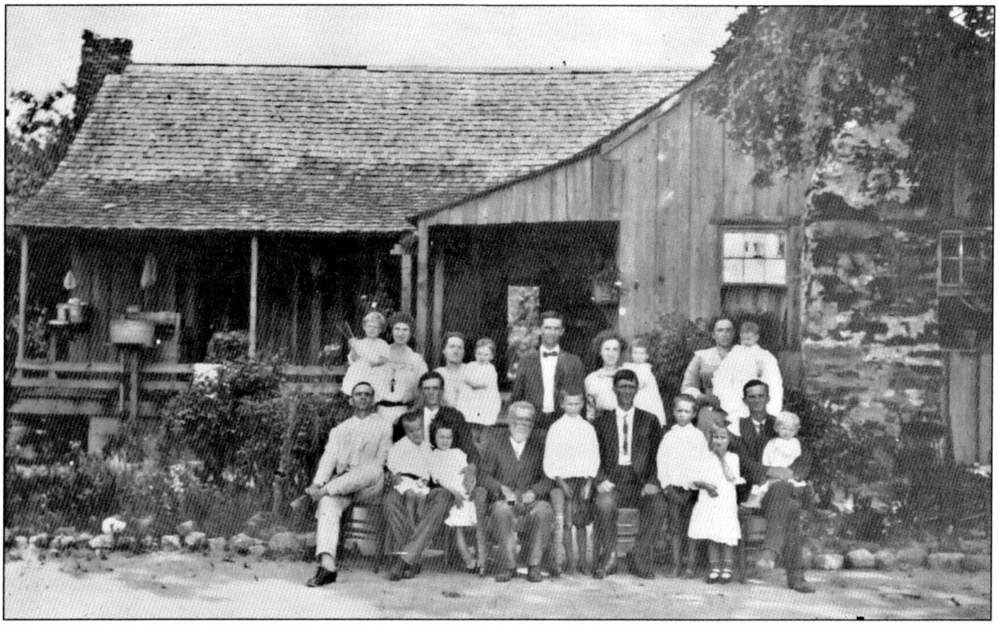

The five sons of Gideon Lazarus Leverett and their families gather for the photographer at the home of Bob Leverett on Leverett Mill's Road west of LaFayette around 1914. Gideon (seated center) was a Confederate veteran who served in Company A, 62nd Alabama Infantry Regiment. Sons pictured from left to right are Lewis, Bob, Dean, Will, and John. (Courtesy of Harriet Leverett Jones.)

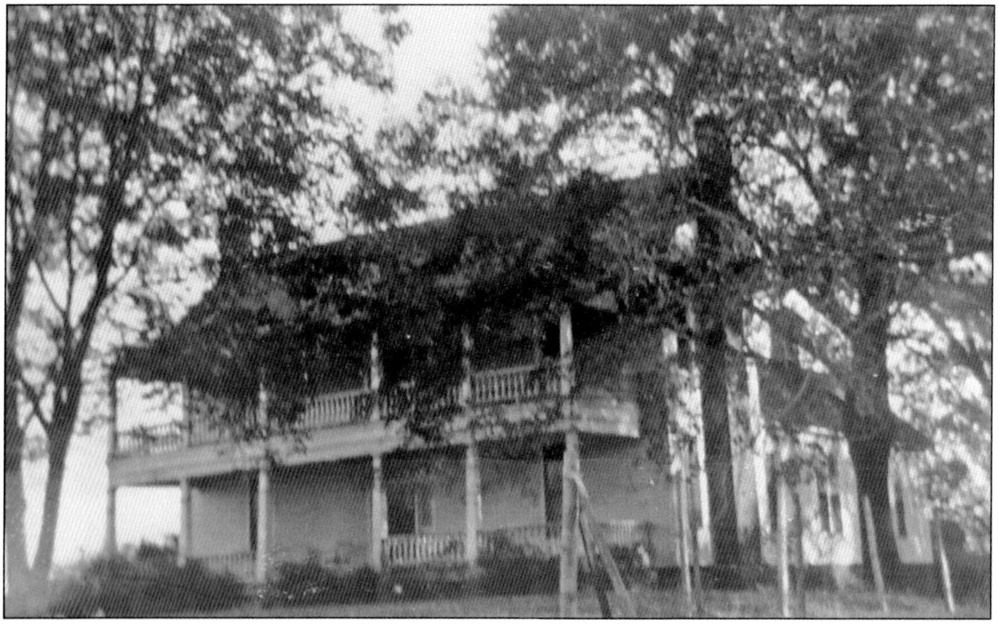

The antebellum residence of Thomas J. Brooks was the center of a prosperous plantation west of LaFayette. Later it was under the ownership of Charles Schuessler, who increased the acreage to over 1,000 acres. The William Farrington family owned the property from 1936 to 1950. Since 1971, the farm has been under the ownership of the Cornelius A. Noordermeer family from Holland. The house burned in 1987. (Courtesy of Kay Farrington Frost.)

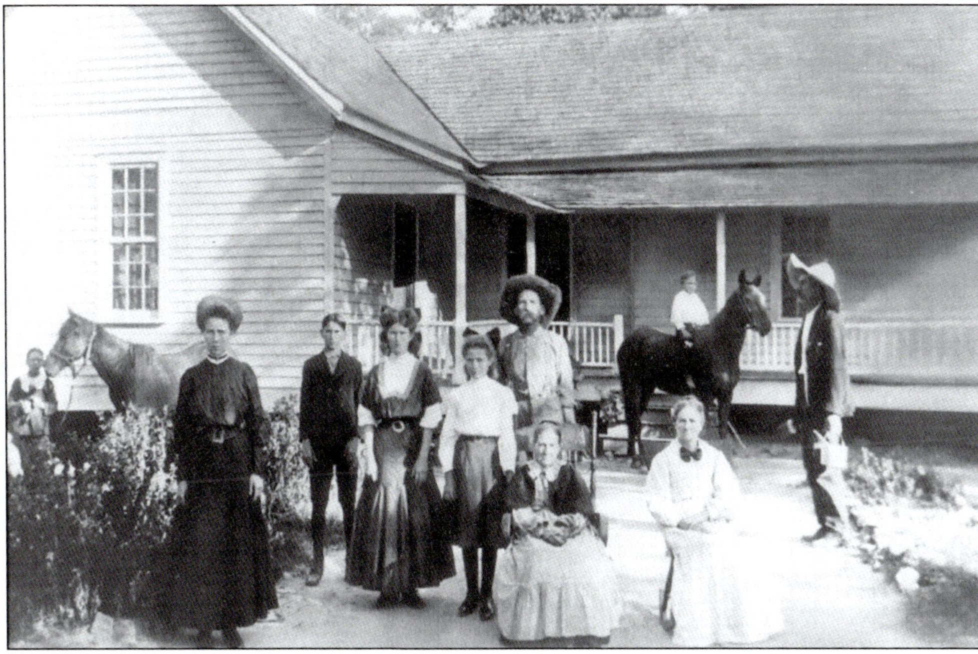

Located west of LaFayette was the attractive farm home of Thomas Abner Still, built in 1899. Pictured from left to right are an unidentified boy with a horse, Sara Savannah, an unidentified son, Janie Pearl, Laura Eugenia, Thomas Abner, Sarah Frances Tucker Still (mother of Thomas A.), Mary Augusta, and two unidentified. (Courtesy of Nina Still Langley.)

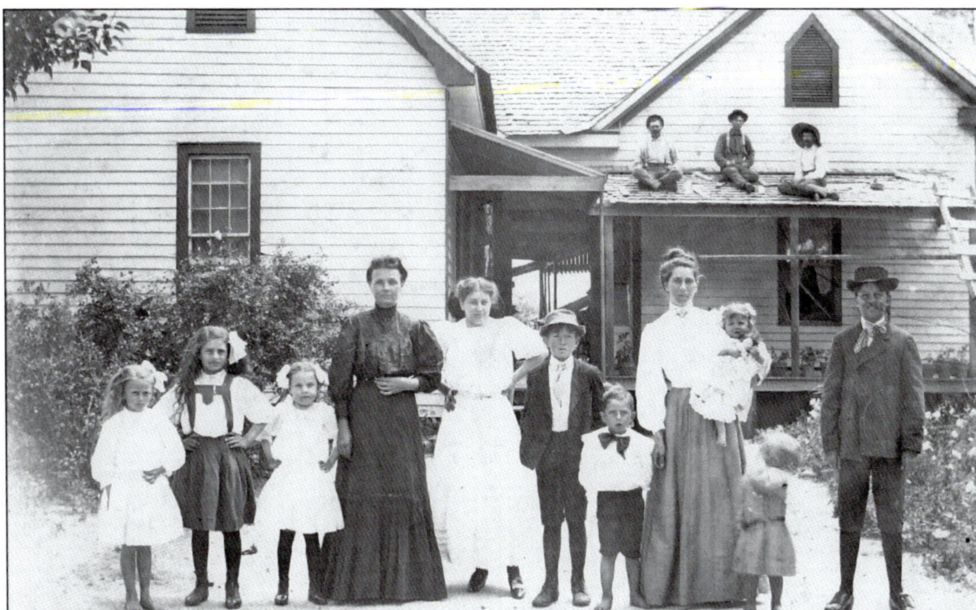

James A. Sanders's house at Ridge Grove is pictured about 1907. Standing from left to right are Floy Sanders, Era Sanders, Bessie Foster, Leila Foster, Eldora Foster, Kennon Foster, Jay Sanders, Lucy Martha Cotton Sanders, Myrtis Sanders (baby), Woodfin Sanders, and Marvin Foster. Working on the roof are James Alonza Sanders, John Foster, and unidentified. The house was later owned by the Foster and Yancey families. (Courtesy of Dinah Moss Estes.)

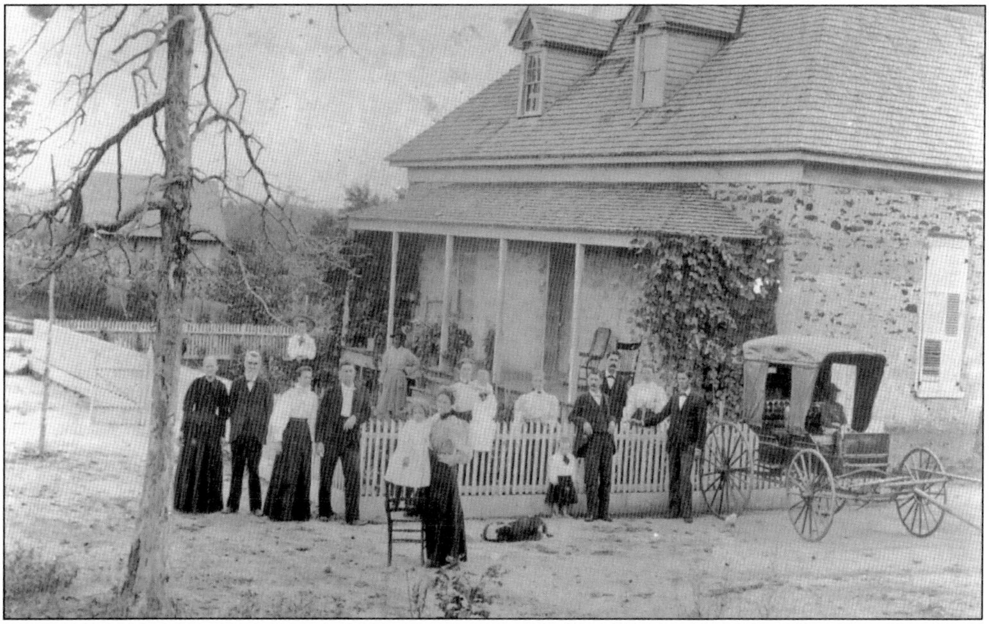

Amaziah Luther McCarley and his wife, Mary Ursula Smith McCarley, pictured at far left, began construction of their rock-walled house about 1895 near Lebanon Presbyterian Church, a short distance from Buffalo. Downstairs were four rooms and a hall, with a separate kitchen in the backyard. Upstairs rooms were in the large attic. This house later burned. (Courtesy of Jean Spence Nunn.)

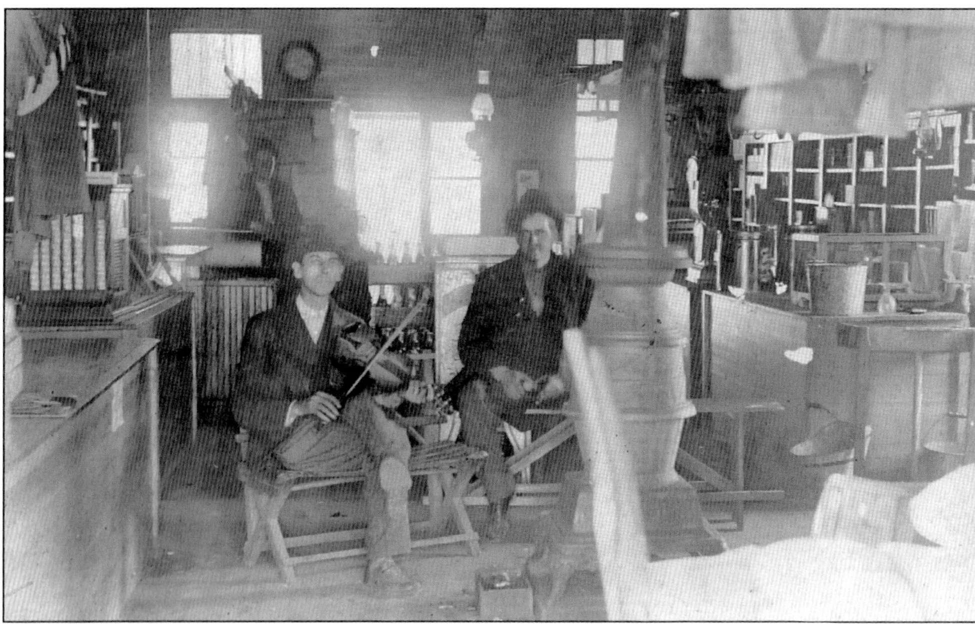

Webster Donelly Aldine Hunter, pictured with a violin, was the proprietor of Hunter's Store and postmaster at Buffalo from 1900 to 1925. To the right is Mack Thompson, and in the background is Morgan Spence. The store later burned but stood near the railroad and across from the Buffalo Depot. An interesting comment was written on the original cabinet card photograph, "Here many lies are told." (Courtesy of Eley C. Frazer.)

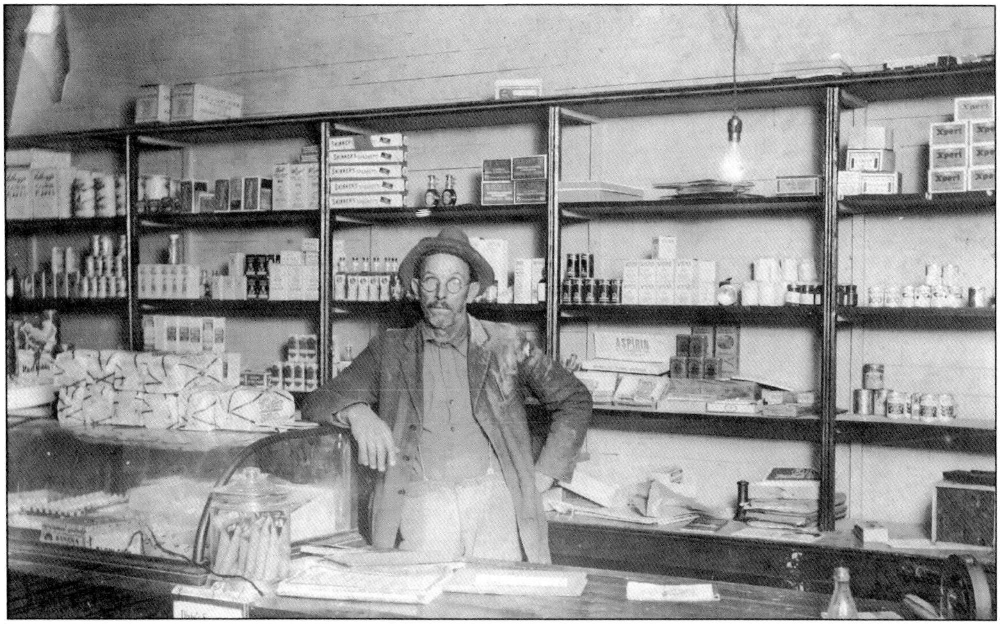

William Allie Harmon, a native of the Marcoot community, farmed and operated a mercantile business for a number of years. Prior to 1920, he sold out and moved his family to White Plains, where he opened another store. Allie Harmon's merchandise sales often came with free quotes of scripture, as he was quite knowledgeable of the Bible as well as family history. (Courtesy of the Nell Tomlinson Leverett.)

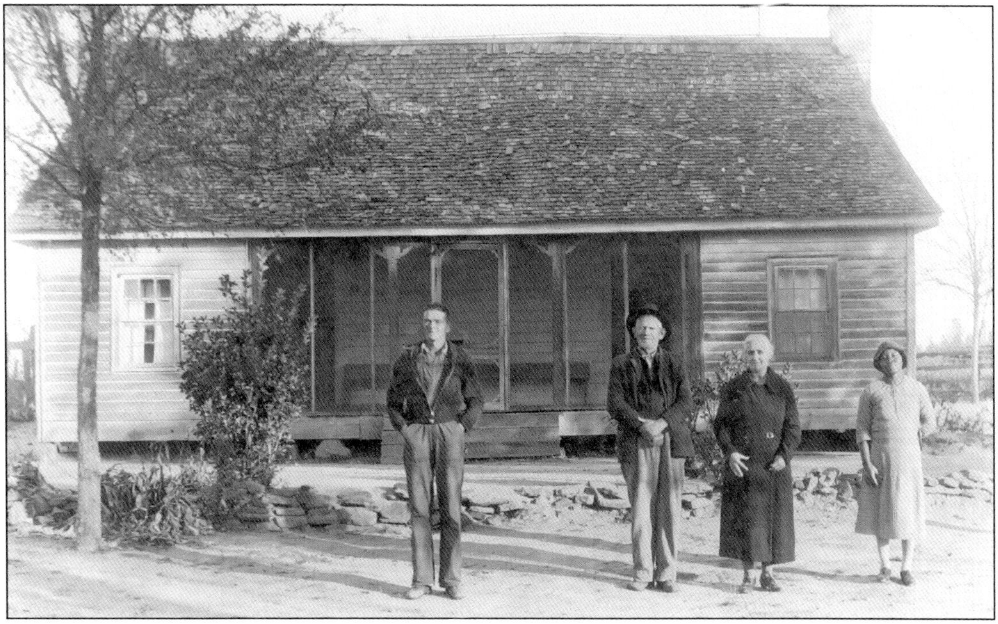

Located west of Penton was the home of George Washington and Neomie Eloise Hanson Turnham, pictured in the center of this photograph. The other people are unidentified. The Turnham house is typical of many rural dwellings built in the mid-19th century, with large middle rooms and smaller unheated shed rooms at the ends of front and rear porches. (Courtesy of Carolyn Edge Wheeler.)

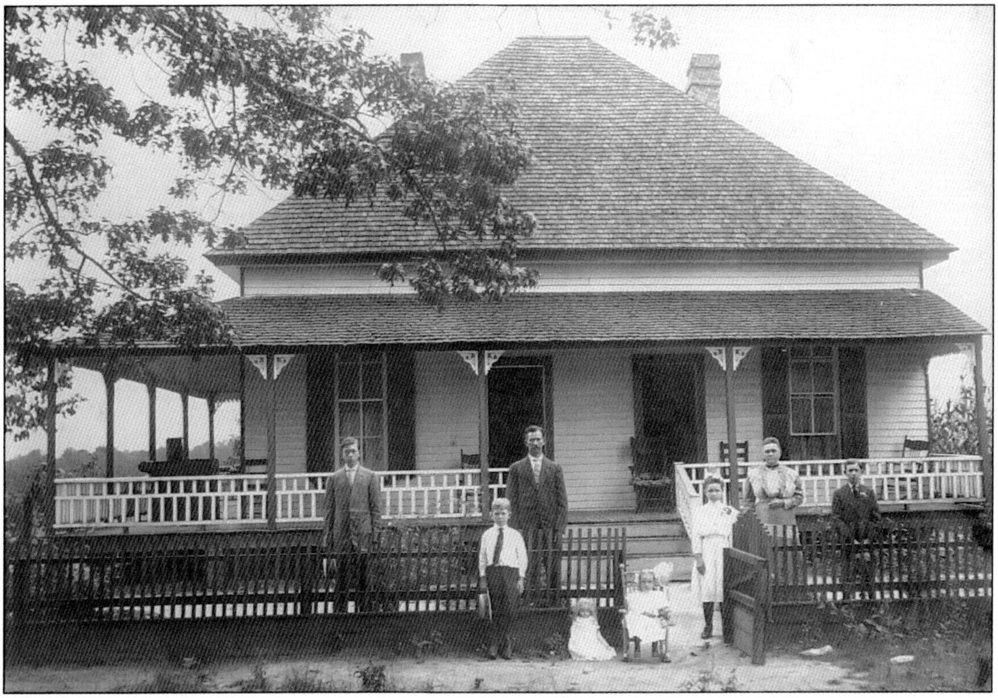

The comfortable and attractive home of the Stephens family was located a short distance south of New Harmony Church in northern Chambers County. In this *c.* 1910 image, from left to right are William Richmond, Kenon Irwin, Marion Richard, Eris Adelle, Bettie Mae, Martha Jane Muldrew and Vernie Hilt. This house no longer exists. (Courtesy of Laura Stephens Patterson.)

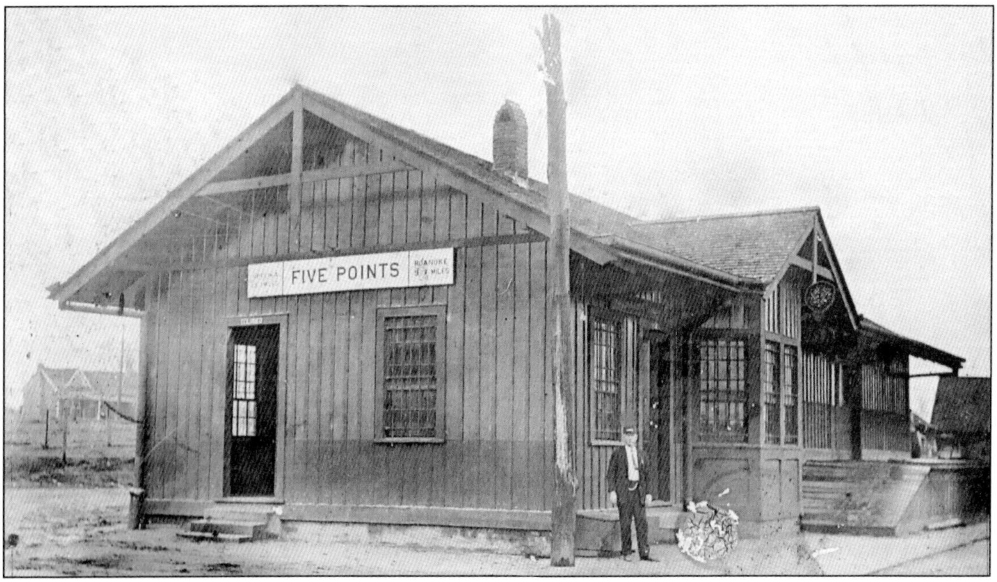

The Five Points Depot was built when the Central of Georgia extended its rail line northward from Buffalo to Roanoke in the 1880s. Pictured is George Washington Sorrell, who was the Five Points depot agent/telegraph operator for many years. A sign on the wall reads "Opelika 18.1 miles and Roanoke 9.7 miles." This building was later moved to Roanoke. (Courtesy of Freddie Pool Hill.)

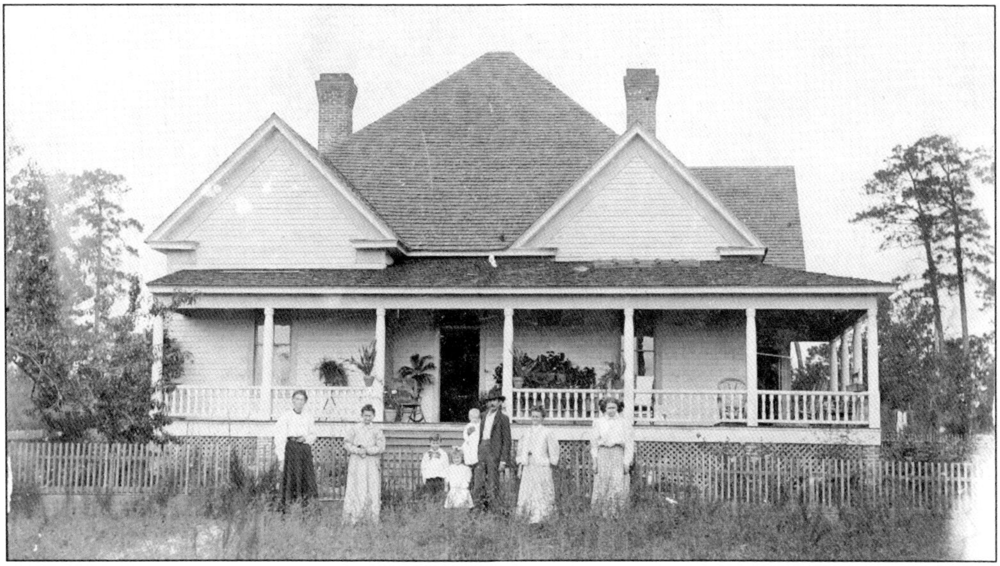

Successful cotton farmers at the turn of the 20th century were eager to demonstrate their good times in the construction of their homes. In 1903, Charles Elmore Higgins of Doublehead had this large multi-gabled, pyramidal-roofed house built by E. A. Zobel, noted architect and builder, for his family. Chambers County was described by an architectural writer as having the largest number of dwellings constructed with this architectural design. (Courtesy of Ann Higgins Rist.)

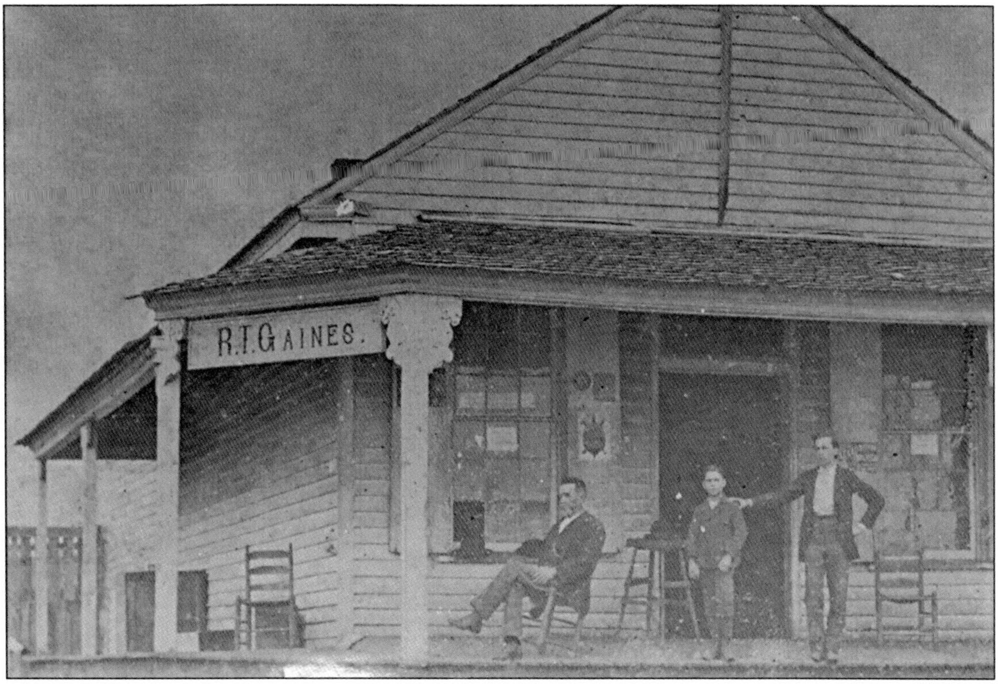

Milltown was once a thriving community with stores, mills, churches, and a school. Robert T. Gaines was a Confederate veteran whose mercantile business prospered in the 19th century. He is shown here seated with sons Curtis (who died in 1910) and Kenon H. Gaines (right). Kenon "Ken" Gaines also became a merchant and well-known figure in the community. (Courtesy of Frank Gaines.)

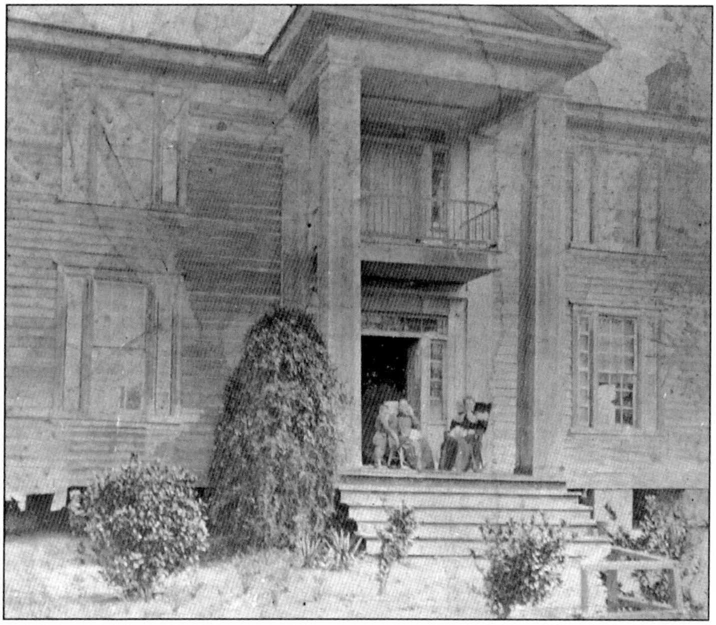

At Milltown stands the antebellum home built by William Whatley Carlisle and wife Elizabeth Evans Carlisle about 1840. The Dr. DeVaughan family later owned this property. When photographed around 1890, the Robert T. Gaines family were the owners. The John D. Denney family lived in this house in the 20th century. Houses of this design dotted the landscape of Chambers County when cotton was king. (Courtesy of Frank Gaines.)

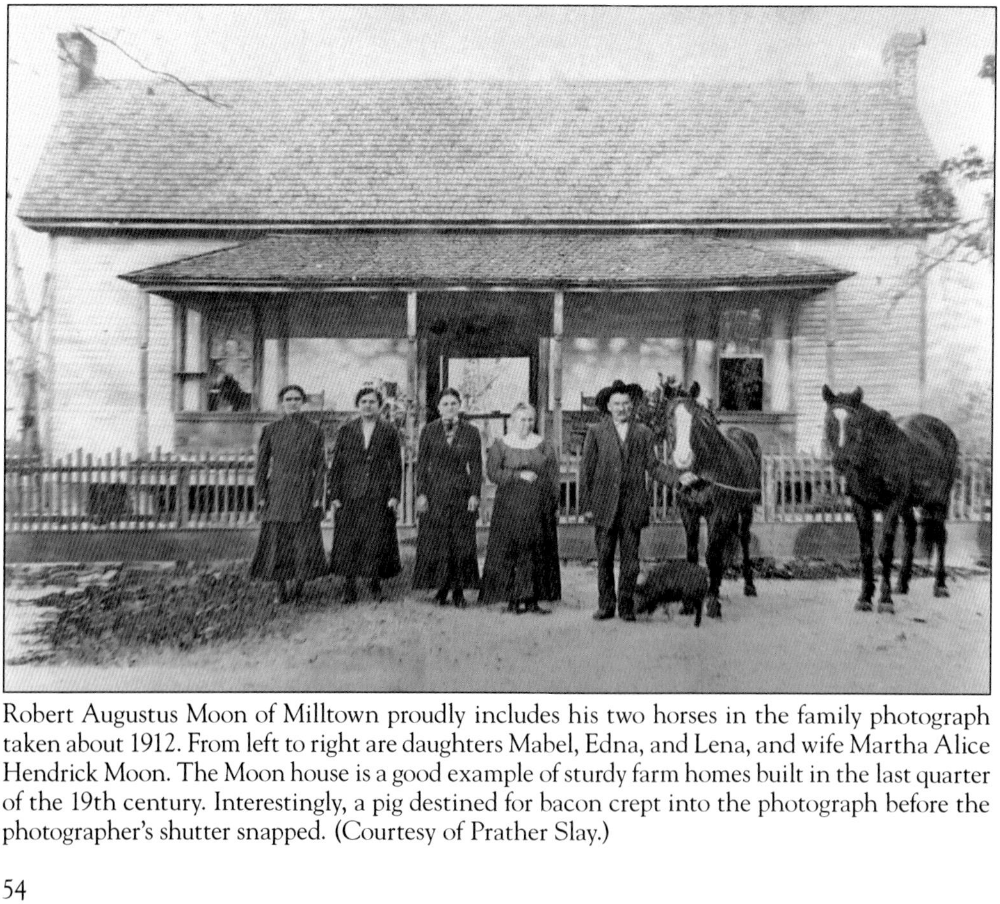

Robert Augustus Moon of Milltown proudly includes his two horses in the family photograph taken about 1912. From left to right are daughters Mabel, Edna, and Lena, and wife Martha Alice Hendrick Moon. The Moon house is a good example of sturdy farm homes built in the last quarter of the 19th century. Interestingly, a pig destined for bacon crept into the photograph before the photographer's shutter snapped. (Courtesy of Prather Slay.)

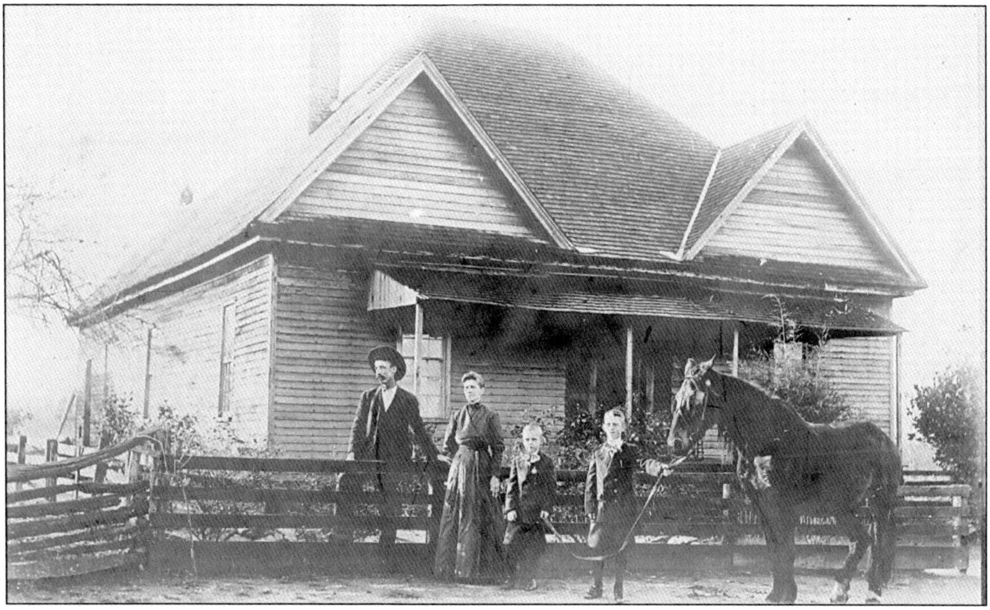

In the Stroud community, approximately 1 mile west of Mount Pisgah Church, was the Burkes farm. In this c. 1913 photograph, James Nathaniel Burkes is pictured with his wife, Susan Elizabeth "Dollie" Pinckard Burkes, and sons Greene Jackson and George Bonner. Bonner (right) holds the reins to a horse that was sired by the famous racehorse Dan Patch. (Courtesy of Carolyn Nunnelly.)

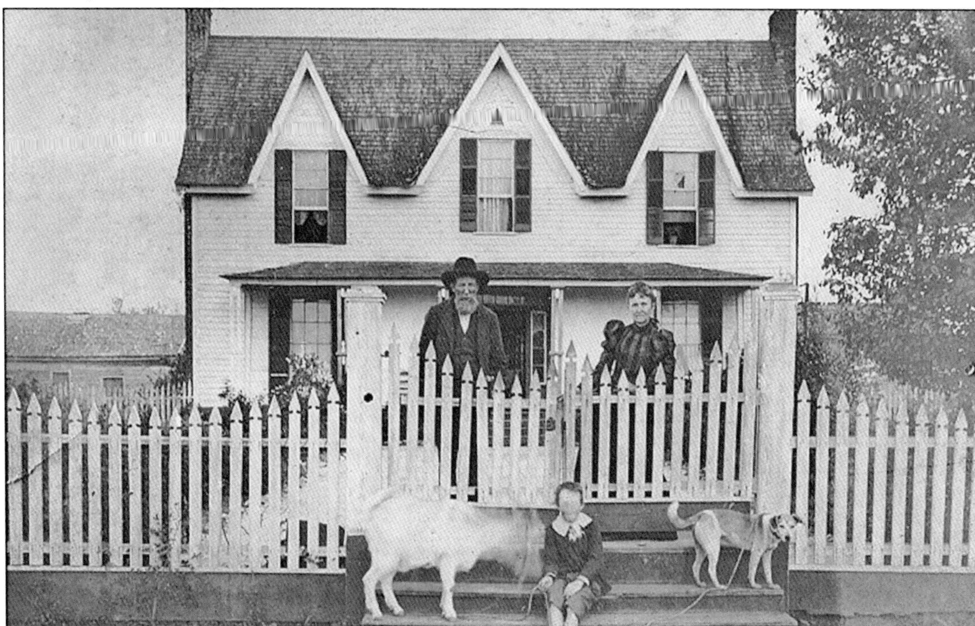

The Gothic Revival residence of Archibald Daniel Wilkinson and wife Mary Virginia Philpott Wilkinson was located in the Fredonia community. Son George Maley Wilkinson is seated on the steps with his pets. Mary Wilkinson purchased the house, which was adjacent to land owned by her husband, from D. K. Breedlove around 1886. The Wilkinson and Philpott families were early settlers of Chambers County and Troup County, Georgia. (Courtesy of Diane Cox.)

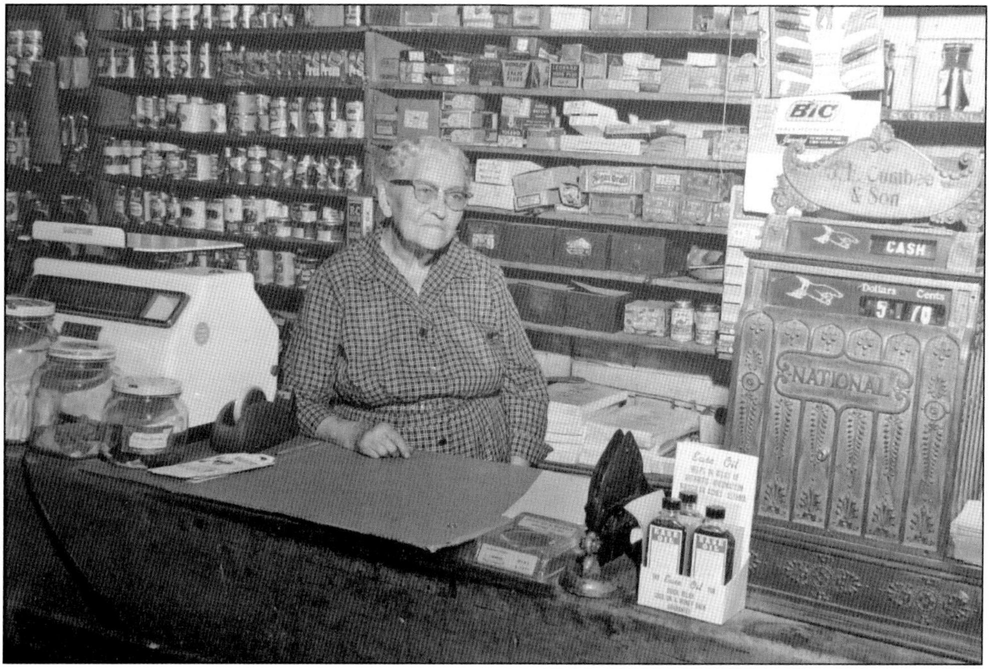

Aileen Andrews Cumbee, daughter of John Golightly Andrews and Emily Ann Cotton Andrews, stands behind the counter at Cumbee's General Store, a landmark since the early days of Fredonia. Rural general stores were a major source of supplies and credit for plantations and farm families in the 19th and early 20th centuries, when a trip to town by wagon was an all-day event. (Courtesy of C. A. Spence Jr. Collection.)

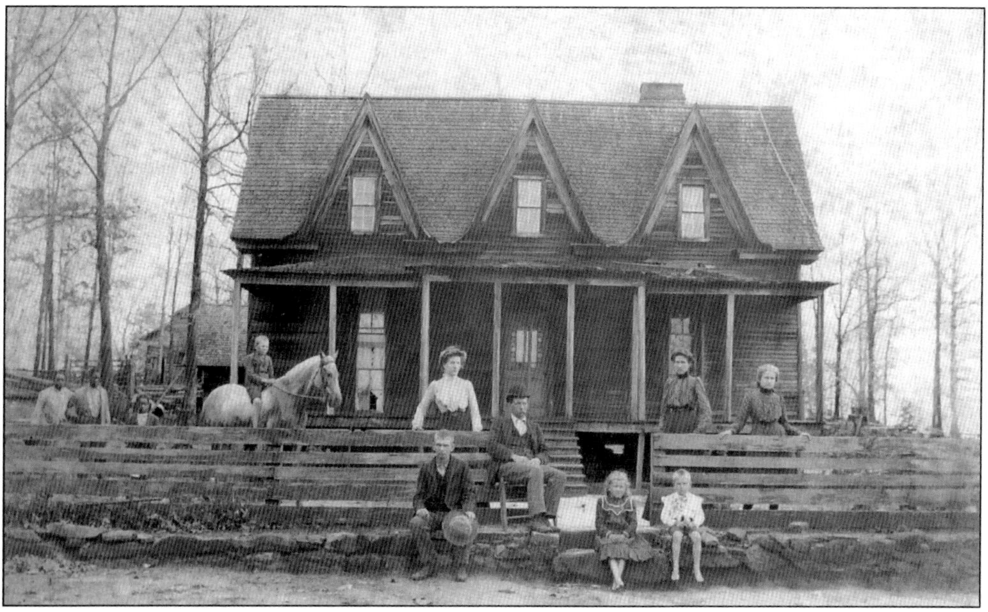

James Hardy Durham is pictured with his family in front of their home in Standing Rock. Seated in front from left to right are Marvin Leon, James Hardy, Emily Lucille, and Clarence Eugene. From left to right behind the fence are three unidentified wage hands, Samuel Reid on horse, Georgia Belle, Molly Arrington, and Ellie May. (Courtesy of Elaine Durham White.)

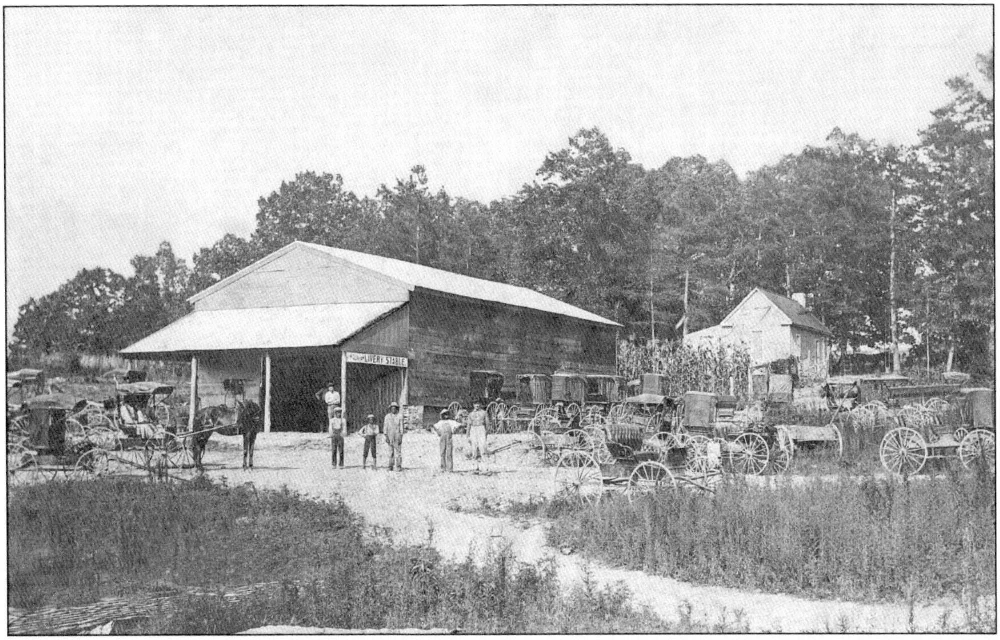

Durham Livery Stable, located at Standing Rock, was under the proprietorship of James Mabry Durham. This business was very important to a community before the days of automobiles. Town residents were able to board their horses, and visitors could easily rent a horse and buggy as needed. Durham obviously enjoyed a lucrative trade, as evidenced by the number of buggies in his yard. (Courtesy of Elaine Durham White.)

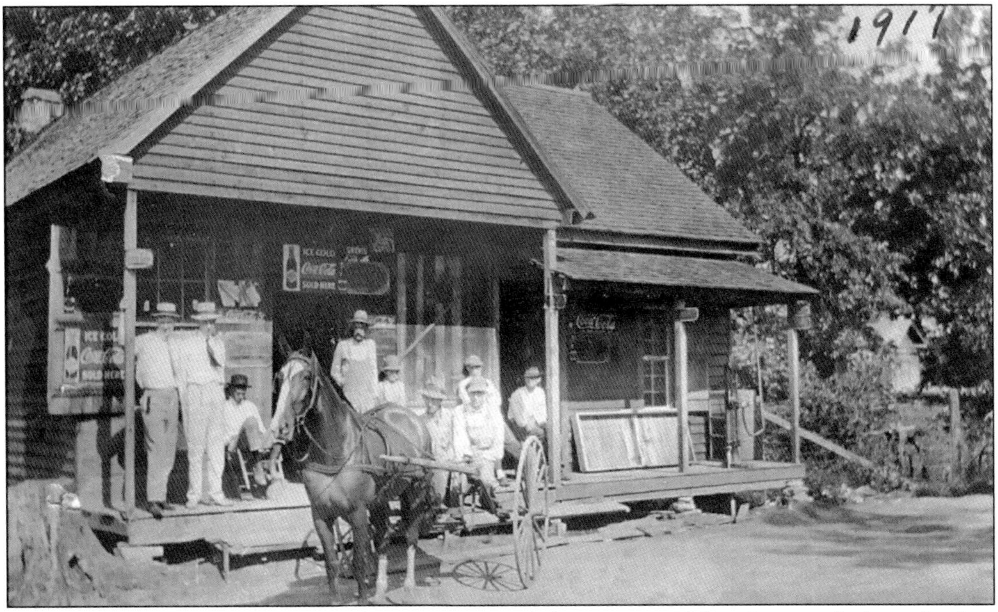

J. F. Johnson and son Isom were the proprietors of this store at Tiller Crossroads from the late 1890s until about 1921. The post office, established in 1879, had three postmasters during its existence: Richard Aycock, Tabitha Williams, and Isom Johnson. Stephen Hubbard Tiller and his wife, Amanda McCowan King Tiller, had been merchants at the crossroad location bearing their family name. (Courtesy of Jason Sanders.)

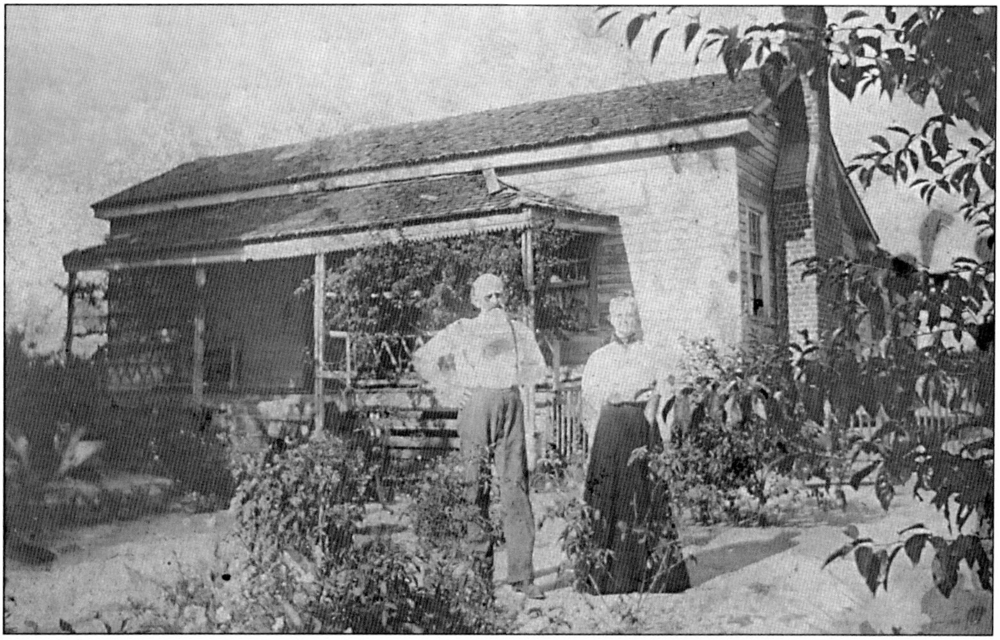

Confederate veteran Rufus Franklin Sanders enlisted as a private with the LaFayette Guards in 1861. After the war, he became a prosperous cotton farmer and raised a large family with his wife, Almedia Aycock Sanders, south of Tiller Crossroads and adjacent to the Emmaus Primitive Baptist Church property. Their home is believed to have been built by her father, John Aycock. (Courtesy of Dinah Moss Estes.)

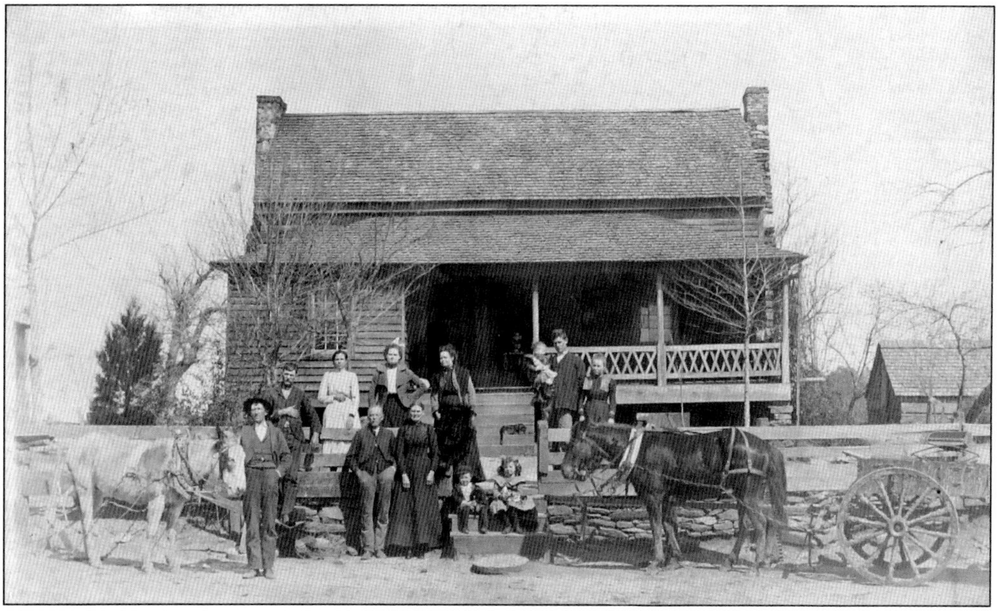

This substantial pioneer residence of the Lett family was located in western Chambers County north of Ripville and was once served by an early post office known as Ireville. Farmer and miller Thomas Jefferson Lett and wife Louisa Abernathy Lett are pictured at left of the steps with other family members. Neighbor Tom Welch holds the mule steady for the photographer. (Courtesy of Teresa Owens.)

Three

Churches and Schools

Pioneer families, later settlers, and their descendants valued spiritual and educational development. In the 1830s, Baptist preachers on horseback traveled through the wilderness in the county ministering to the small, recently formed congregations. Elder John M. Gray helped organize churches at Welch and Fredonia in 1833 and in LaFayette in 1834. Other pioneer Baptist ministers and church organizers were Francis Calloway, John R. Humphries, Benjamin Lloyd, Fredrick Swint, and John Blackstone. In the 1830s, doctrinal differences caused the Baptists to divide into two groups, the Primitives and the Missionaries. Some of the early ministers became prosperous cotton planters and slave owners.

The Methodist movement dates from 1833, when its first church was founded at Fredonia. Rev. Evan G. Richards, who organized the Fredonia Church, requested the Alabama Conference to send two missionaries to help establish churches in LaFayette, Standing Rock, Cusseta, and Oak Bowery. Just as the pioneer Baptist and Methodist churches were the mother churches for the many churches established in the county in the 19th century, New Hope Congregational Christian Church was the mother church for Christian churches in Alabama. This church was organized under a brush arbor near Clacksville in 1850 by Rev. Wyche Malone Jenkins Elder. Other denominations established churches in the county throughout the 19th century, but the Baptist, Methodist, and Christian churches enjoyed the largest memberships.

Log cabin schools were established in the frontier communities at the same time the first churches were being established. The school term was limited to winter months when labor from the farm could be spared. Later, prosperous communities would establish academies for young men and young women. Throughout the 19th and 20th centuries, improvements would be made in the physical buildings and the curriculum of the county schools. The community school and the community churches created social relationships, beyond family ties, which sustained individuals and families during periods of personal and collective crisis.

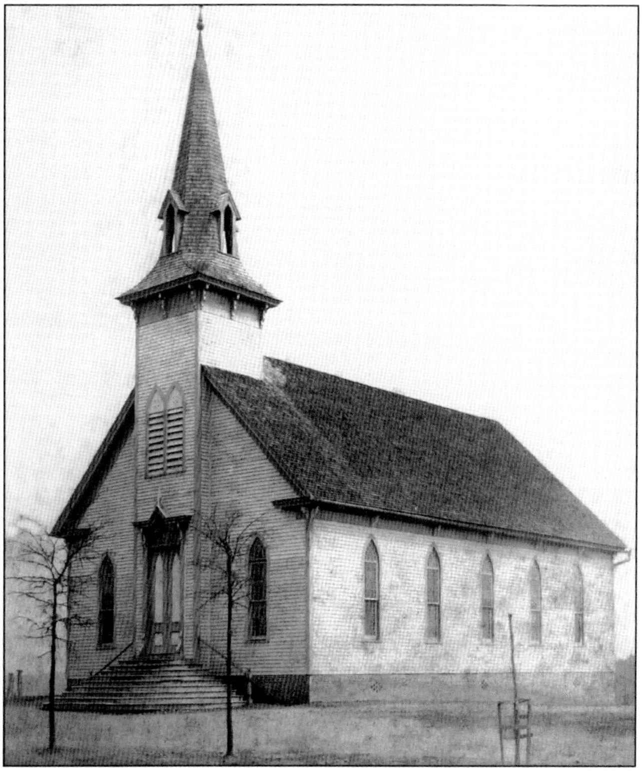

LaFayette (now First United) Methodist Church can trace its origin back to 1833, when Evan G. Richards, a young minister/lawyer, attended the Methodist Episcopal Conference in Montgomery and was granted permission to form a mission in Chambers County. The building presented here was constructed in 1890 and used until the present brick structure was built in 1914. (Courtesy of First United Methodist Church.)

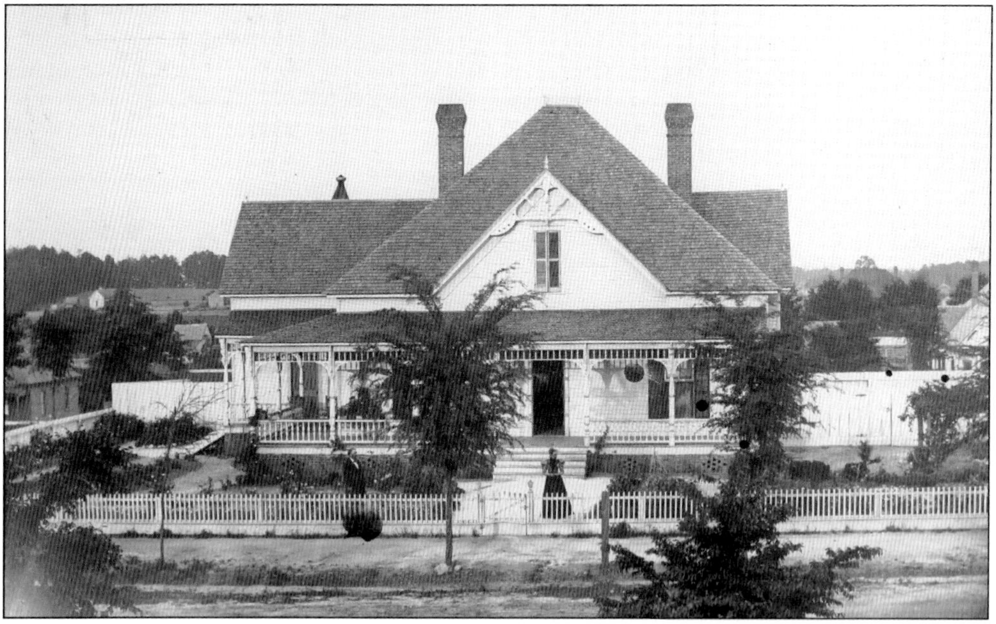

In 1896, a handsome pyramidal-roofed parsonage was constructed for the LaFayette Methodist Church. The dignified appearance of the residence would no doubt have captured the eye of admiring travelers as they passed through LaFayette. Later this house was used as a private residence until purchased and razed by Home Federal Savings and Loan. (Courtesy of First United Methodist Church.)

Chambersville Baptist Church was constituted on May 21, 1834. A year later the name was changed to LaFayette (now First) Baptist Church. The church was originally located where the LaFayette Community House now stands; an old cemetery can be found there. The congregation moved to the present location in 1890 after completing the building shown here. This building has been brick veneered and is still used today. (Courtesy of CCM.)

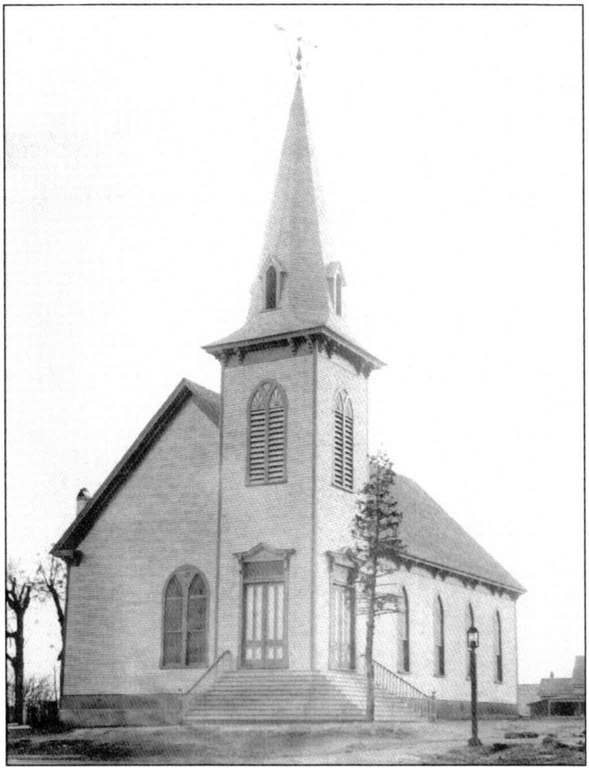

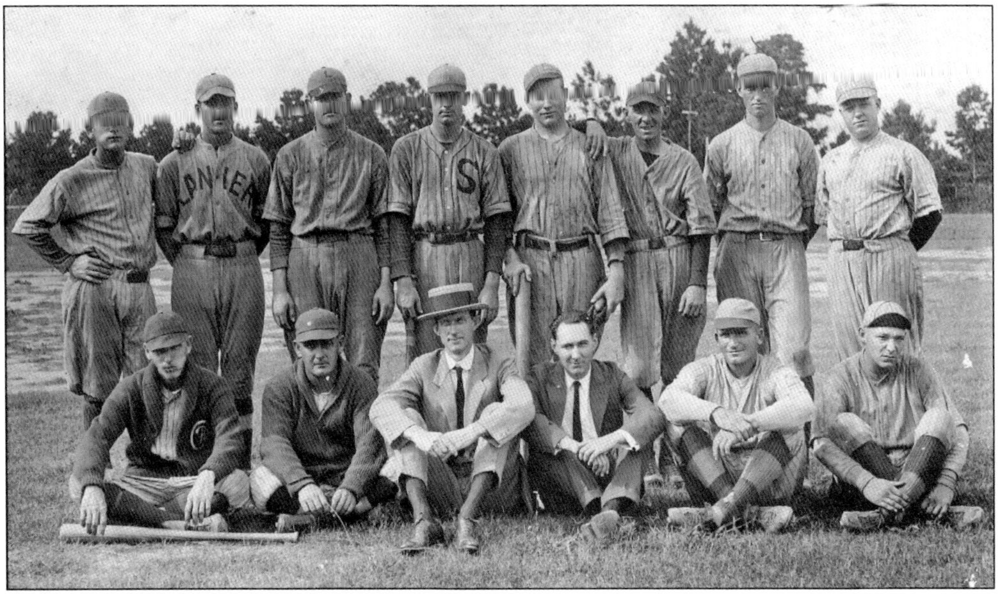

The 1924 LaFayette baseball team included, from left to right, (first row) Charlie Miller (third base), Zach Schuessler (pitcher), Julian Hollingsworth (manager), Bud Wood (business manager), Sam Frazer (second base), and Bill Buckner (first); (second row) Dan Miller (captain and third base), Dick Wallace (center field), Dan Hurst (catcher), Wilbur Brown (shortstop), Guy Dobbs (right field), Battle Moon (left field), Speedy Spear (pitcher), and John Thomas Frazer (catcher). (Courtesy of Bill Bowling.)

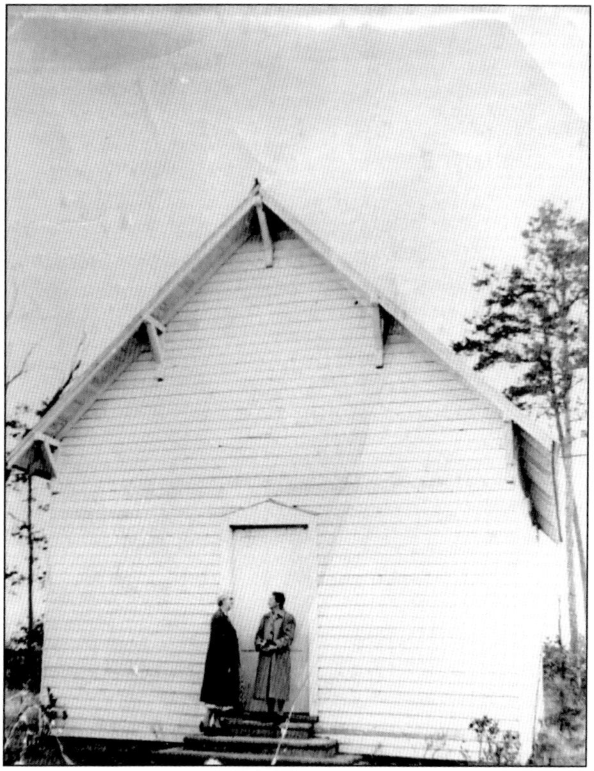

Harrell's Chapel Methodist Church in the Moorefield community was organized in 1892 and built on land donated by A. L. Harrell Sr. It was named in honor of his invalid mother, who never was able to enter the building. Minnie Wyche Barber (left) and Myrtle Adams Jones are shown in this early 1950s photograph. The church no longer exists. (Courtesy of Allen Jones.)

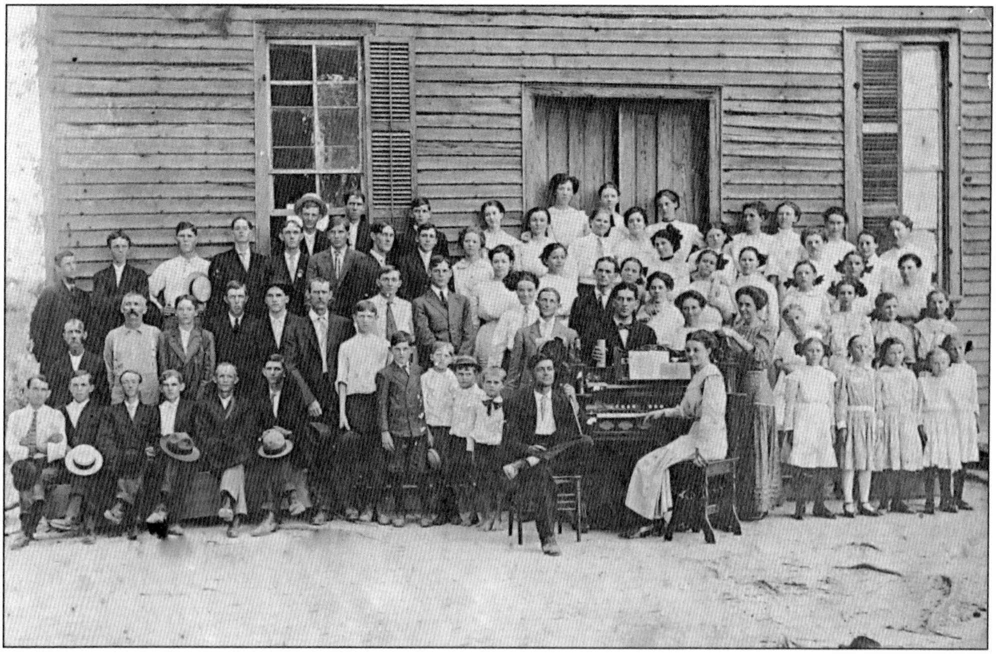

Students, teachers, and possibly trustees are shown in this early 1900s photograph of Sturkie School. A pump organ has been brought into the yard, perhaps to show that the school was able to afford such an amenity. Students periodically rendered programs of recitation and song, and this was possibly one of those times. (Courtesy of Allen Jones.)

A crowd gathers on the banks of Sandy Creek near Gold Hill in the 1920s to witness the baptism of a young convert. This event could be found on almost any weekend during the warm weather months in the days before churches had indoor baptismal pools. Accounts record ice being broken on the water for the ordinance. (Courtesy of Miriam Ann Kirkwood Syler.)

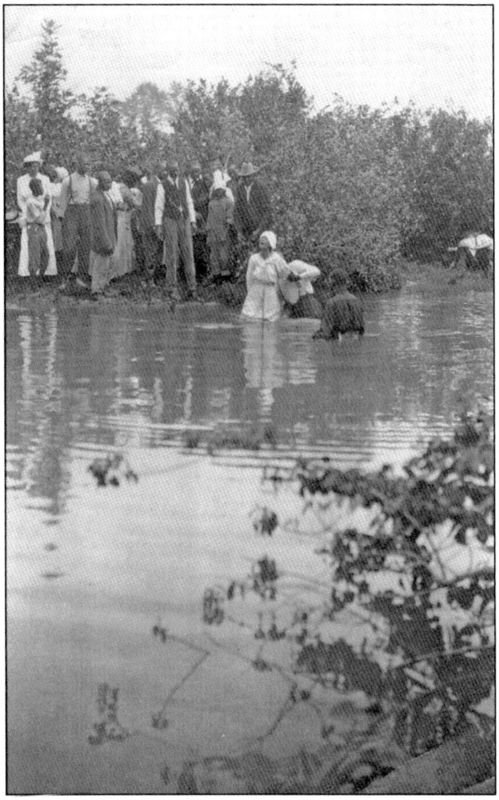

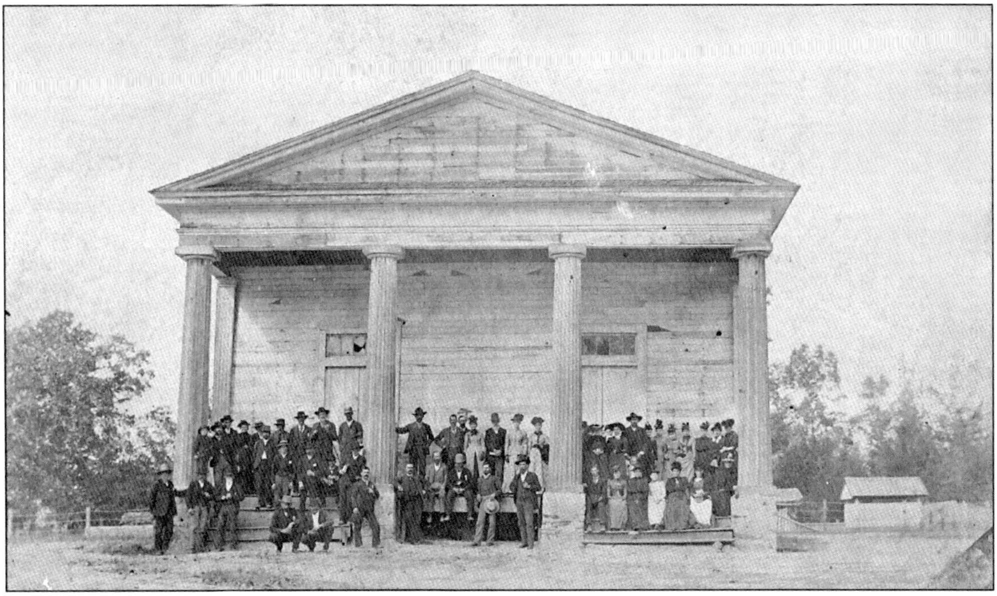

This Greek Revival building was originally built at Oak Bowery for Sardis Baptist Church. When that church disbanded, the building was dismantled and moved to the Antioch Church lot west of LaFayette, where it served the congregation until 1910. Once again the building was taken apart, and much of the framing was used to construct the present structure. This cabinet card photograph dates from the 1890s. (Courtesy of Mary Yates Lowe.)

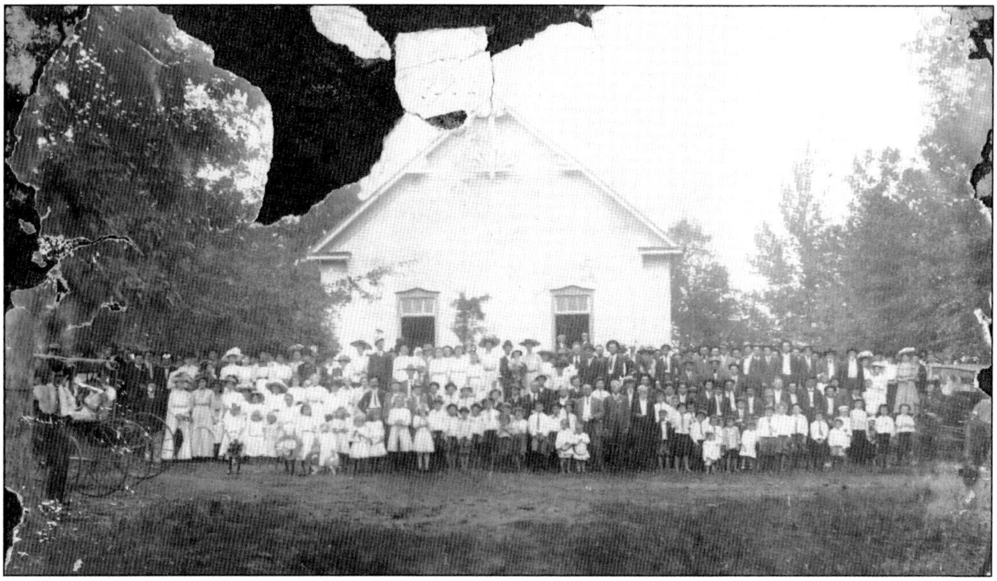

Located near Dudleyville, County Line Baptist Church was organized on May 5, 1835, by a presbytery consisting of Elders Francis Calloway, Henry Perkins, and Benjamin Lloyd at the home of William C. Morgan. The handsome building pictured here was erected in 1890 and was typical of many rural churches of that era. The building is lovingly cared for by the current membership. (Courtesy of Betty Barrett.)

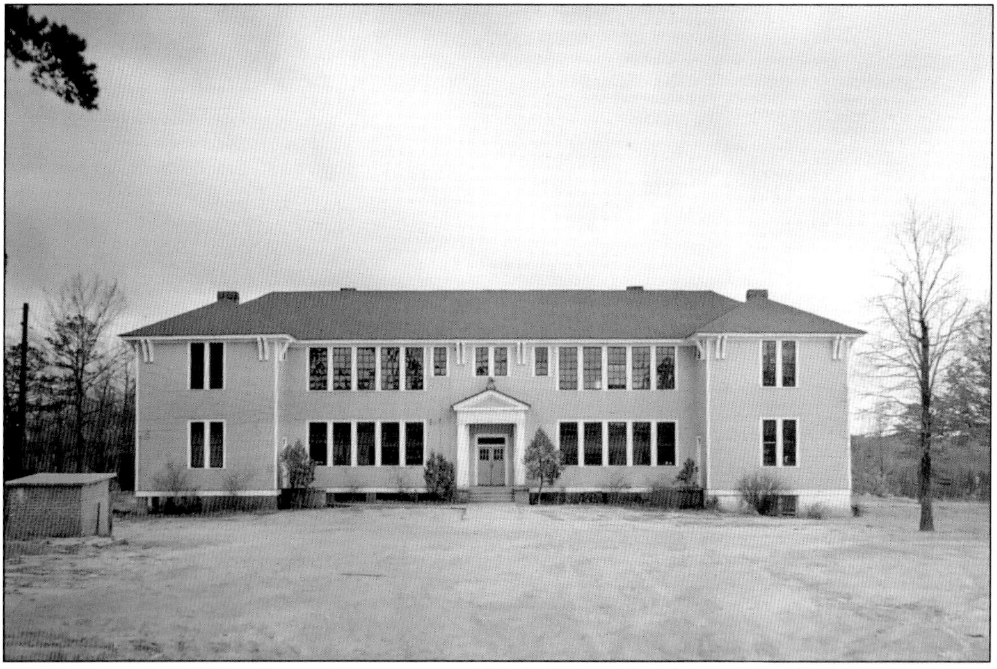

In 1921, trustees of Woodlawn, Harmony, and High Point schools united to build Ridge Grove Consolidated School with Houston Yancey and James Sanders donating land. The school opened in 1922, with 10 grade levels. By 1925, there were 12 grades of classes available. The school had wood-burning heaters and a Delco lighting system, a gasoline-powered DC generator with storage batteries, that was modern for the time. (Courtesy of C. A. Spence Jr. collection.)

Cusseta Baptist Church was constituted at the house of James Taylor Sr. on April 18, 1835, and originally named Bethesda, with elders Gideon Leverett, Henry Perkins, and John W. Cooper comprising the presbytery. In 1840, a building was constructed at Flint Hill, and in 1856 a final move was made to the village of Cusseta. (Courtesy of Ann K. Alsobrook.)

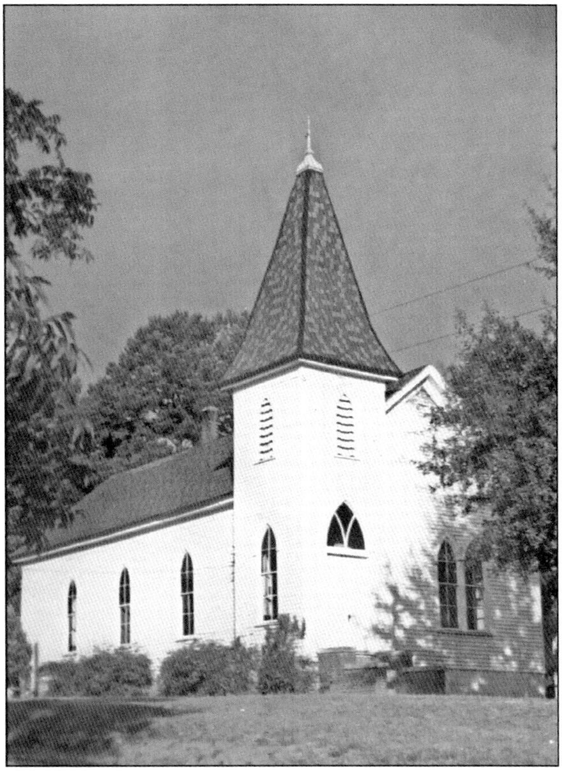

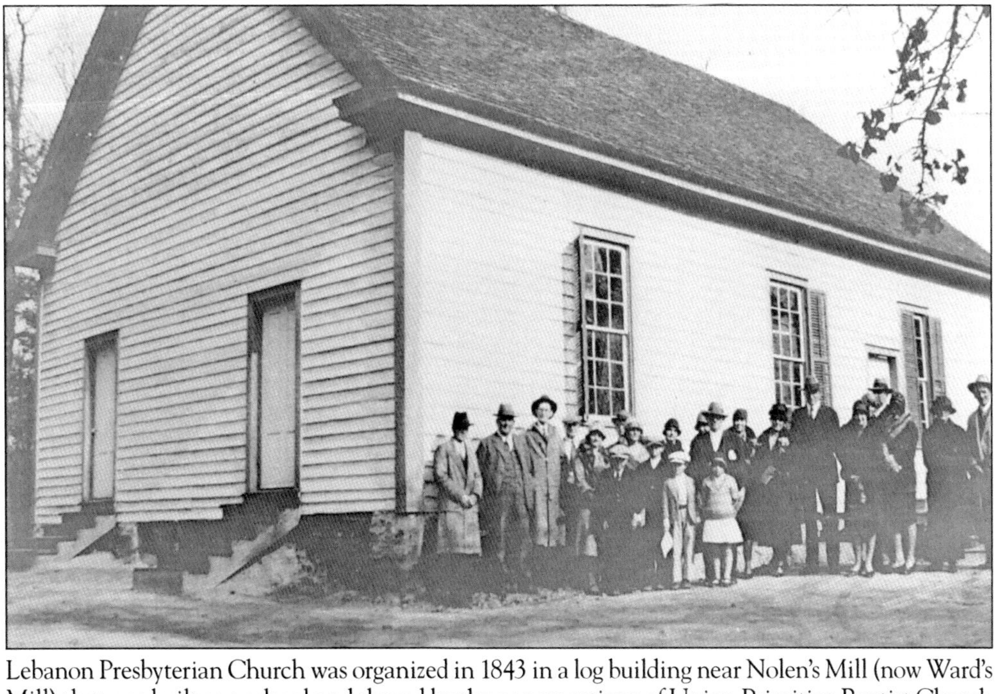

Lebanon Presbyterian Church was organized in 1843 in a log building near Nolen's Mill (now Ward's Mill) that was built as a school and shared by the congregations of Union Primitive Baptist Church and Sweet Home Methodist Church. Some years later, the church moved to a site near Buffalo, and the present house of worship was erected in 1870. (Courtesy of Jean Spence Nunn.)

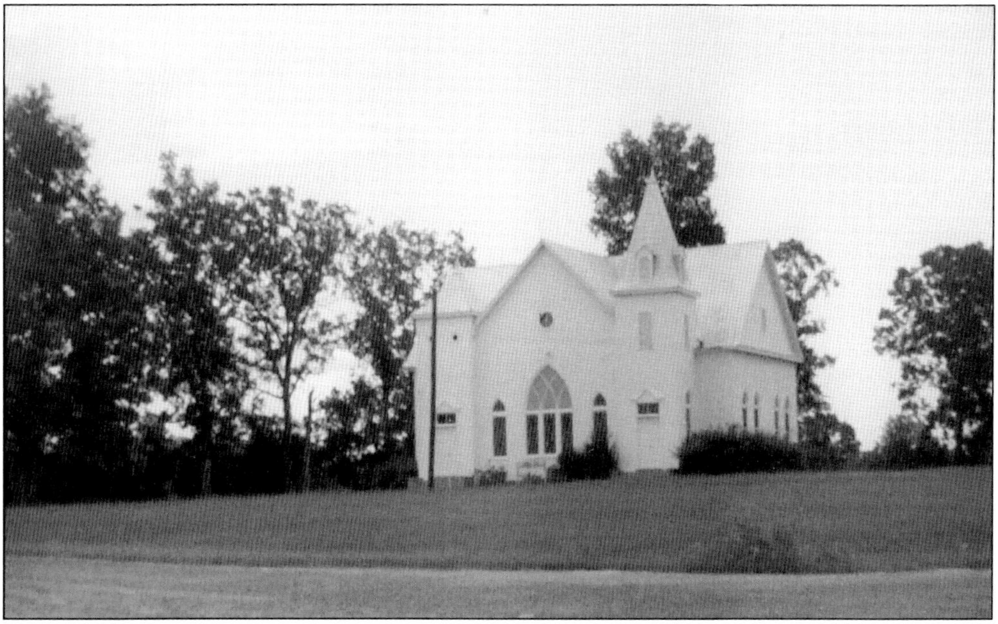

Chapel Hill Methodist Church, organized in 1911 a few miles west of White Plains, can trace its origin to an earlier church named Mount Zion at Penton. The congregation sold this building to the Pentecostals (now Penton Church of God) and relocated at the crossroads midway between Penton and White Plains in 1911. There they erected this handsome building, which was destroyed by fire in 1984. (Courtesy of Greg Farrar.)

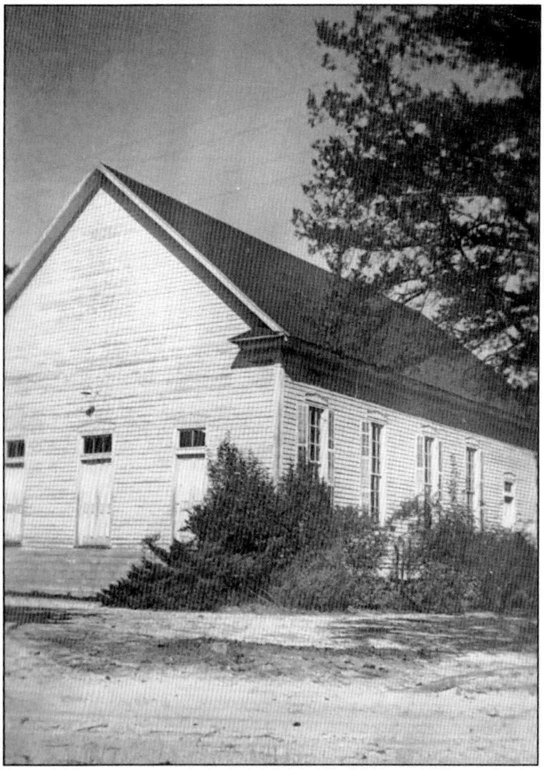

The Rock Spring Baptist Church was organized on April 24, 1839, with 12 charter members. Elder William Lacy was the first pastor and Abner Webb was the clerk. An older cemetery is at the site of the first church. The congregation moved to the present location in the 1850s and built the second building on that site in 1881. Photographed in 1938, this building is still used but has been extensively remodeled. (Courtesy of CCM.)

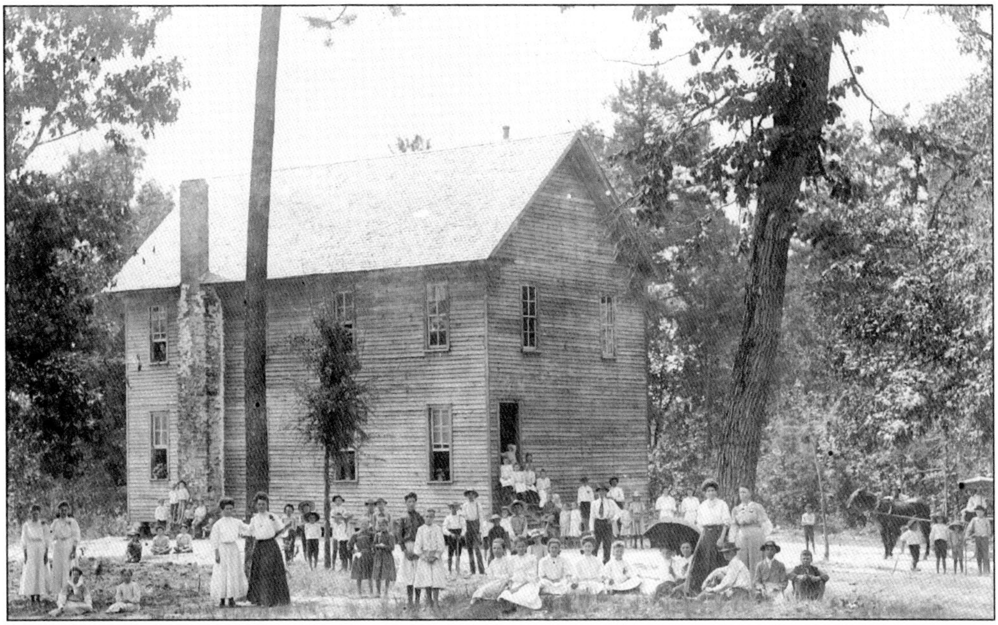

Rock Spring School appears in church records as early as 1874. At least two buildings burned during the school's existence. This photograph from about 1908 shows a two-story building. The upper floor was used by the Rock Spring Masonic Lodge No. 479. Mollie Beaty, a fondly remembered teacher, read from the Bible at the start of each school day, usually from the Book of Proverbs. (Courtesy of CCM.)

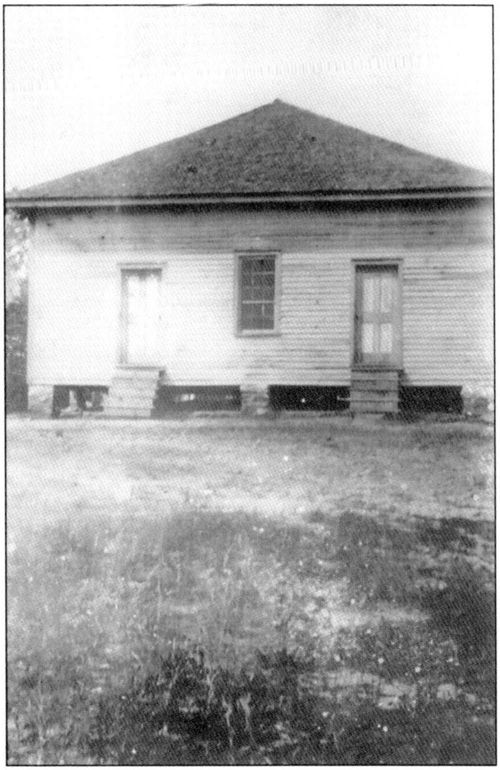

This 1920s photograph is of Macedonia Primitive Baptist Church at Marcoot. Constituted in 1835 as Mount Paran, the church relocated from its original site near the old Yarbrough Cemetery in 1841. This building was swept away by a tornado on Easter Sunday 1932. The present building was built back on the same foundation and floor. (Courtesy of Nell Orr.)

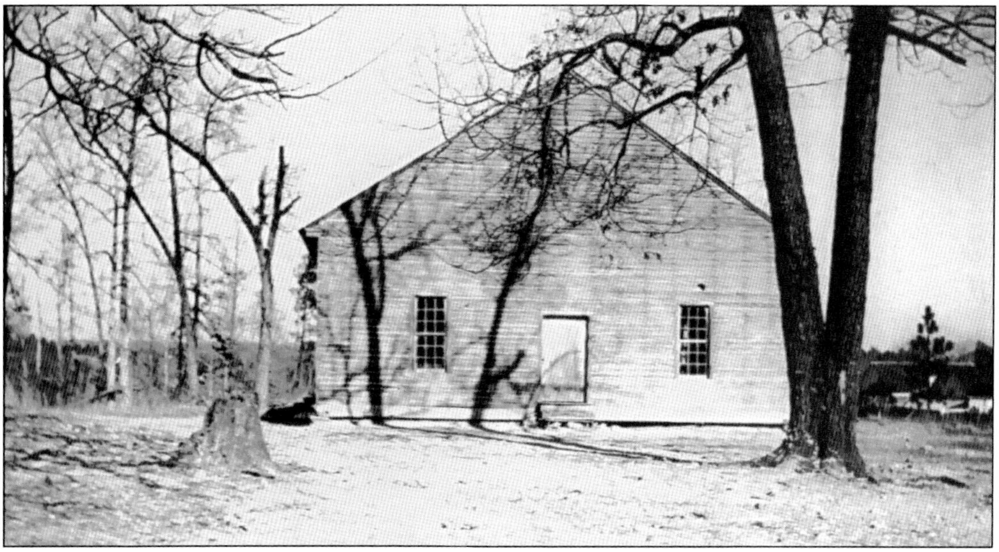

Photographed in the 1920s, Mount Olive Primitive Baptist Church was located north of the Shiloh community. Although officially constituted on August 14, 1884, the building has an earlier appearance, and the nearby cemetery has burials from the 1830s. The church disbanded in the 1930s, and the building stood vacant for many years afterwards until it was razed. (Courtesy of Etta Sims Hall.)

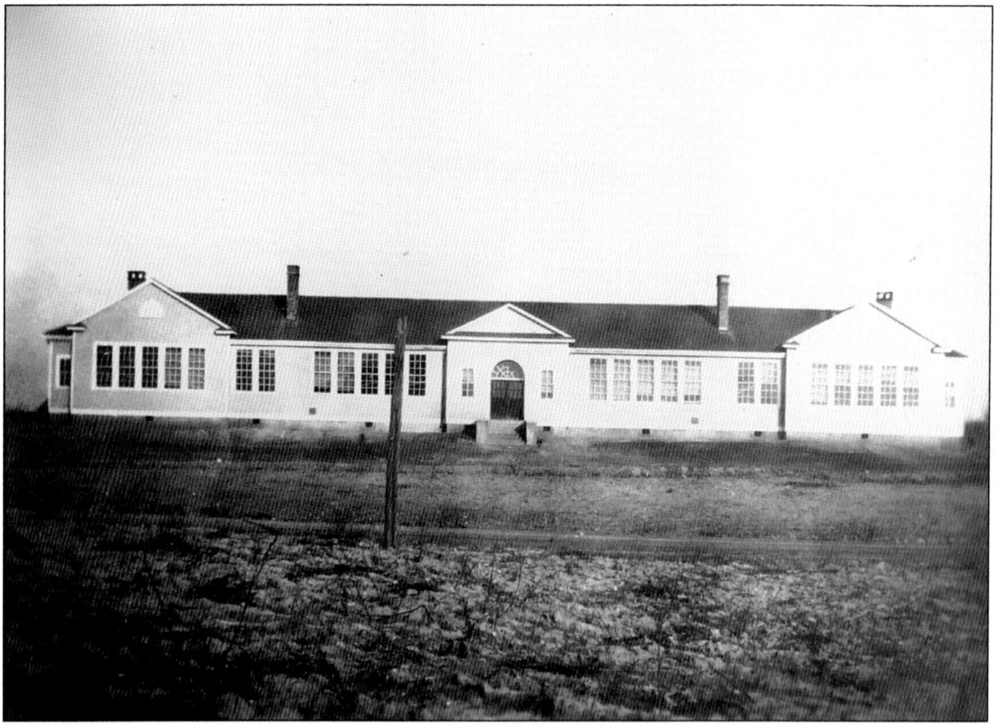

Union Hill School was formed with the consolidation of Union, Red Hill, Shiloh, and Ebenezer schools in 1929. The school was 12 grades for a short period and later had classes only through the sixth grade. It was a fine rural school and was known for its excellent basketball team in the 1930s. In 1962 the school was closed. (Courtesy of Mary Reeves Alsobrook.)

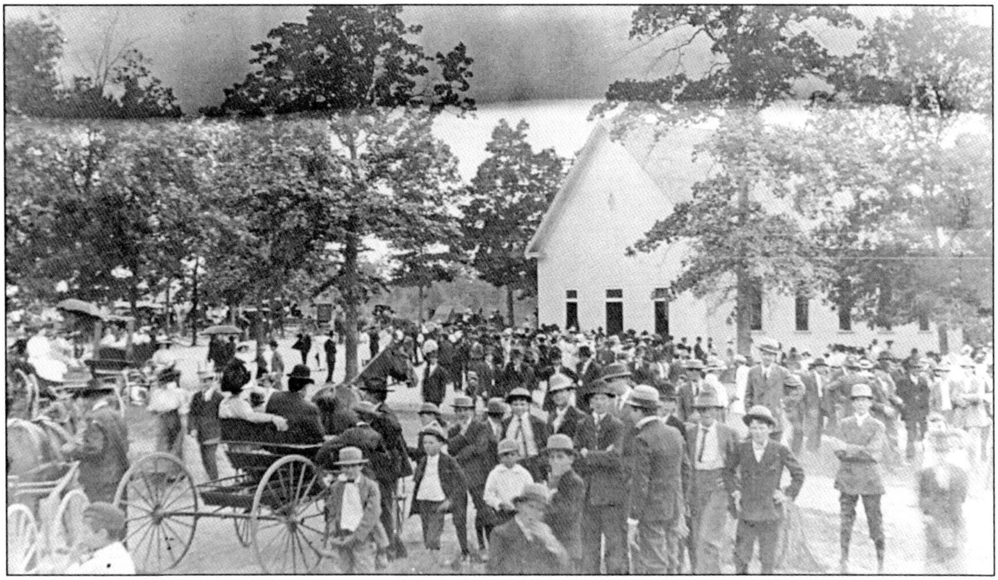

People, horses, and buggies abound on the grounds of Pleasant Grove Congregational Christian Church in this early-1900s image made by local photographer Warner M. Phillips. Located in the Union Hill community, the church was organized in 1886. This building has been replaced with a brick structure, and the pleasant grove of hardwood trees no longer stands. (Courtesy of Cenus Phillips Heptinstall.)

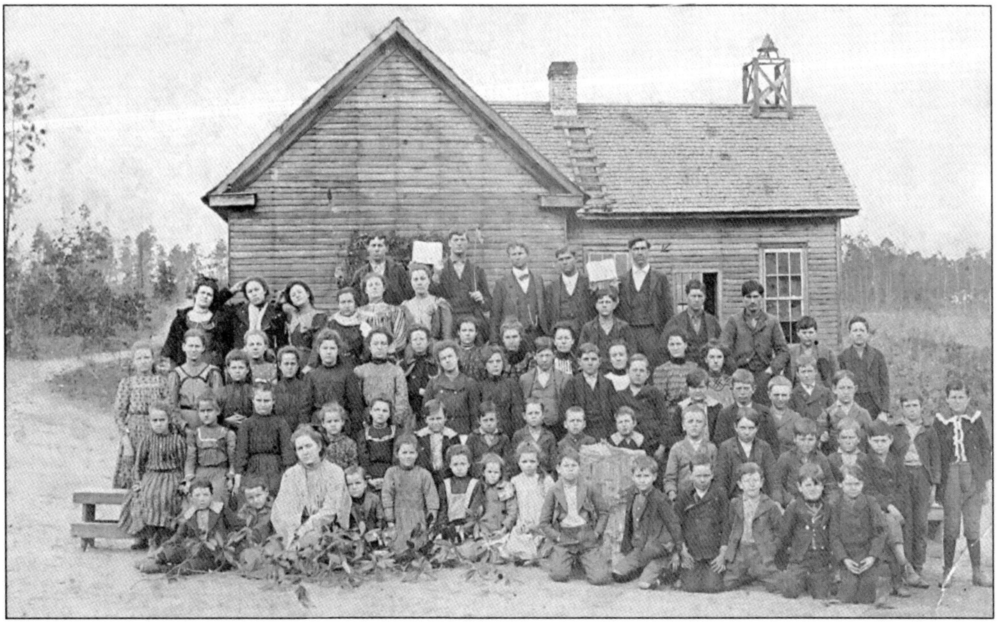

Liberty School was located a short distance southeast of Union Hill at the intersection of Foster Cross Roads. Originally built as one room, an addition was added later. A fireplace in each room served as the only source of heat. A large bell mounted on the roof was used to summon students to class. Lurie Griffin was the teacher in the early-1900s photograph. (Courtesy of Andrew O. Redmon.)

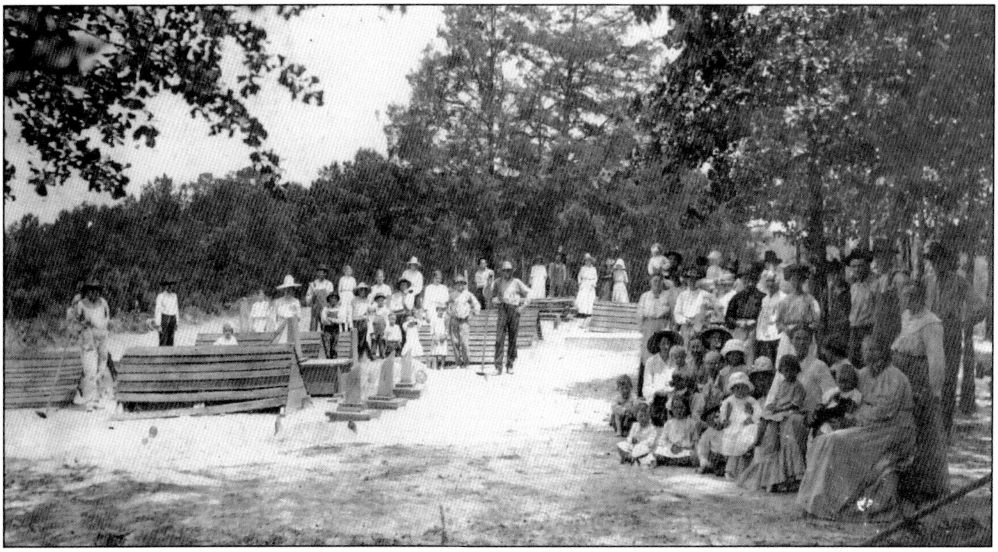

Family and friends gather at the Megginson Cemetery, located west of Penton, to clean up the graveyard around 1912. Wooden structures that resemble chicken coops were built over some of the graves to prevent animals from disturbing the soil. Samuel Megginson, the family patriarch, is among the 50 or more people buried here. Local photographer Warner M. Phillips made the image. (Courtesy of Cenus Phillips Heptinstall Collection.)

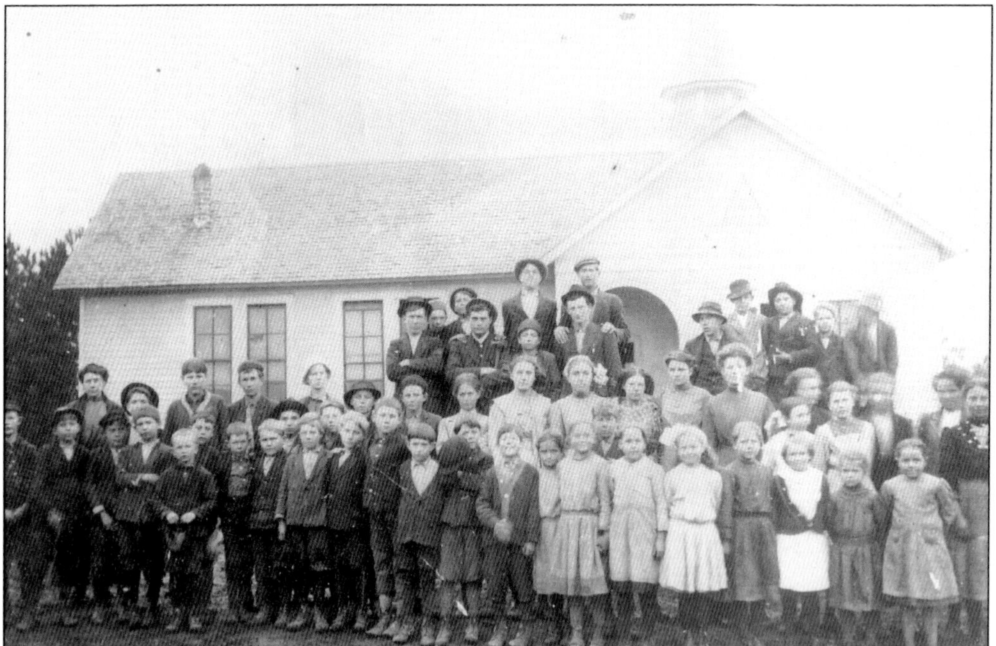

Red Hill School, northwest from LaFayette, was built when two earlier schools, Friendship and Liberty, were closed. The attractive school building with cupola was built from plans designed by the School of Architecture at Alabama Polytechnic Institute (API), now Auburn University. Later, a third room was added, giving the building a T-shaped plan. This photograph is from around 1910. (Courtesy of Alma Harmon Clark.)

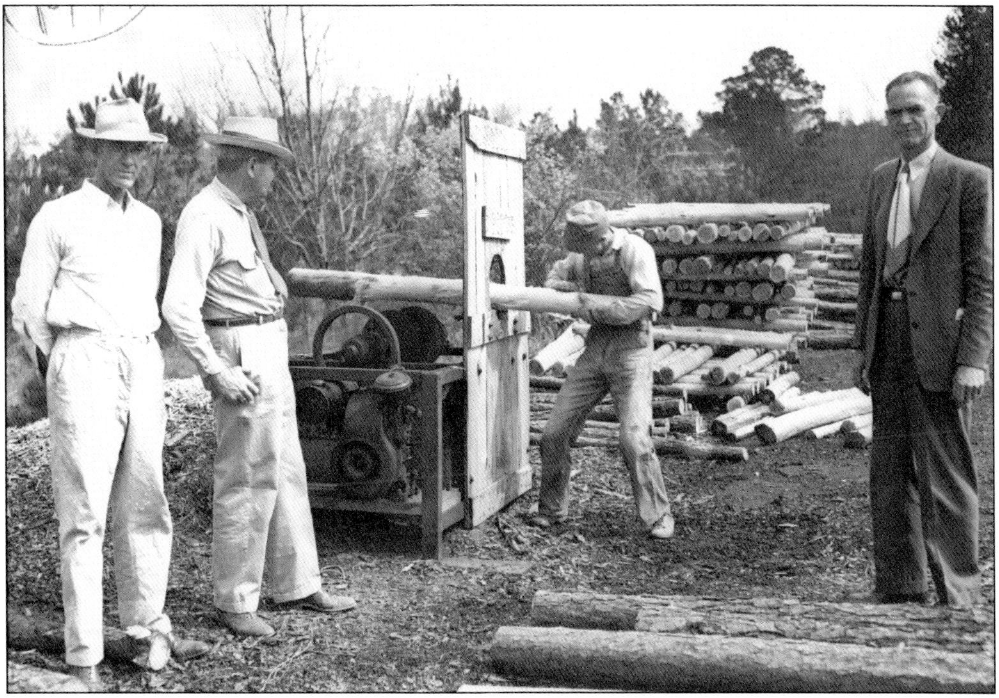

From left to right, Escar Carden, Earle Thomas, and principal Max Johnston look on as an unidentified vocational agriculture student at Chambers County High School in Milltown wrestles with a fence post in a debarking machine. According to one former student with firsthand knowledge, a young man could get a real workout with this piece of equipment. (Courtesy of William Earle Thomas.)

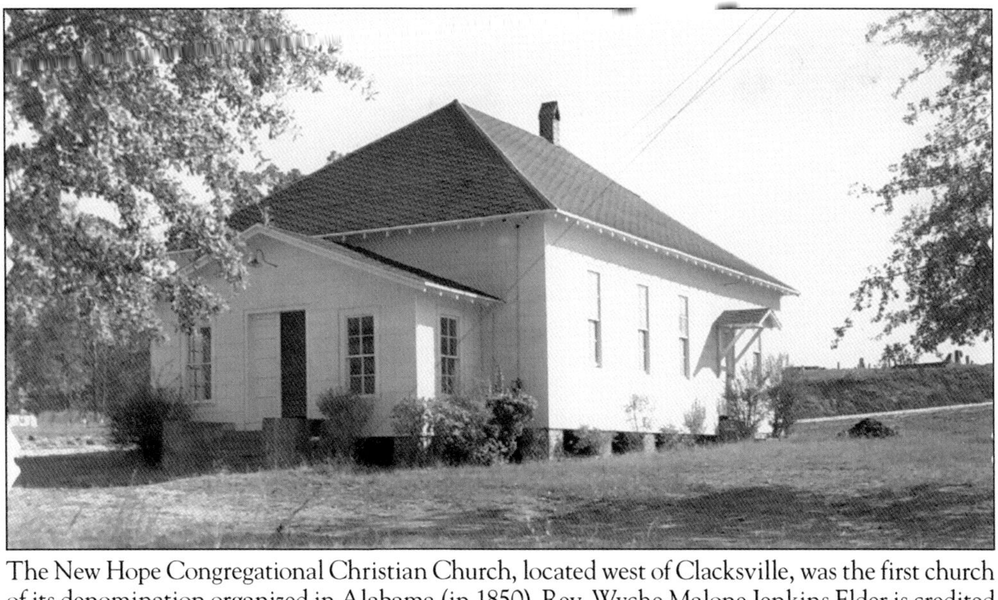

The New Hope Congregational Christian Church, located west of Clacksville, was the first church of its denomination organized in Alabama (in 1850). Rev. Wyche Malone Jenkins Elder is credited as the primary minister in the constitution. Several earlier buildings prior to the 1934 structure pictured here were destroyed by storms and fire. The building has since been brick veneered and reroofed. (Courtesy of Mount Olive Community Club Scrapbook.)

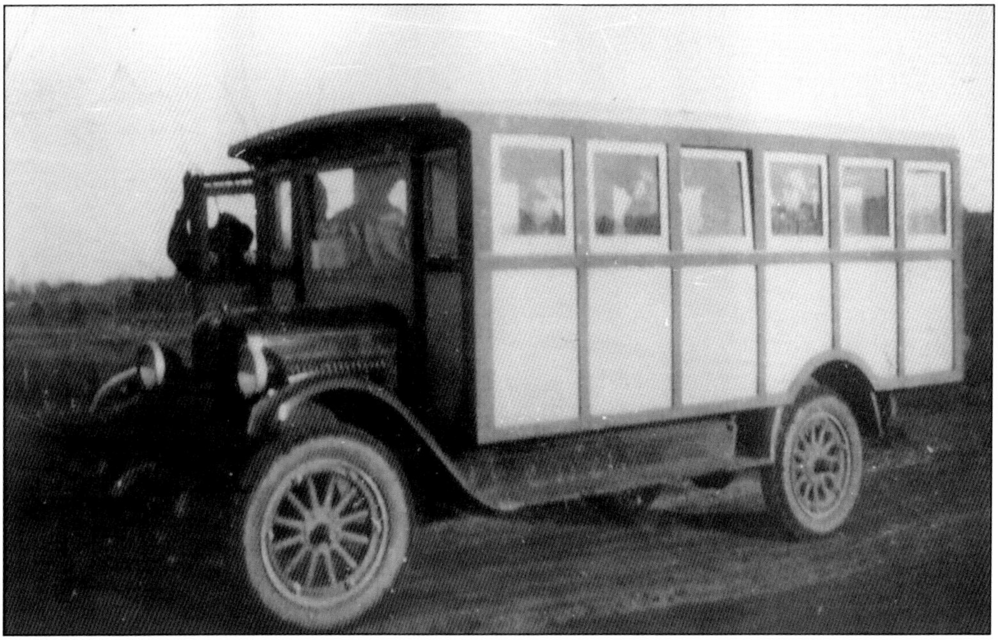

With the consolidation of Five Points School in 1916, Nathaniel Alfred Claud Piper was contracted to modify farm wagons into vehicles for transporting students. Piper was a blacksmith and furniture craftsman living in Five Points. He later built wooden buses on a Model T chassis with hardwood frames covered in sheet metal. Seams were covered with wood battens and the top covered with canvas. (Courtesy of CMA.)

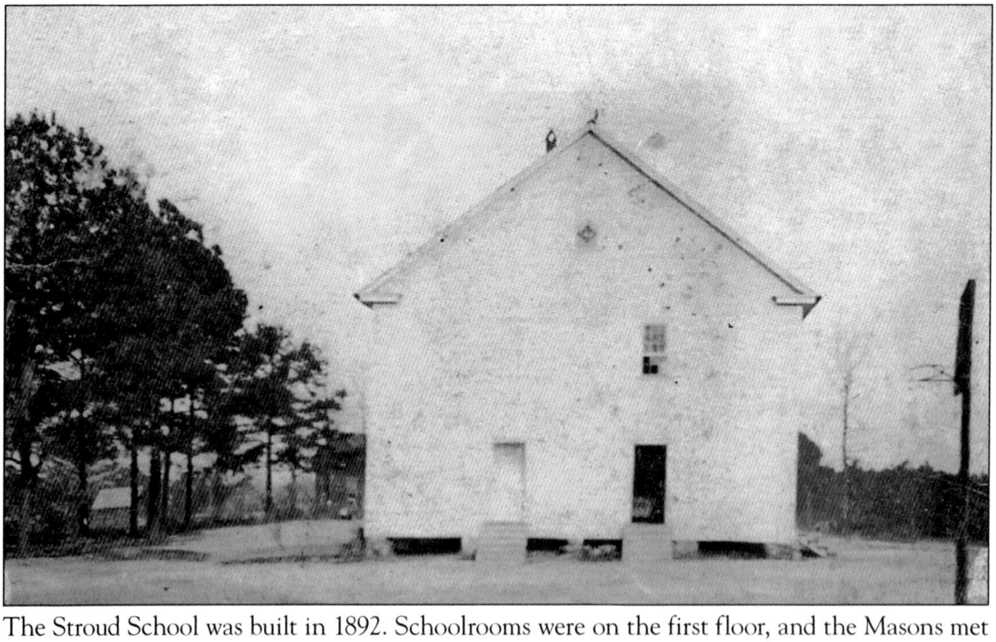

The Stroud School was built in 1892. Schoolrooms were on the first floor, and the Masons met on the second floor. Some of the teachers were George Burks, Payne Moody, John Will Johnson, Marshall Hurst, Myrtle Trimble, Ruby Grady, Helen Grady, Pearl Holderfield, and Ava Holderfield. Stroud School was closed in 1929, and its students were sent to the consolidated Five Points School. (Courtesy of Horace McLean Holderfield.)

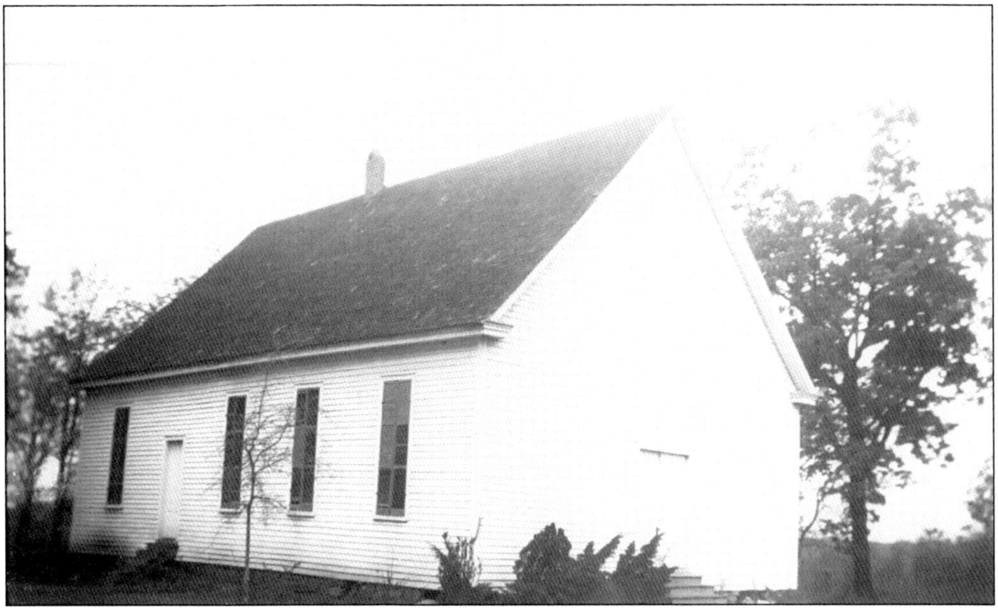

On August 4, 1837, elders John Blackstone, Frederick Swint, Moses Gunn, and Benjamin Lloyd formed the presbytery in constituting Mount Pisgah Primitive Baptist Church. The church moved from the original location near Five Points to Stroud prior to 1855, with the present building erected in 1884. The large cemetery includes veterans from the Revolutionary War, the War of 1812, and the Civil War. A large slave cemetery is also on the property. (Courtesy of Don Clark.)

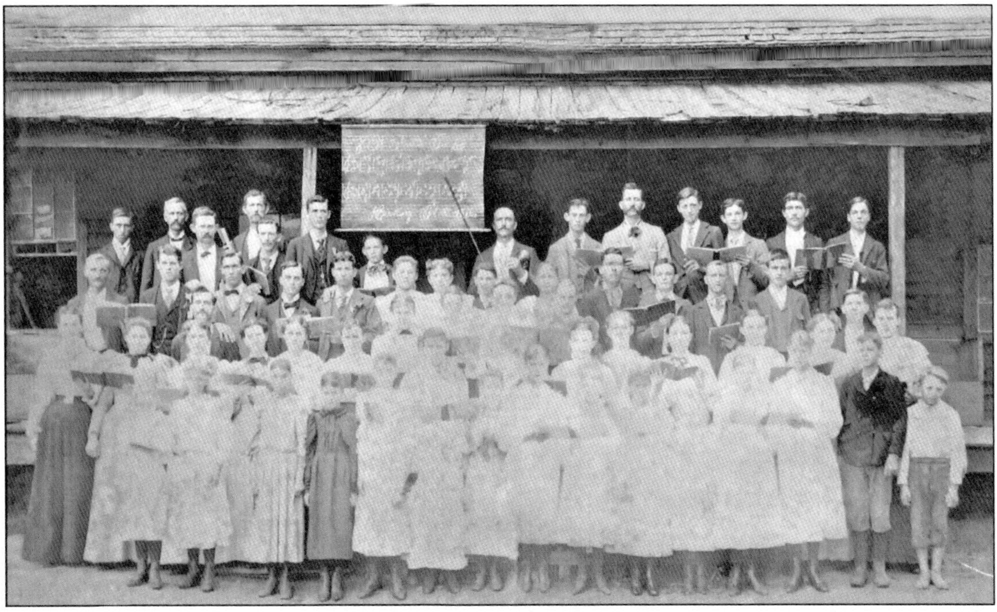

In 1896, Prof. Jerry Walker Pearson, who was considered a singing master among his peers, taught a shaped note singing school from *The Sacred Harp* at Hickory Flat School. Students learned to sing the shapes *fa*, *sol*, *la*, and *mi* before the poetry and without musical instrument. Singing schools such as this were held in almost every community throughout the county. (Courtesy of Laura Densmore.)

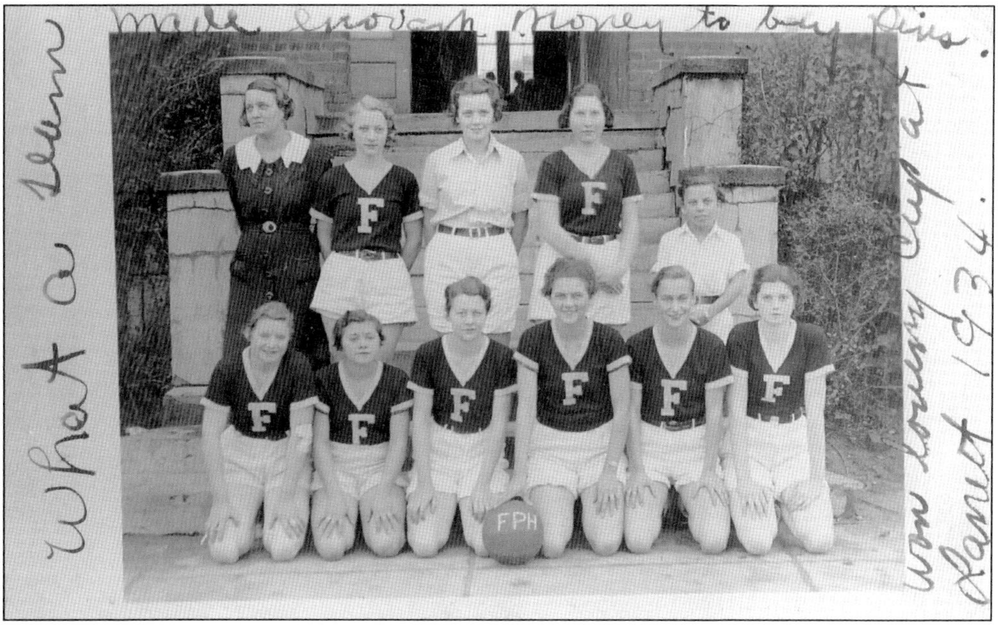

The Five Points Girls basketball team of 1934, pictured from left to right, are (first row) unidentified, Katie Williamson, Louise Littlefield, May Finney, Frances Cumbee, and Mary Eleanor Finney; (second row) Lena Horn (teacher), Bonnie Anglin, Dora Mae Ramage, Georgia Belle Sorrell, and Boveen Hamlin (manager). Written on the photograph is, "We won the loving cup at Lanett 1934." (Courtesy of Mary Helen Benford.)

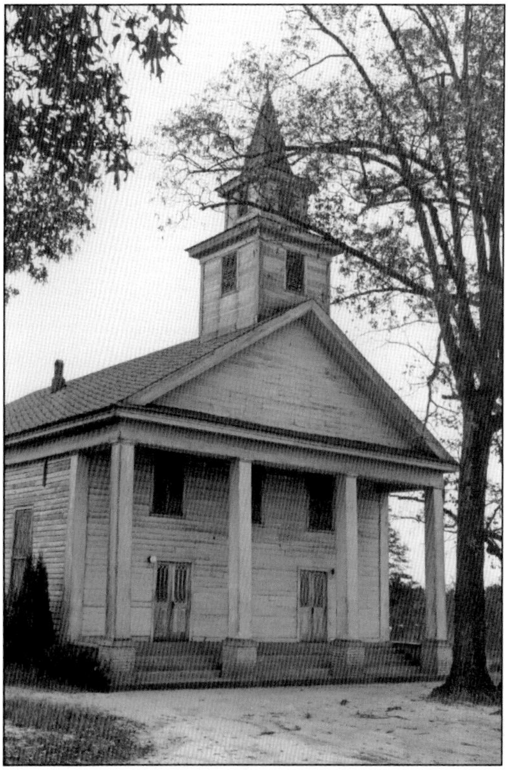

The Fredonia Methodist Episcopal Church is believed to have been established around 1833. This 1850s building with four square columns is typical of rural Greek Revival church architecture. The windows above the doors gave ventilation to the slave gallery. In 1954, this building burned and was replaced with the present brick structure. (Courtesy of C. A. Spence Collection.)

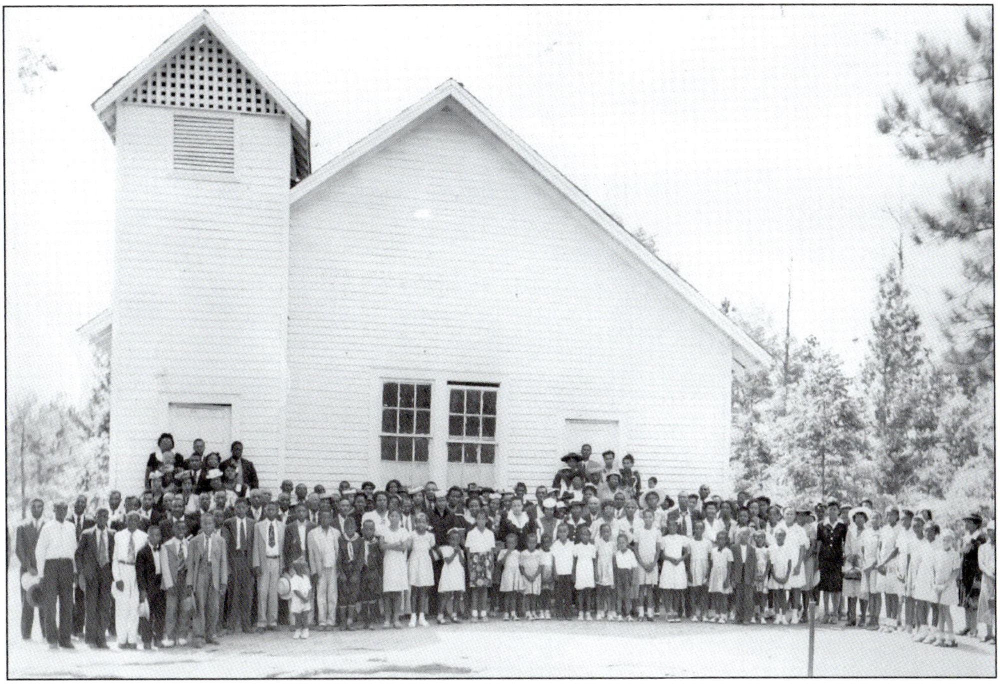

Organized in 1874, the congregation of New Hope Missionary Baptist Church at Fredonia gathered for a group picture in 1938 during the pastorate of Rev. Roosevelt Vines. Family names remembered from that time include Griggs, Davis, Hogg, Trammell, Brooks, Mellon, Patterson, Copeland, Moreland, James, Cooper, and Cofield. The congregation remains active in the community. (Courtesy of Florine Griggs.)

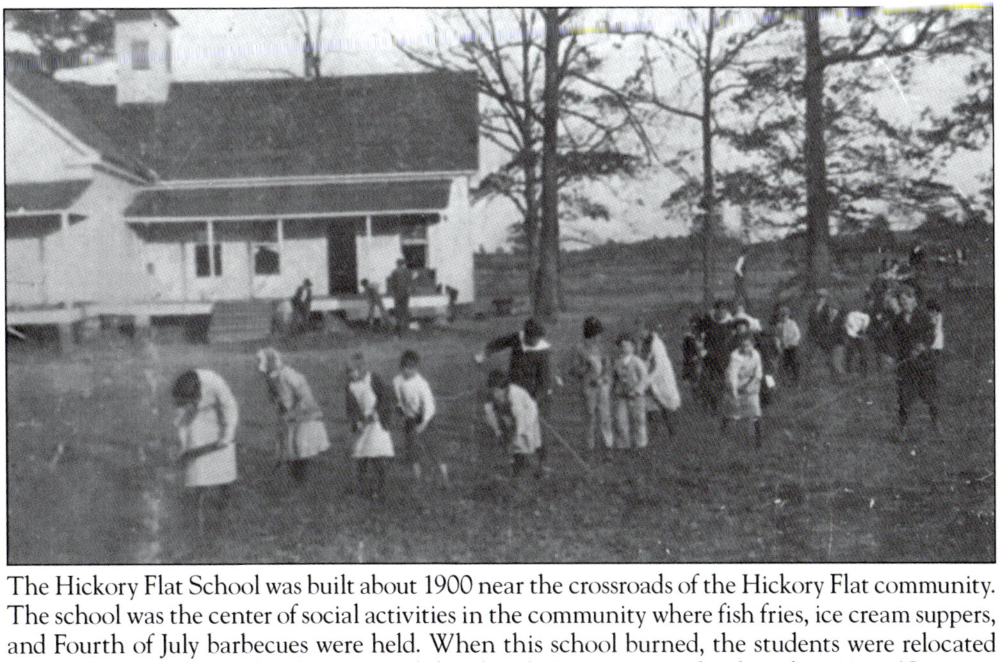

The Hickory Flat School was built about 1900 near the crossroads of the Hickory Flat community. The school was the center of social activities in the community where fish fries, ice cream suppers, and Fourth of July barbecues were held. When this school burned, the students were relocated to a church until the school was consolidated with Five Points School in the 1920s. (Courtesy of Marjorie Newell.)

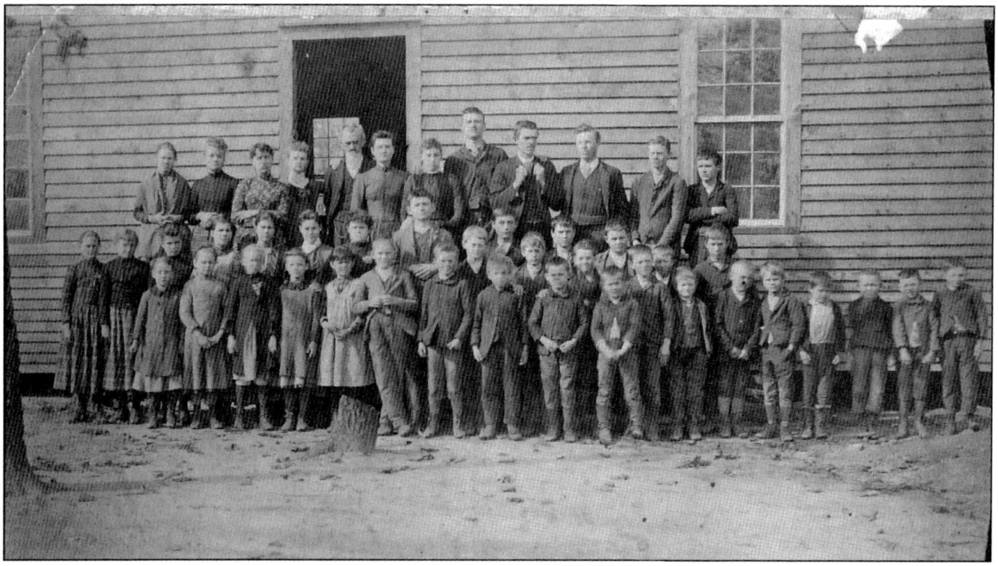

This 1888 photograph presents the student body of Slipstraw School, located near Post Oak Forks. The only students identified are (first row) Annie M. Holderfield (first girl), Lena Lee Holderfield (fourth girl), and Robert Lee Newell (second row, third from right). The teacher standing in the doorway is Marshall B. Hurst, a Confederate veteran and principal musician for Company C, 14th Alabama Infantry Regiment. (Courtesy of Horace McLean Holderfield.)

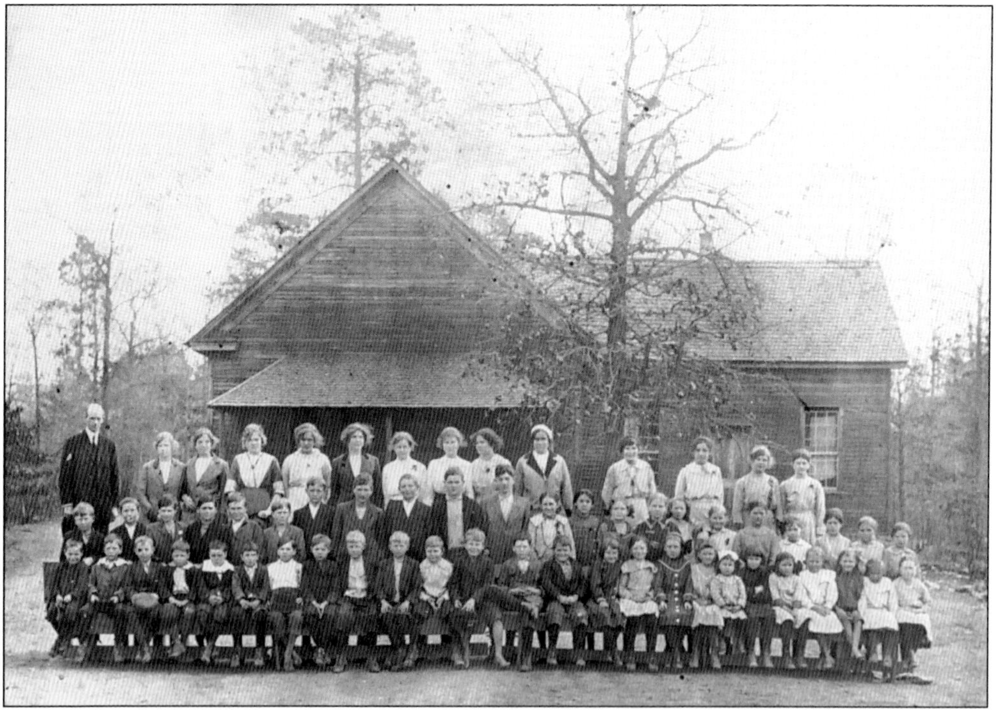

Mountain Spring School was located in the extreme northwest corner of the county. Similar to other rural schools, it originally was one room with a room added to the side making it L-shaped. Across the back of the original room was a wide stage with the teacher's table and chair. This photograph is from around 1913. (Courtesy of Claire Bishop Caldwell.)

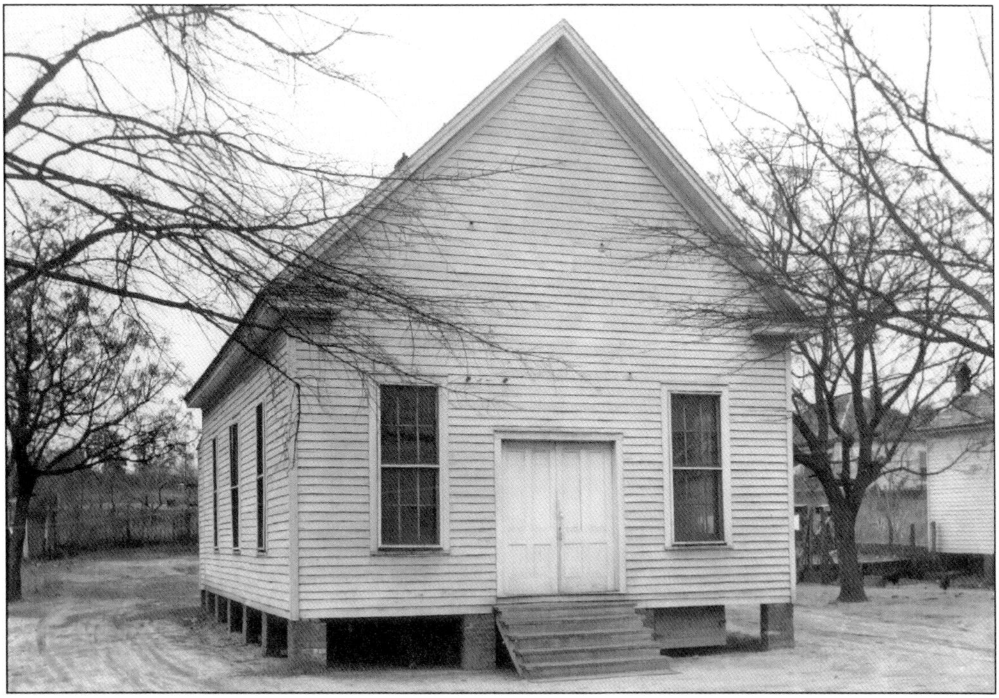

The Lanett Primitive Baptist Church was constituted on February 15, 1903, with the following members: J. C. Arnett and his wife, Mary E. Arnett, Moses Hollis, J. J. Jordan, Jesse Kirby, J. D. McGuirk, Lucille Still, and elder H. J. Redd. A permanent house of worship was built three years later, as shown in this 1936 photograph. The congregation disbanded in recent years, and the building was sold to the Freedom Worship Center. (Courtesy of CMA.)

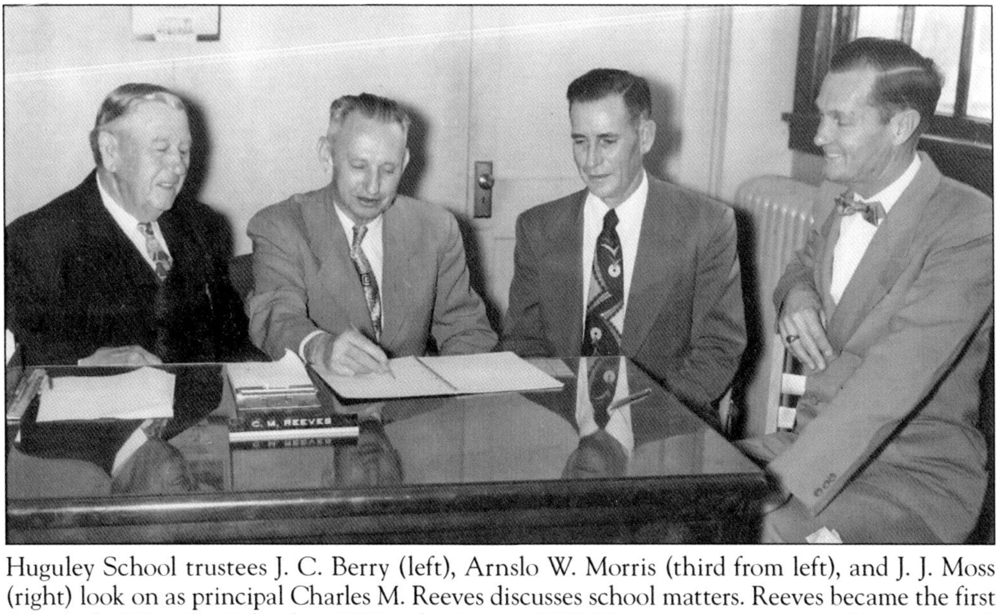

Huguley School trustees J. C. Berry (left), Arnslo W. Morris (third from left), and J. J. Moss (right) look on as principal Charles M. Reeves discusses school matters. Reeves became the first principal of Huguley School in 1938 and retired in 1957. The trustees were men of integrity and prominence in the community who acted as the governing board for the school. (Courtesy of Mary Reeves Alsobrook.)

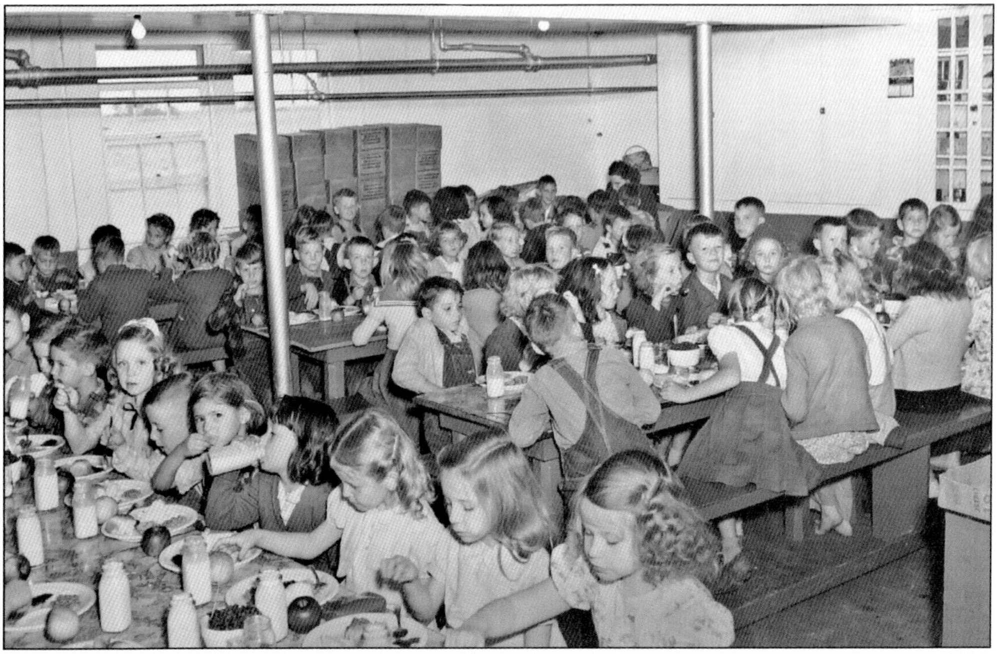

The photograph of the children in the Huguley School lunchroom was taken about 1950. The lunch scene was a common experience for children across the county. The 25¢ lunch provided a pint of milk, meat, two vegetables, and fresh fruit. Children were proud to be asked to help the staff with simple tasks in the lunchroom. (Courtesy of Mary Reeves Alsobrook.)

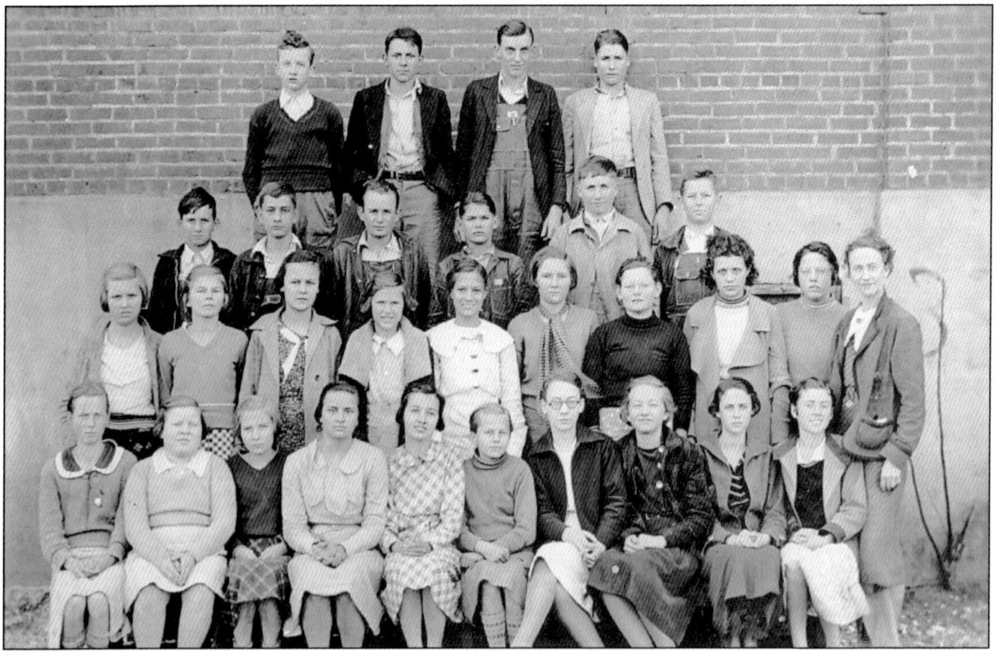

Teacher Addie Anita Cumbee stands on the right in this 1934 photograph of a class of Five Points High School students. This image survived with the names of all 29 students written on the back of the photograph by Edna Jo Lee, the small girl sitting sixth from the left in the front row. (Courtesy of Cathy Burnett Sellers.)

Four

The Valley

In the early 1830s, the first settlers frequenting the frontier trading stores of West Point, Georgia, on the west side of the Chattahoochee River were hardly aware of the boundary between Alabama and Georgia. The commercial district of West Point, Georgia, developed on the Alabama side of the river on a narrow strip of land less than 50 acres adjacent to the river. Most importantly for commercial growth, the Atlanta and West Point Railroad met the West Point and Montgomery Railroad here in 1854. The car shed, station depot, and warehouses were constructed west of the river and near the Chambers County boundary. Since the two railroads used different gauges of track, all freight and passengers were required to change trains at the West Point depot. This inconvenience for the people and businesses using the railroads served as an immediate stimulus to the local economy. From 1854, the people of Chambers County, especially the county's most productive cotton plantations, had rail connections with the manufacturing cities and seaports in the eastern regions of the nation. The presence of this important railroad stimulated the production of cotton on plantations and farms in Chambers County as well as the development of the local textile industry for 100 years following the Civil War.

The village of Bluffton, which was later rechartered as Lanett, developed adjacent to and southwest of West Point. Many merchants operated stores in West Point but lived in Lanett in Chambers County. The first textile mill and village was built in Riverview, followed by mills in Bluffton-Lanett, Langdale, Shawmut, and Fairfax. These five locations were in Chambers County, where the mills were incorporated, but corporate offices were located in West Point. At some point during the 19th century, people began to refer to West Point and these Chambers County towns and villages as simply "the valley" because of their location by the river and the many economic and social interrelationships resulting from the single textile employer, the West Point Manufacturing Company.

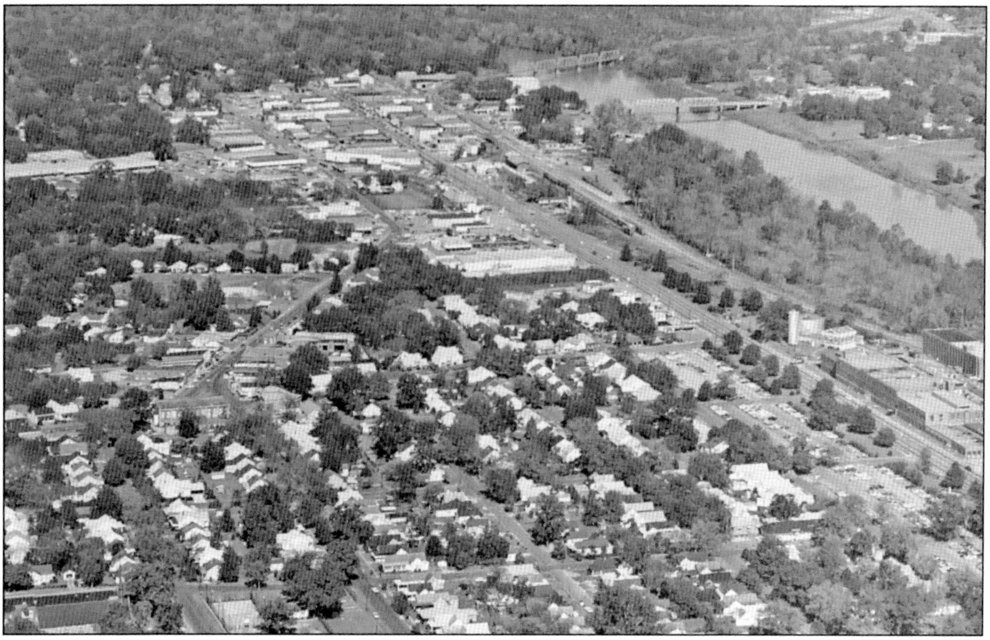

This 1950s aerial view of Lanett and West Point reveals a blending of streets. The business district of West Point, Georgia, situated in the center of the photograph, stimulated the economic and social development of the eastern areas of Chambers County. Lanett Bleachery and Dye Works is located on the lower right in the photograph with the Lanett mill village laid out on the left. (Courtesy of CMA.)

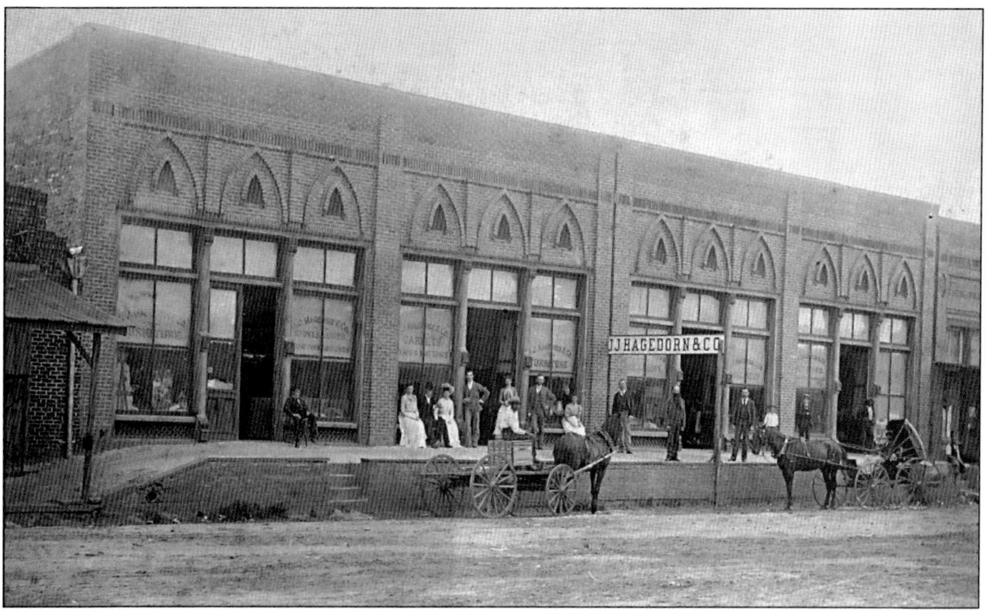

J. J. Hagedorn and Company was founded in 1872, although this photograph dates from 1900. The Hagedorns developed a reputation for providing quality merchandise to families and farms in the region. Their business included a funeral parlor with chapel and ambulance service. The Hagedorn family and then the Herzberg family, who inherited the business, provided leadership for mercantile growth in West Point and Lanett almost 80 years. (Courtesy of CMA.)

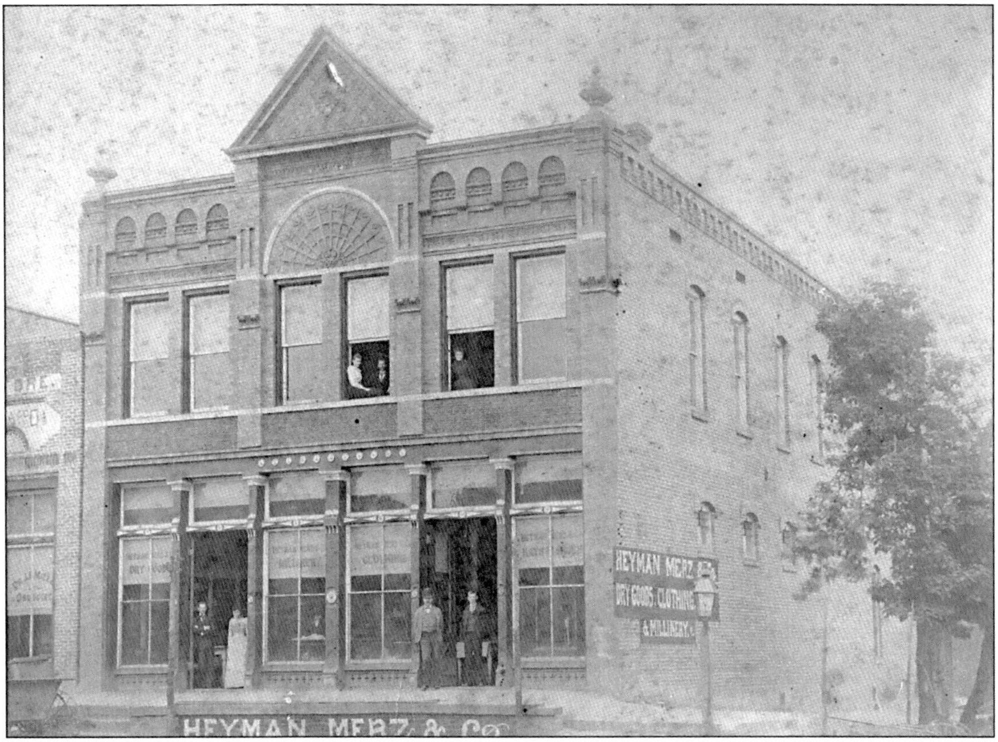

The Jewish community in the valley dates from the 1850s. Herman Heyman established a business with Daniel and Louis Merz to supply farmers and planters as well as townspeople and, during the Civil War, operated a tannery to supply leather to the Confederate army. Louis Merz died at Antiedam in 1862. Members of the Hagedorn, Heyman, and Merz families lived in Bluffton, later Lanett, in Chambers County. (Courtesy of CMA.)

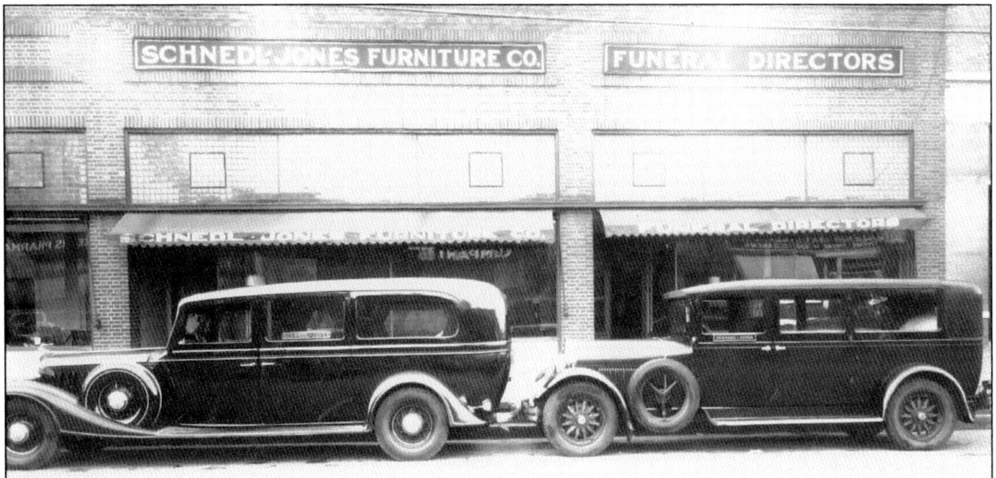

In 1935, these two hearses belonged to the Schnedl–Jones Furniture Company and Funeral Directors, which was established in 1919. The company from West Point served the citizens of Chambers County with various lines of household items such as Hoosier kitchen cabinets, Majestic ranges, Romeagle stoves and ranges, Berkey and Gay bedroom furniture, Statton early American furniture, and the full services of a funeral home. (Courtesy of CMA.)

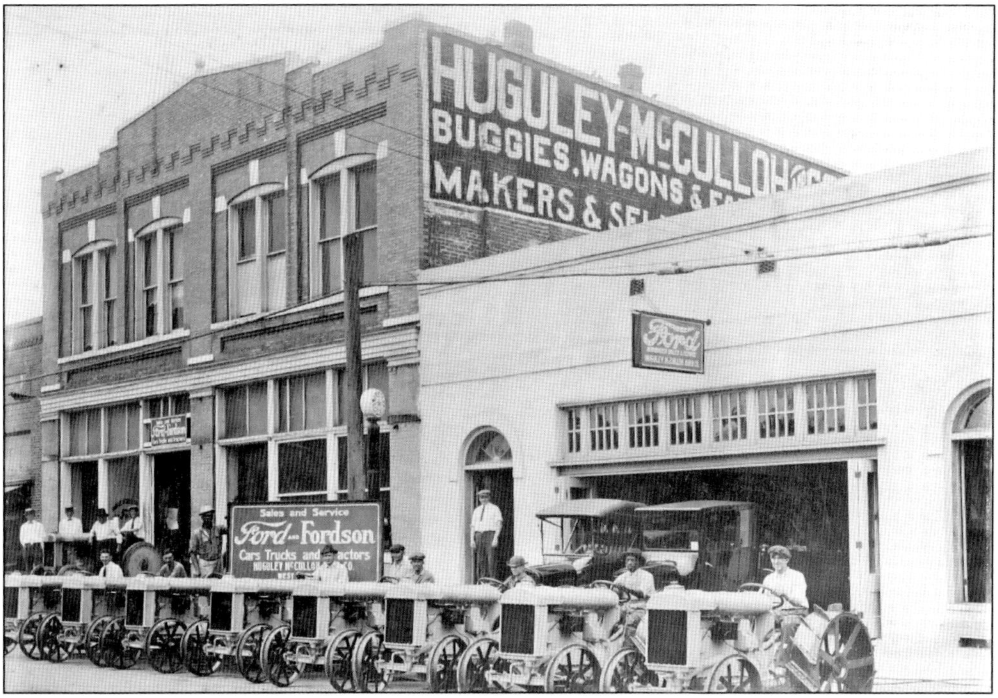

In 1905, Mark McColloh, W. H., and Amos Huguley established a farm supply store that in 1921 became an agent for Ford automobiles. In 1924, the name changed to the Huguley-Scott Automobile Company. In the first 15 years of its existence in West Point, the automotive company sold more than $4 million in new and used cars. The photograph displays Fordson tractors and Model T Fords about 1922. (Courtesy of CMA.)

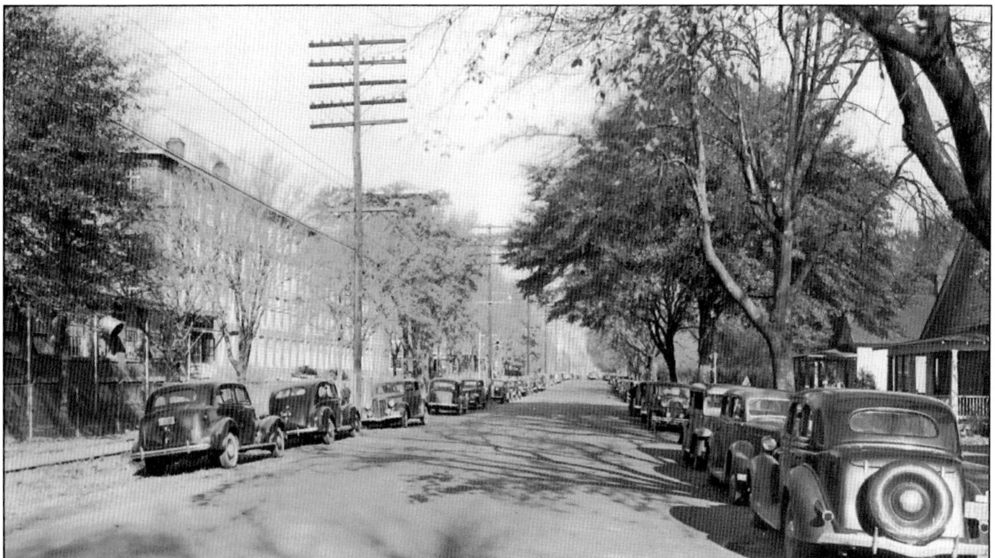

This 1939 photograph is a view of Gilmer Avenue (US Highway 29) looking south in front of the Lanett Mill. Cars are parked parallel on both sides of the highway as far as the eye can see. A railroad track runs between the mill and the cars on the left side of the road. (Courtesy of CMA.)

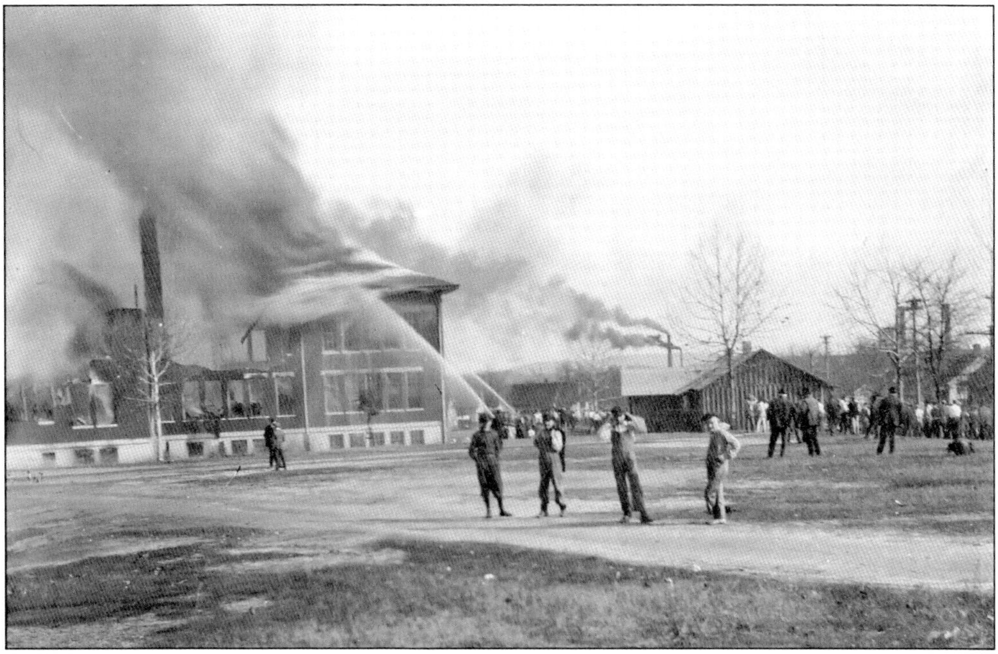

On January 3, 1923, the three-story 20-classroom brick Lanett School burned. In this photograph, the West Point Fire Department answered the alarm and was forced to run a pump line to the Chattahoochee River to get adequate water to fight the fire. All efforts failed to save the 1909 brick structure. (Courtesy of CMA.)

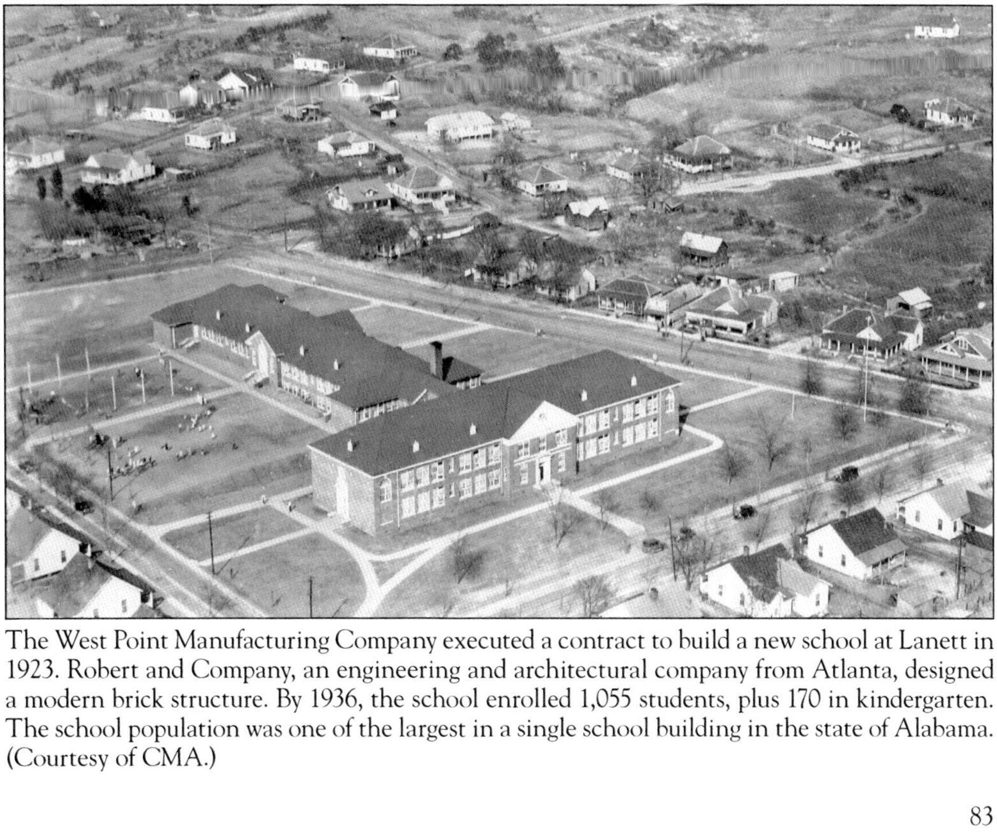

The West Point Manufacturing Company executed a contract to build a new school at Lanett in 1923. Robert and Company, an engineering and architectural company from Atlanta, designed a modern brick structure. By 1936, the school enrolled 1,055 students, plus 170 in kindergarten. The school population was one of the largest in a single school building in the state of Alabama. (Courtesy of CMA.)

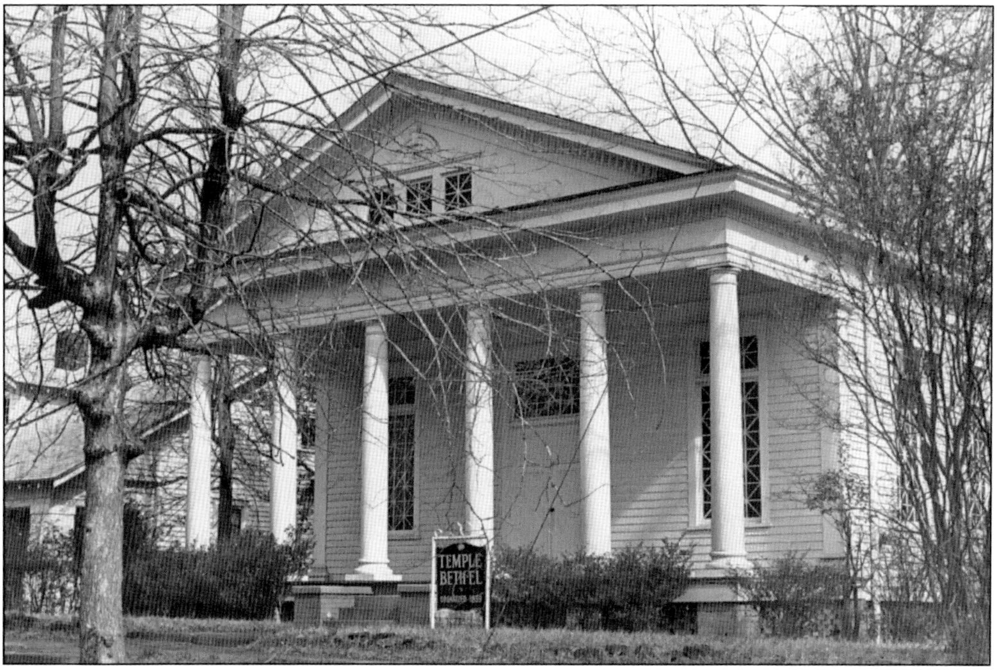

The Jewish community, which was important to the development of the valley area, built Temple Beth-El in 1909 in Lanett. Earlier religious services were conducted in homes by a guest rabbi from Atlanta. The Heyman family provided leadership in the religious life among the Jewish families, who lived primarily in Bluffton-Lanett. (Courtesy of CMA.)

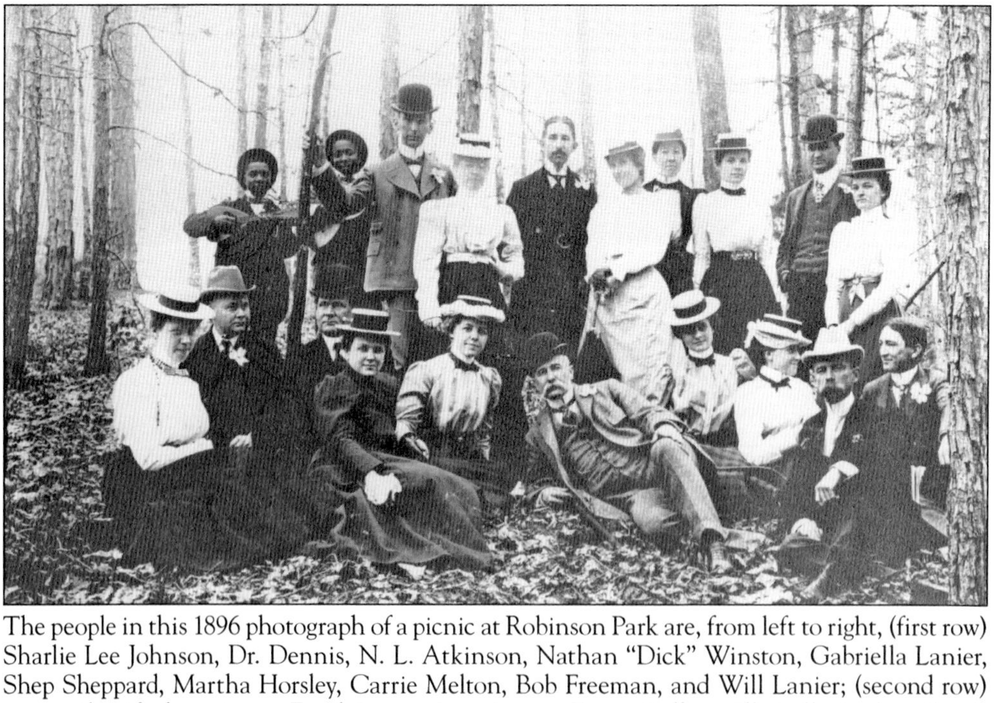

The people in this 1896 photograph of a picnic at Robinson Park are, from left to right, (first row) Sharlie Lee Johnson, Dr. Dennis, N. L. Atkinson, Nathan "Dick" Winston, Gabriella Lanier, Shep Sheppard, Martha Horsley, Carrie Melton, Bob Freeman, and Will Lanier; (second row) two unidentified musicians, Frank Lanier, Lucy Lanier, Erwin Collins, Ella Belle Booker, Florrie Johnson, Eunice Horsley Winston, Phil Lanier, and Gillian Lanier. (Courtesy of CMA.)

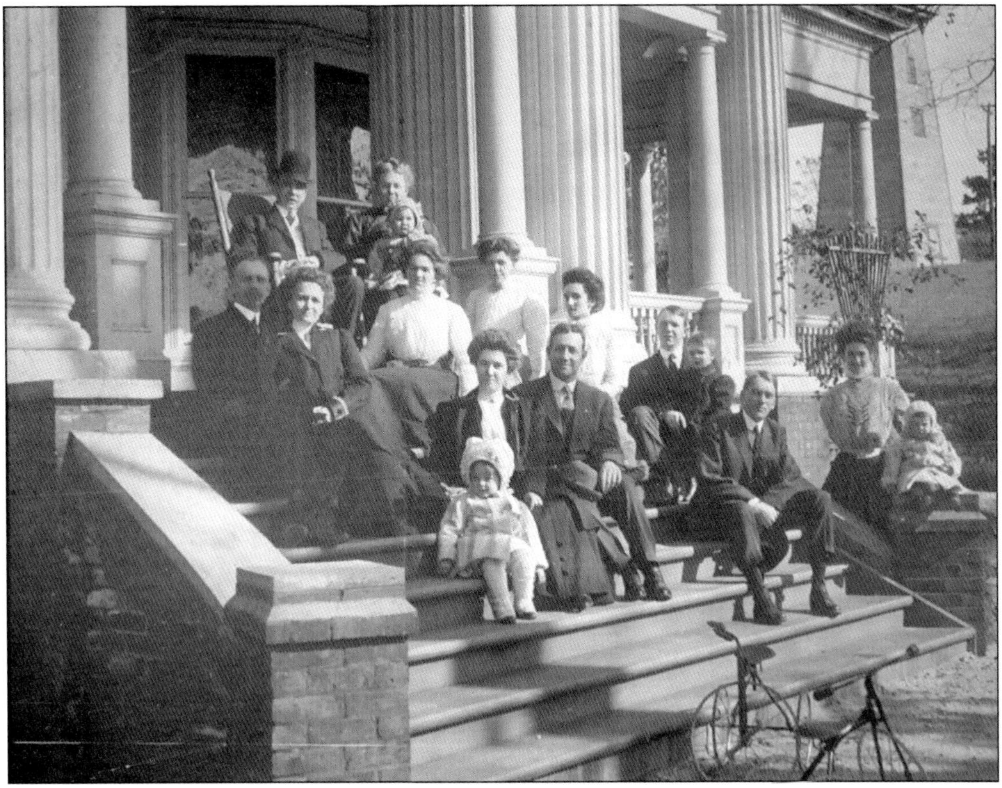

This photograph, taken before 1911, shows LaFayette and Ida Huguley Lanier seated in chairs at the top of the steps at their home, which burned in 1917. Adults seated on the lower steps are, from left to right, (first row) Louise Lanier Dixon, Bryant Dixon, and Joseph Lanier; (second row) Robert Freeman, Gillian Lanier Freeman, Alice Lanier Hinton, Gabriella Lanier Hunnicutt, Marie Lamar Lanier, and George Lanier. Annie Laurie Jones Lanier is standing on the far right near the bottom of the stairs. (Courtesy of CMA.)

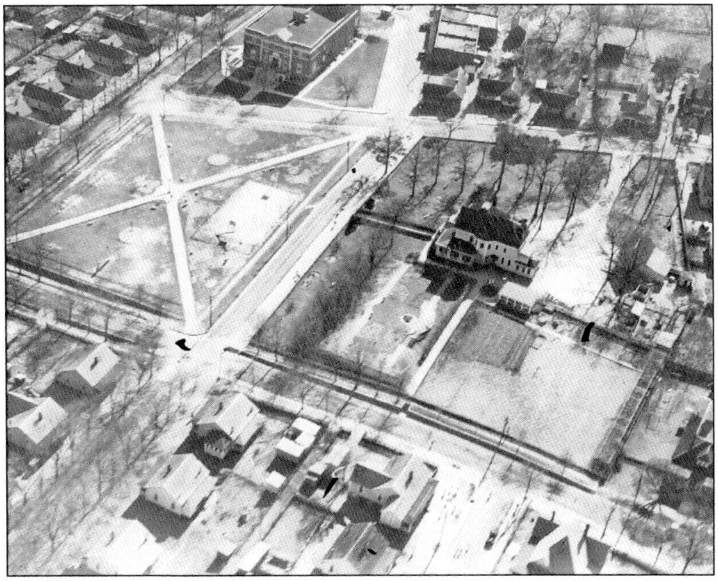

The large house in the center of this 1928 aerial photograph is the home provided to R. W. Jennings, the Lanett Mill superintendent from 1920 to 1950. To the left of this home is a playground and recreation area for the mill children. The large building at the top of the picture is the Lanett Athletic Hall used by teams from the Lanett Mill and Lanett High School. (Courtesy of CMA.)

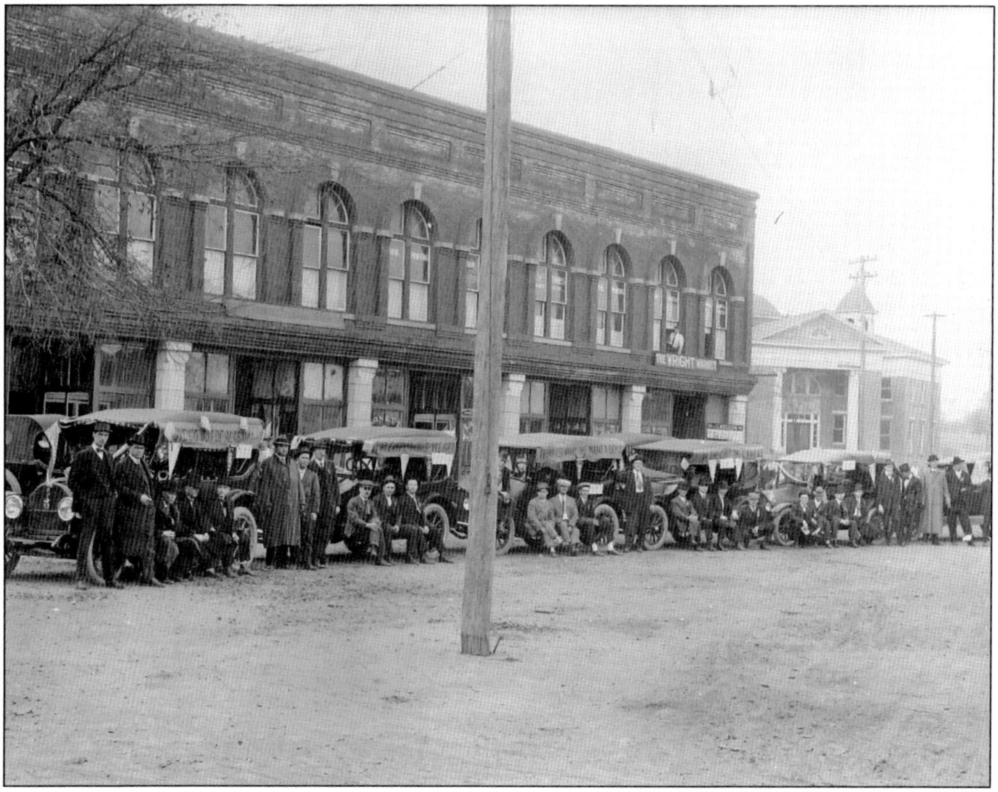

In 1921, businessmen of Lanett organized a rally to petition the railroad to locate a depot in Lanett. Banners on the first four cars read, "We go out of Alabama/ For every thing we get/ That is why we want a Depot/ In the city of Lanett." The cars are parked in front of the Lanett Fraternal Hall built in 1906. (Courtesy of CMA.)

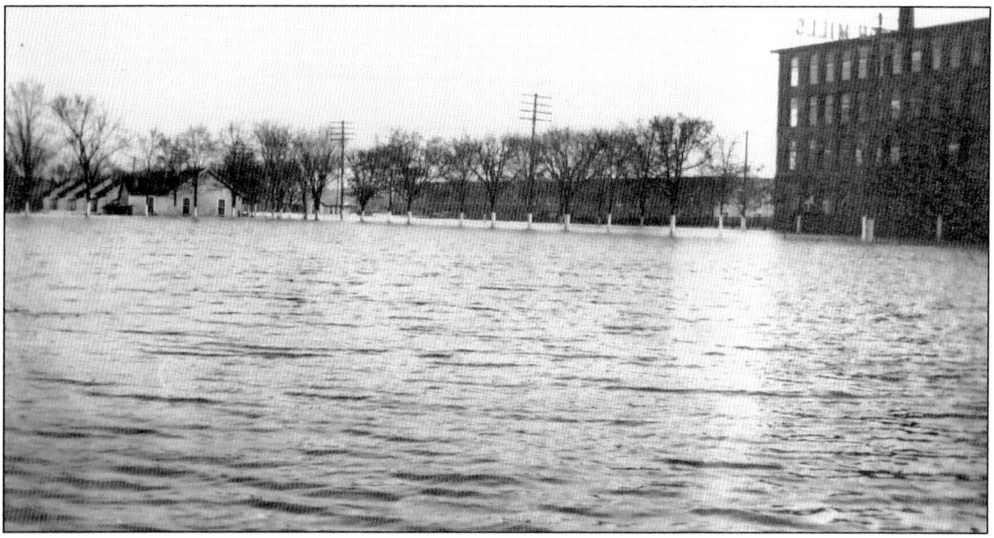

The flood of 1919 created a lake around the Lanett Mill and caused severe damage to houses and businesses. From 1901 until 1971, when the dam was built on the Chattahoochee River above West Point, the river rose above flood stage 32 times. The 1919 flood, the worst flood, was 10.5 feet above flood stage. (Courtesy of CMA.)

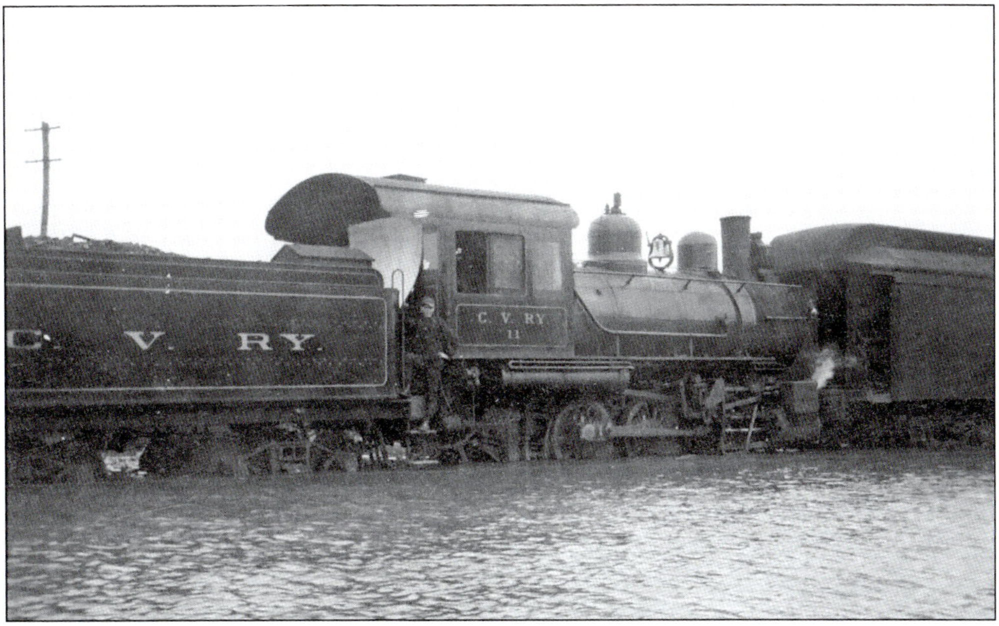

This 1919 photograph shows the water above the tracks of the locally owned Chattahoochee Valley Railway. By 1916, the railway was 45 miles long, stretching from Standing Rock in the north to Bleeker in Lee County to the south. The five mills initially used mules and wagons, then river barges, and finally this railway to move raw cotton, finished products, and passengers. (Courtesy of CMA.)

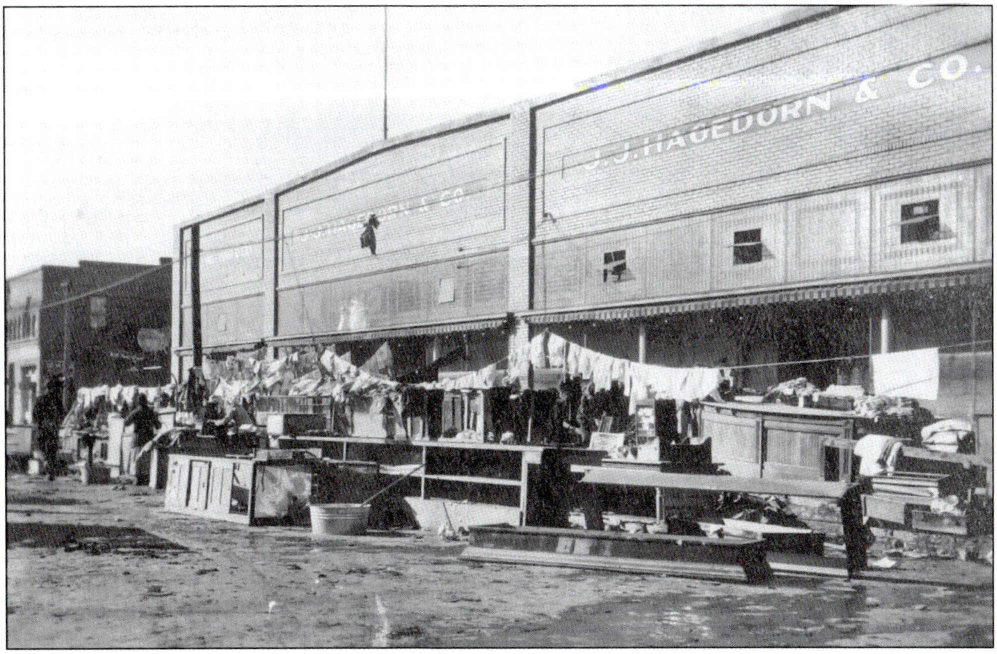

Following the big flood on December 9, 1919, J. J. Hagedorn and Company in West Point moved their inventory and furniture into Gilman Street (now Third Avenue) to dry. The floodwaters reached the top of the windows on the store's facade. The bridge across the Chattahoochee River was only washed away twice, in 1886 and in 1919. (Courtesy of CMA.)

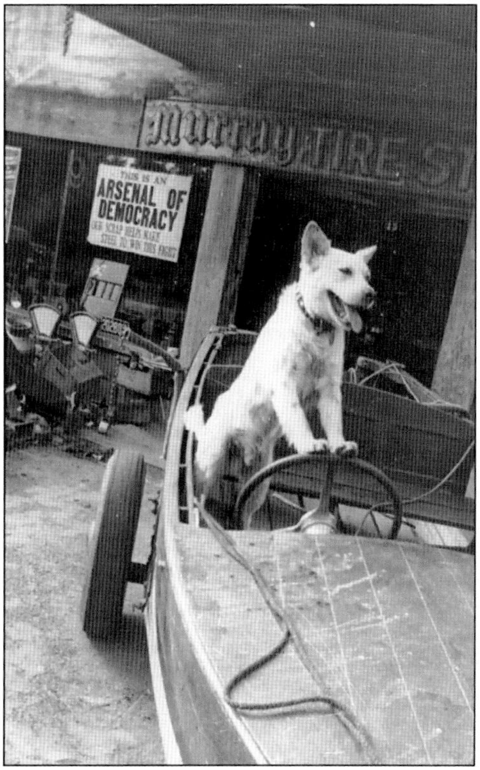

The Chattahoochee River provided mechanical power and later hydroelectric power for the mills and their villages, as well as a source of entertainment that included speedboat races in the 1930s. The dog, Rebel, and the speedboat belonged to Marion Lee "Pop" Ennis. The Ennis Company began selling Johnson outboard motors in 1938 and managed scrap metal drives during World War II, when this photograph was taken. (Courtesy of CMA.)

John H. Howarth (second from left in the third row) organized the Wedowee Council Daughters of Pocahontas band in the 1920s. The Daughters of Pocahontas was the ladies auxiliary of the Improved Order of Red Men, a national patriotic and charitable society. The Daughters of Pocahontas Wedowee Council was located in Lanett, and the Tocoa Council in Fairfax. (Courtesy of CMA.)

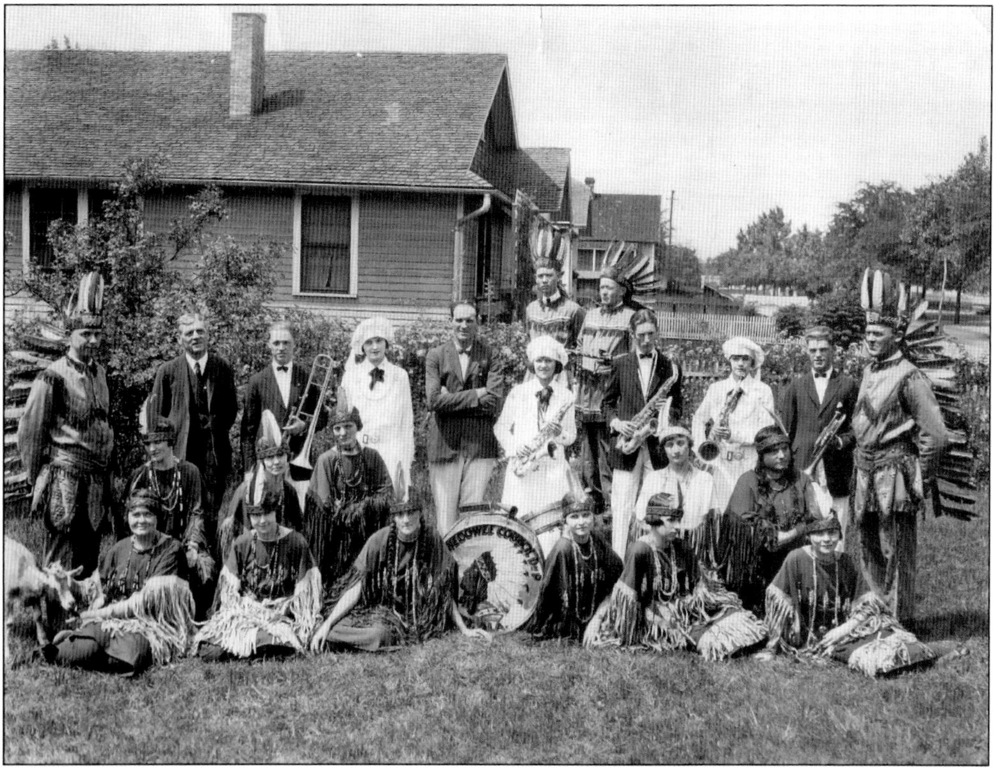

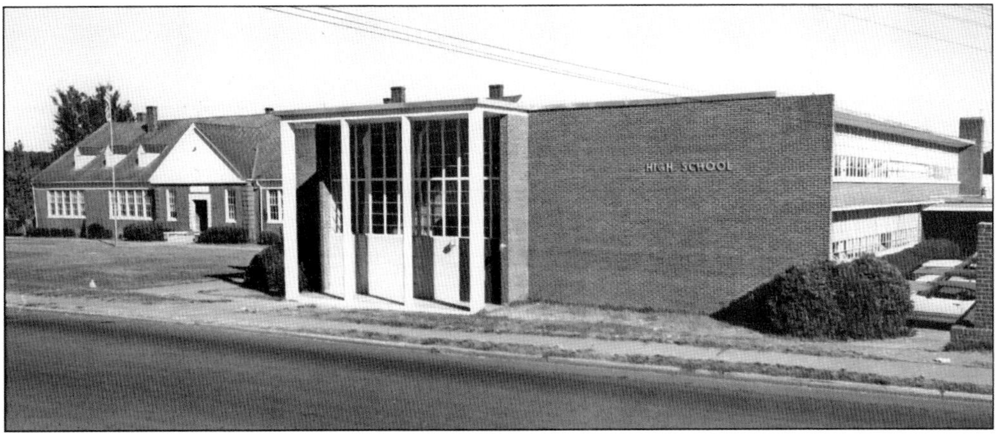

The photograph shows the Lanier High School, built in 1937, on the left, and the annex, built in 1958, on the right. In 1937, the new building housed grades 3 through 12, leaving first and second grades at the Jackson Hill School, which had been established in 1907 as the only high school to serve black students in the valley area. (Courtesy of CMA.)

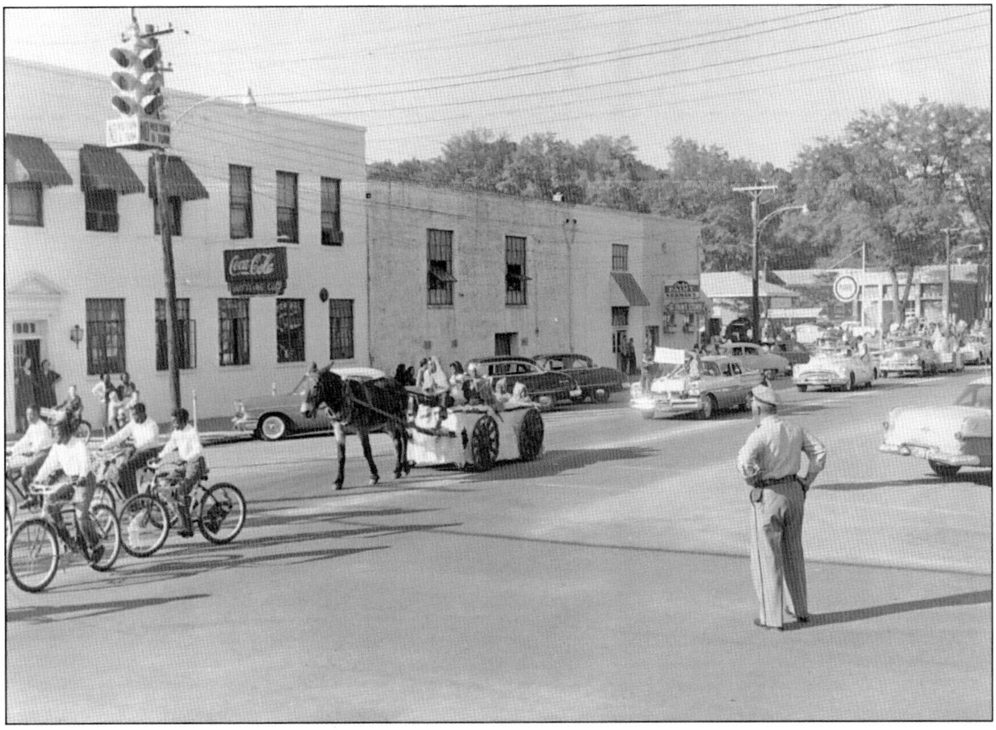

The photograph shows the Lanier High School 1957 homecoming parade. The parade is proceeding south on Third Avenue in front of the Coca-Cola bottling plant. The mule-drawn wagon decorated with white crepe paper is followed by the homecoming queen and her court. The Lanier High School Band (not pictured) led the parade and was directed by John Brooks. (Courtesy of Florine L. Griggs.)

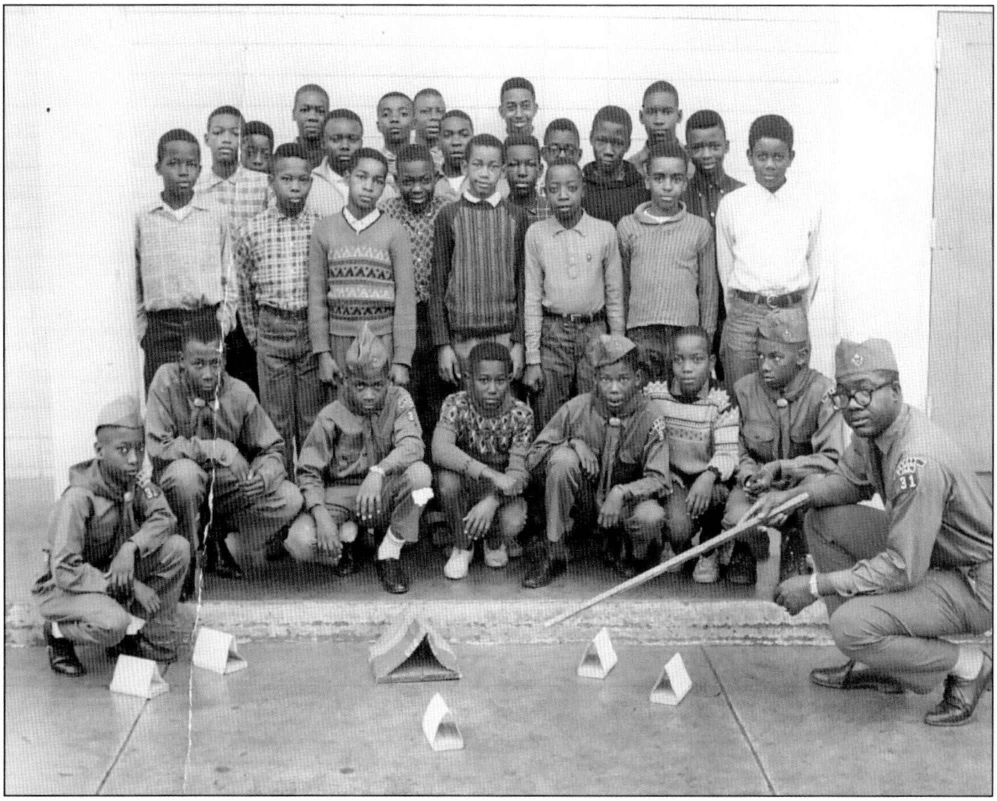

About 1960, scoutmaster Wesley Oliver instructs a Boy Scout troop from Lanier High School in how to set up a camp site. Three Boy Scouts identified are, from left to right, Buck Davis (second row, second scout), Jimmy Fears (second row, fifth scout), and Phillip Fears (third row, third scout). (Courtesy of Florine L. Griggs.)

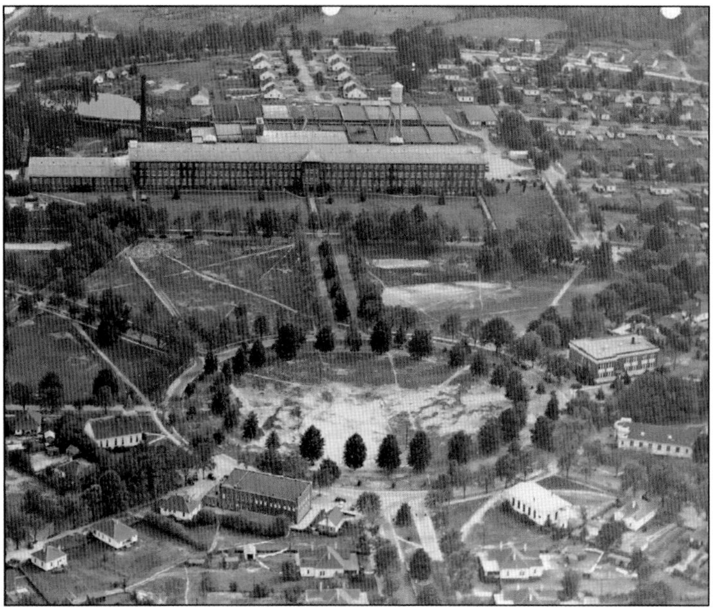

The Shawmut Mill, facing the center hub of the new village, was photographed about 1915. The mill began manufacturing in 1908 as an operating division of the parent West Point Manufacturing Company. A landscape architect was employed to design plans for the new village, and George D. Allen, a civil engineer from West Point, carried out those plans. (Courtesy of CMA.)

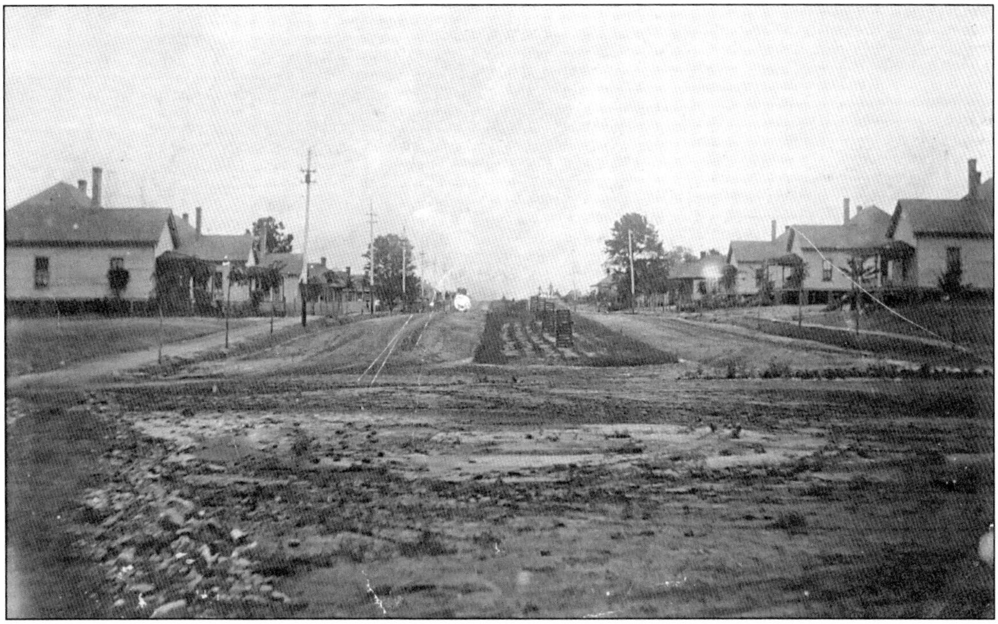

The view from about 1915 is Double Drive (Twenty-third Avenue) north from Shawmut Circle. Tall cages surround young trees that have been planted in the center of Double Drive. The use of professional design services to develop this village reflected a progressive philosophical commitment of the mill owners to provide the employees with a healthy and attractive environment in which to live. (Courtesy of CMA.)

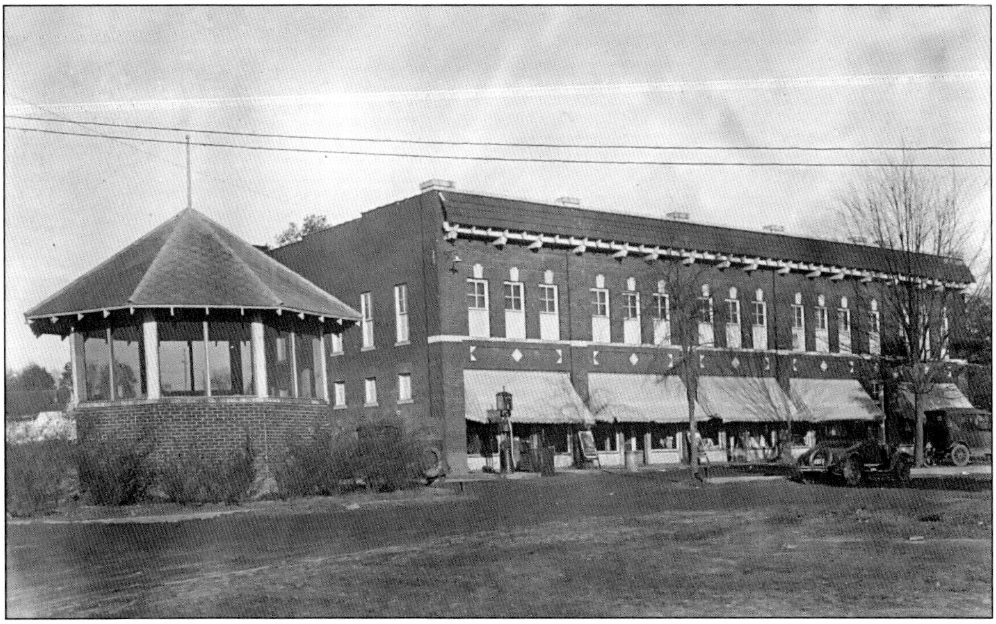

One of the first public buildings constructed on Shawmut Circle was the company-owned, two-story brick building that provided rental space for private businesses on the first floor and space for the Masonic lodge and community group meetings and activities on the second floor. Some of the businesses that were located in this building were McClendon's Drugstore, Whitehead's General Merchandise, and Newby's Barbershop. (Courtesy of CMA.)

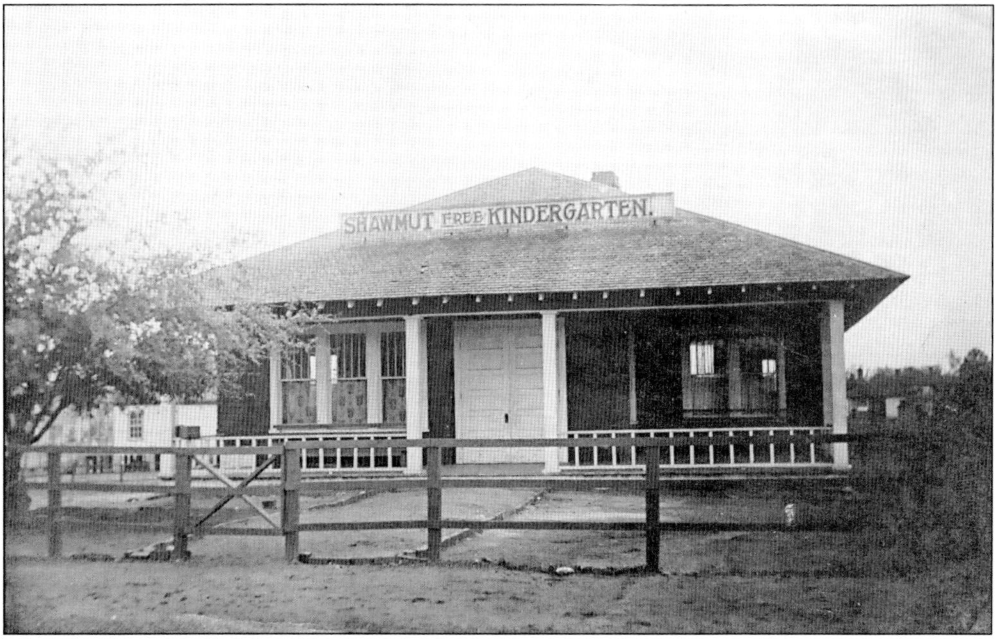

The Shawmut Kindergarten in the photograph began operating in its cottage about 1915 with 60 students. Prior to the construction of a brick two-story elementary and high school building in 1917, students were housed temporarily in a mill cottage next to the brick store building on the circle. (Courtesy of CMA.)

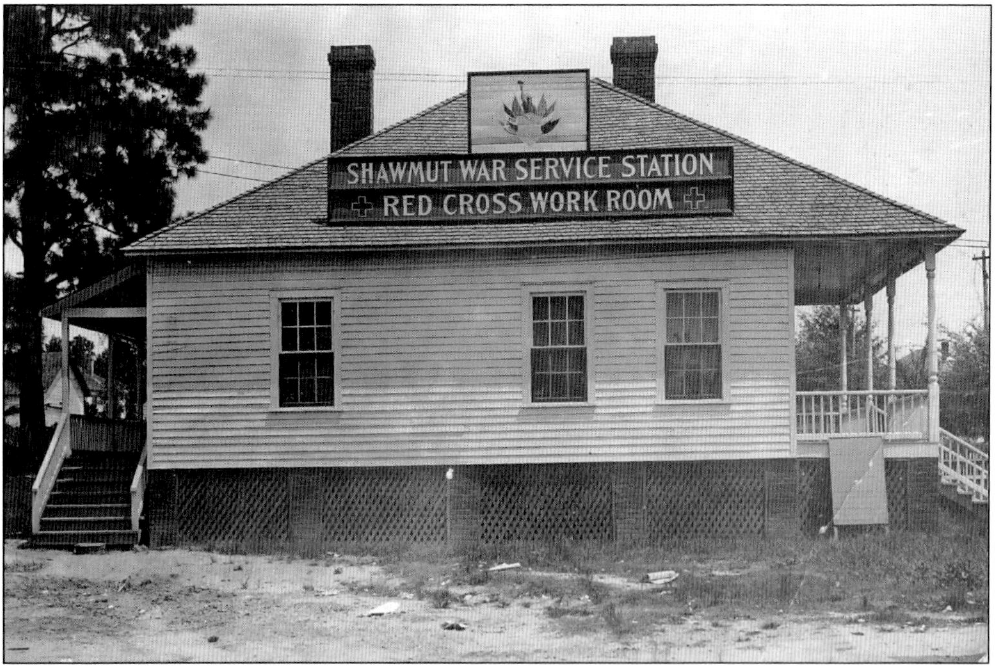

This Shawmut War Service Station Red Cross Work Room photograph dates from 1918. In this cottage, Red Cross workers assisted families in maintaining contact with their soldier relatives and organized activities to assist the war effort. Women were taught to make bandages for the military medical services. (Courtesy of CMA.)

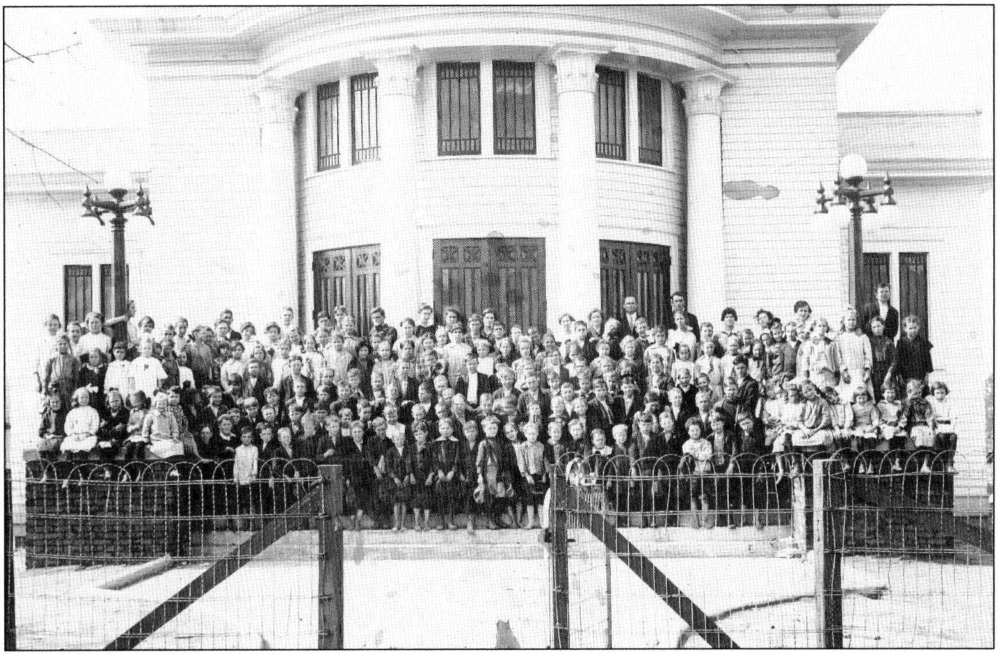

About 1920, the company built the Shawmut Theater, which featured a neoclassical facade, on the circle. The company's athletic association provided motion pictures, plays, and vaudeville acts in this theater. It was also used as an auditorium for the school, as evidenced in this photograph of barefooted school children standing on the theater steps. (Courtesy of CMA.)

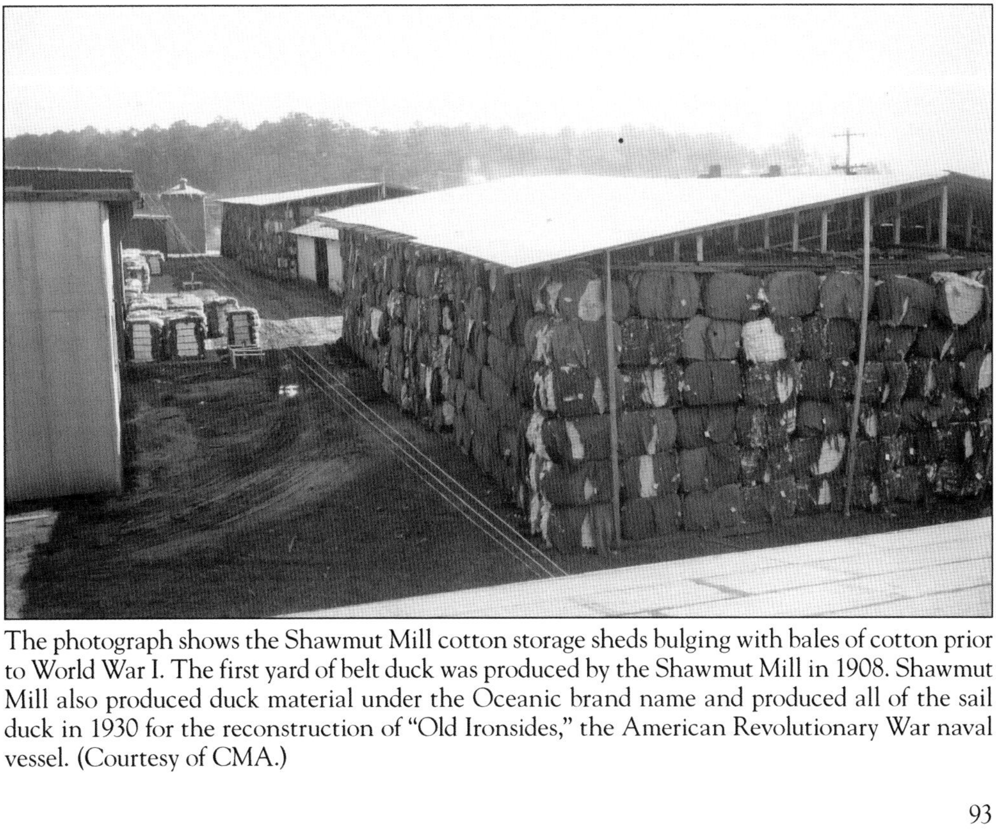

The photograph shows the Shawmut Mill cotton storage sheds bulging with bales of cotton prior to World War I. The first yard of belt duck was produced by the Shawmut Mill in 1908. Shawmut Mill also produced duck material under the Oceanic brand name and produced all of the sail duck in 1930 for the reconstruction of "Old Ironsides," the American Revolutionary War naval vessel. (Courtesy of CMA.)

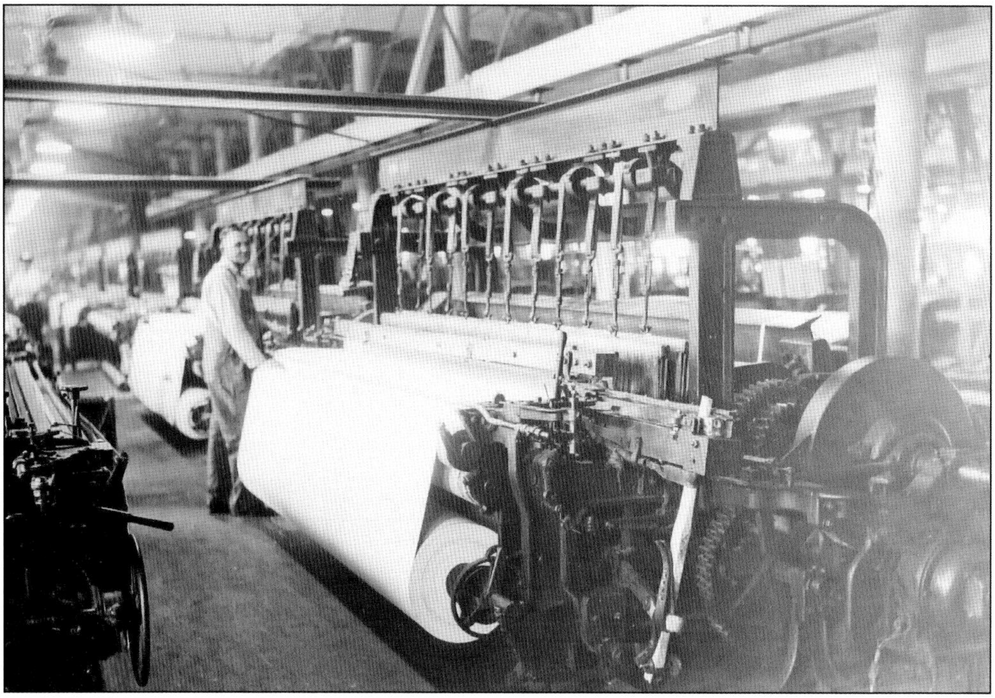

In the mid-1920s, an unidentified weaver is monitoring large looms producing cotton duck cloth in the weave room in Shawmut Mill. In its early period, the company supplied heavy fabric for filters, hoses, and belting to companies such as International Harvester, as well as canvas for marine applications. (Courtesy of CMA.)

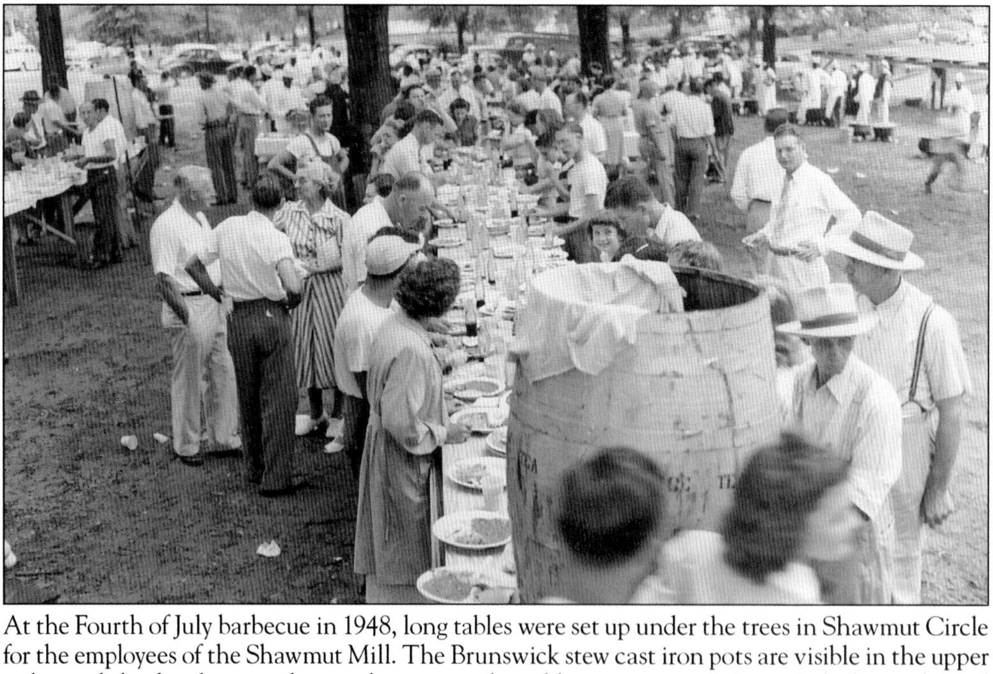

At the Fourth of July barbecue in 1948, long tables were set up under the trees in Shawmut Circle for the employees of the Shawmut Mill. The Brunswick stew cast iron pots are visible in the upper right, and the families standing and eating at the tables are enjoying Coca-Cola (as evidenced by the empty bottles) with their barbecue. (Courtesy of CMA.)

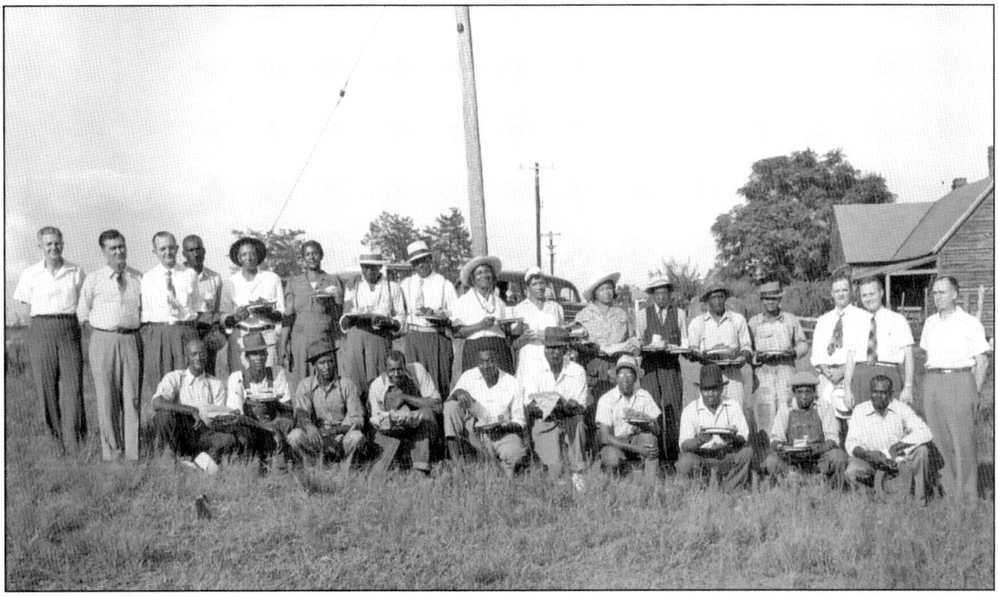

John Ben Jones (Shawmut Mill superintendant), F. L. Underwood, and four unidentified supervisors have joined the group of African American employees at their company barbecue. The Shawmut Mill began with a small number of minority employees, who were provided housing on one side of the Shawmut Village. (Courtesy of CMA.)

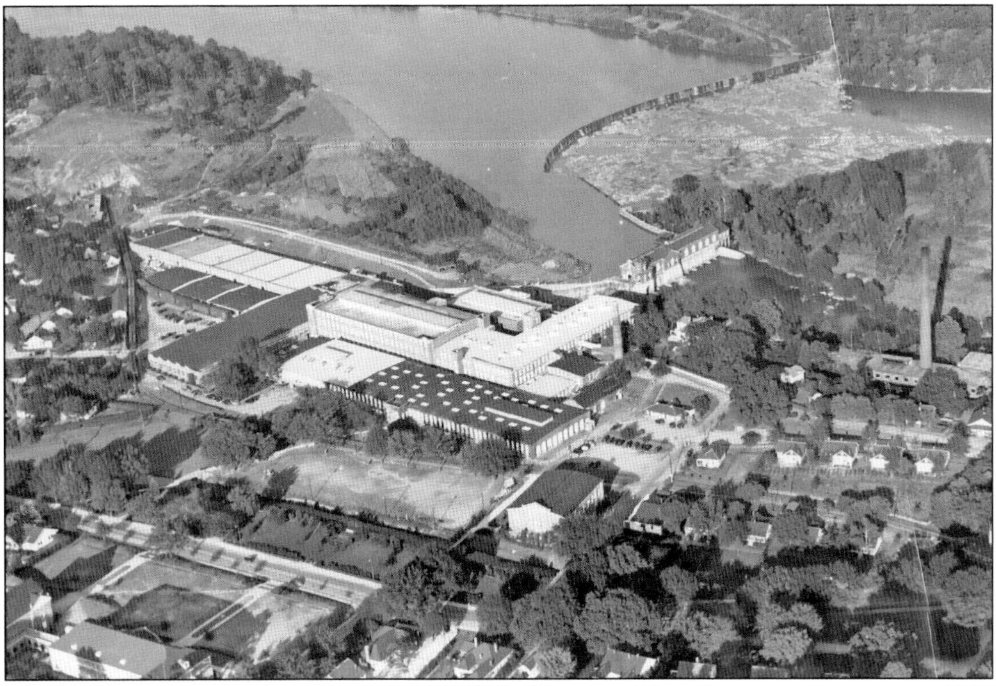

The first mill on this site was founded by Chattahoochee Manufacturing Company in 1866 in a building that was originally the Elisha Trammell gristmill. The 1924 aerial photograph of Langdale Mill clearly shows the dam across the Chattahoochee River, the powerhouse, the mill, and a limited number of homes. In 1954, this mill employed 1,500 people, with 39,752 spindles and 716 looms. (Courtesy of CMA.)

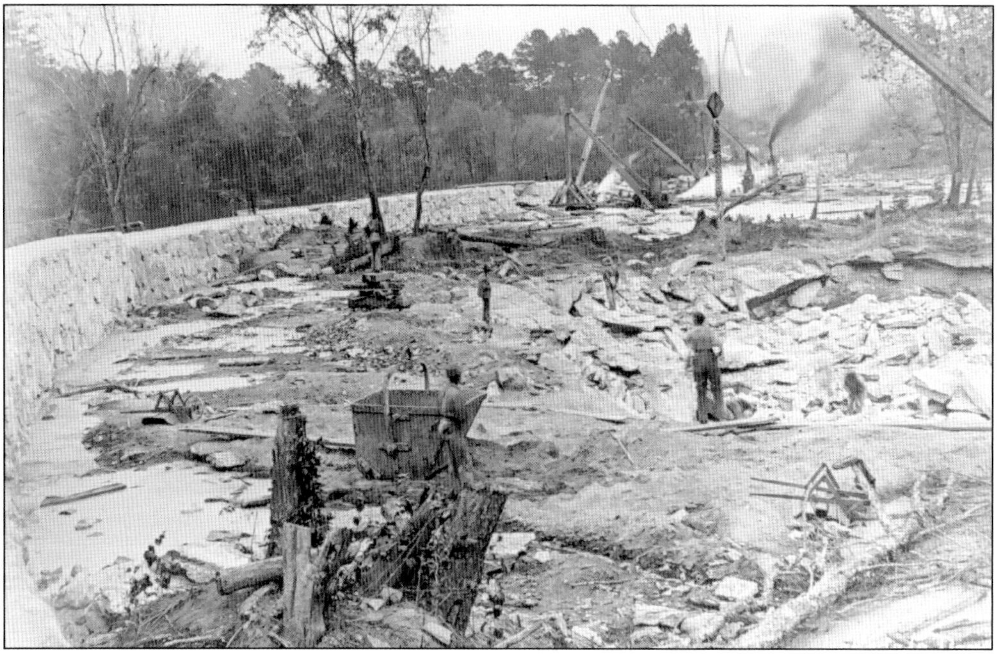

This 1904 photograph taken during the construction of the Langdale dam shows how steam machinery moved granite from the bedrock under the Chattahoochee River into position to build the dam. The powerhouse at the west side of the dam would be sitting in the state of Georgia, since Georgia owned the river to the eastern bank of the river. (Courtesy of CMA.)

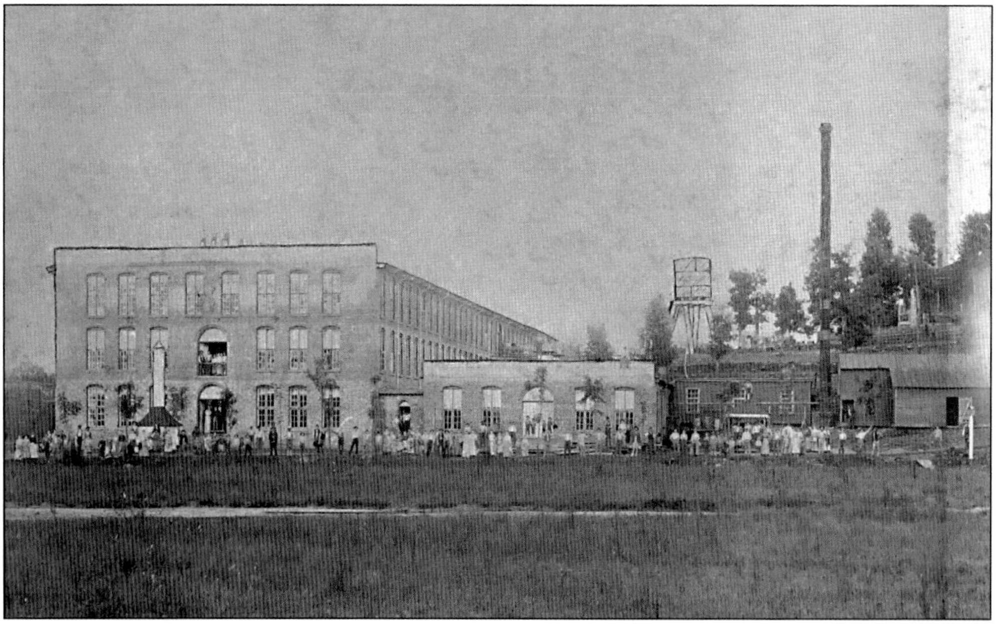

In 1886, a fire destroyed the original mill structure, and the facility in this photograph was built after that date. This is a celebratory photograph. The mill workers (men, women, and children) are lined up in front of the new buildings. Thomas and Elizabeth Lang are standing in the central arched doorway. He is wearing a cutaway jacket, and she is wearing an evening dress. (Courtesy of CMA.)

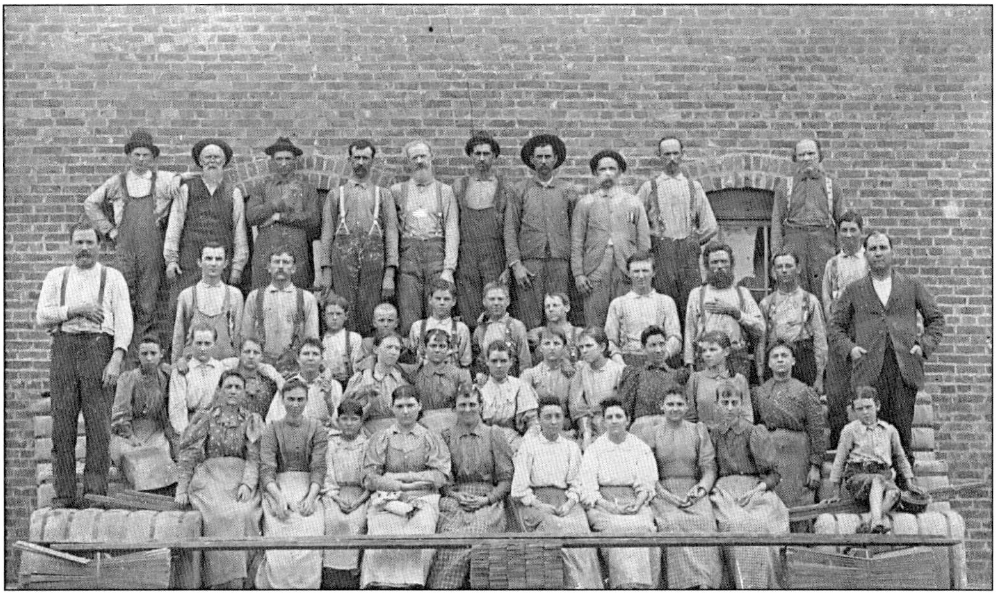

This photograph from the 1880s is one of the earliest taken of operatives at the Langdale Mill. The one identified individual, the man standing on the right wearing a coat with no tie, is believed to be I. B. Morris, who later was the overseer for the card room employees. (Courtesy of CMA.)

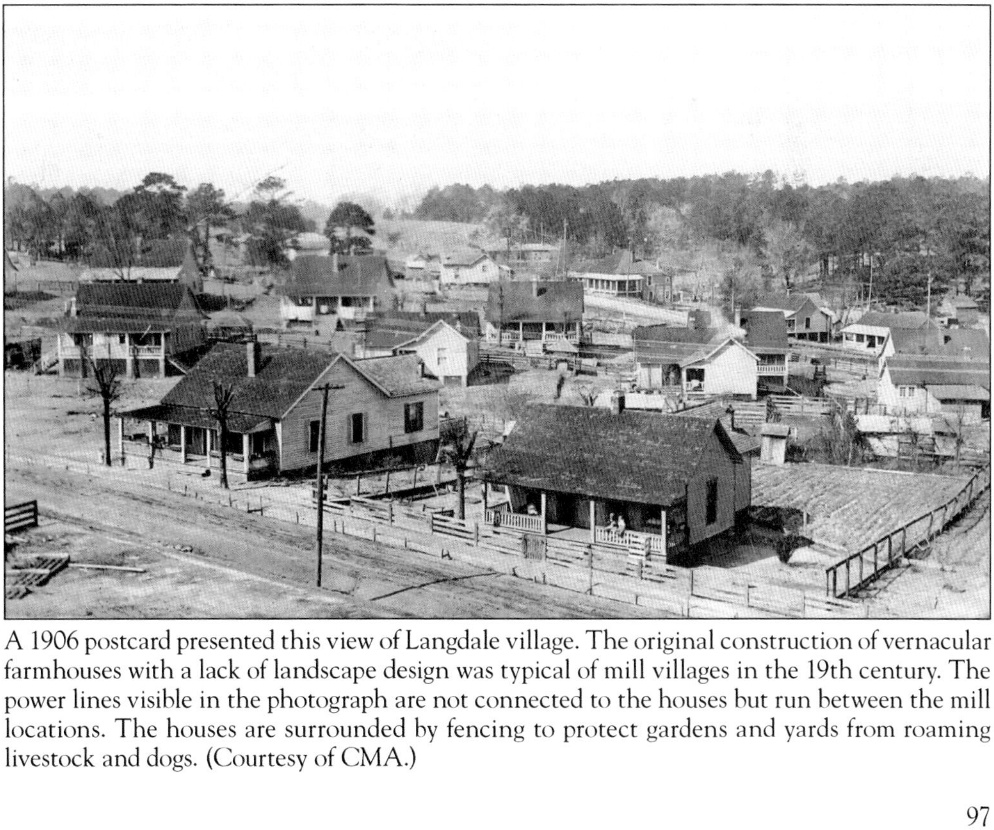

A 1906 postcard presented this view of Langdale village. The original construction of vernacular farmhouses with a lack of landscape design was typical of mill villages in the 19th century. The power lines visible in the photograph are not connected to the houses but run between the mill locations. The houses are surrounded by fencing to protect gardens and yards from roaming livestock and dogs. (Courtesy of CMA.)

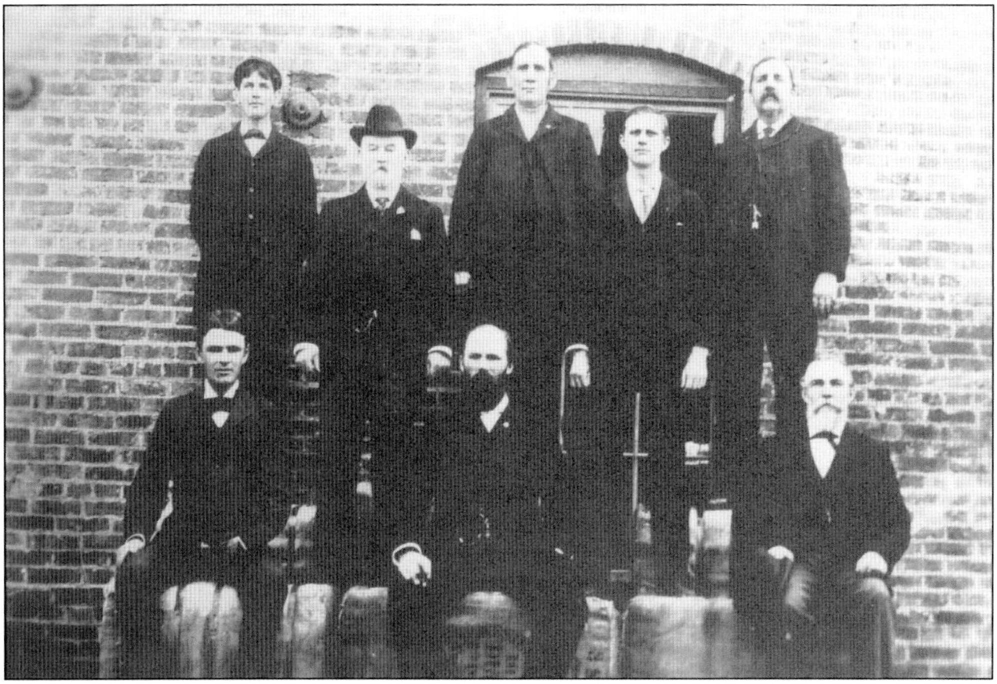

This photograph of the overseers and superintendent of Langdale Mill was taken about 1900. From left to right are (first row) unidentified, Caleb Heard (cloth room overseer), and Isham Stanley (master mechanic); (second row) ? Lanier, Thomas Lang (superintendent), I. B. Morris (carding overseer), Harvey Enloe (spinning overseer), and Joseph Holderbrand (weaving overseer). (Courtesy of CMA.)

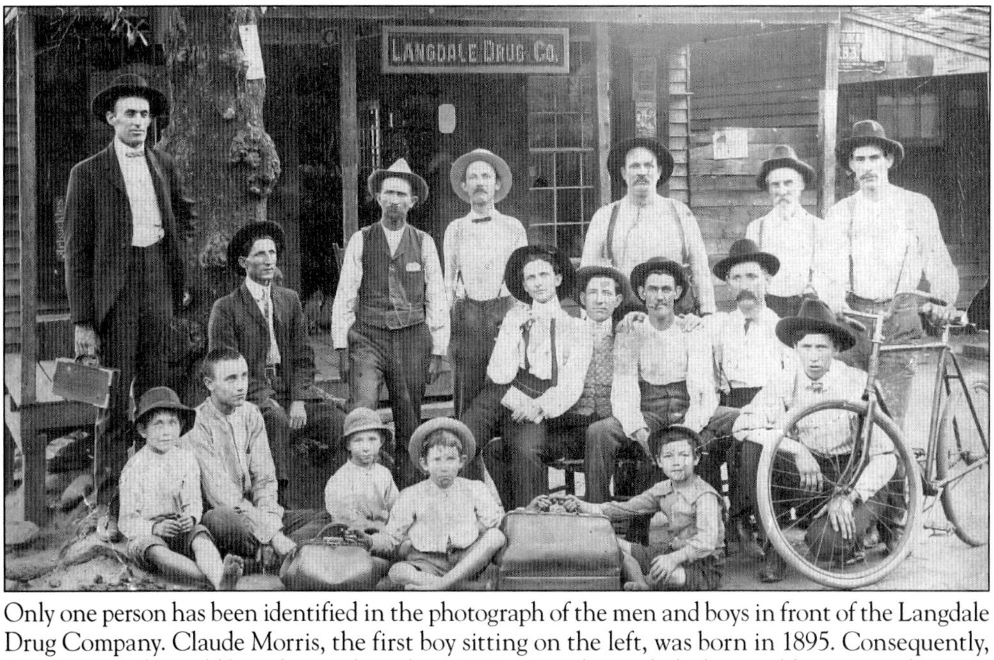

Only one person has been identified in the photograph of the men and boys in front of the Langdale Drug Company. Claude Morris, the first boy sitting on the left, was born in 1895. Consequently, the photograph would have been taken about 1903. Note the satchels that could suggest a physician or possibly a traveling salesman is in the photograph. (Courtesy of CMA.)

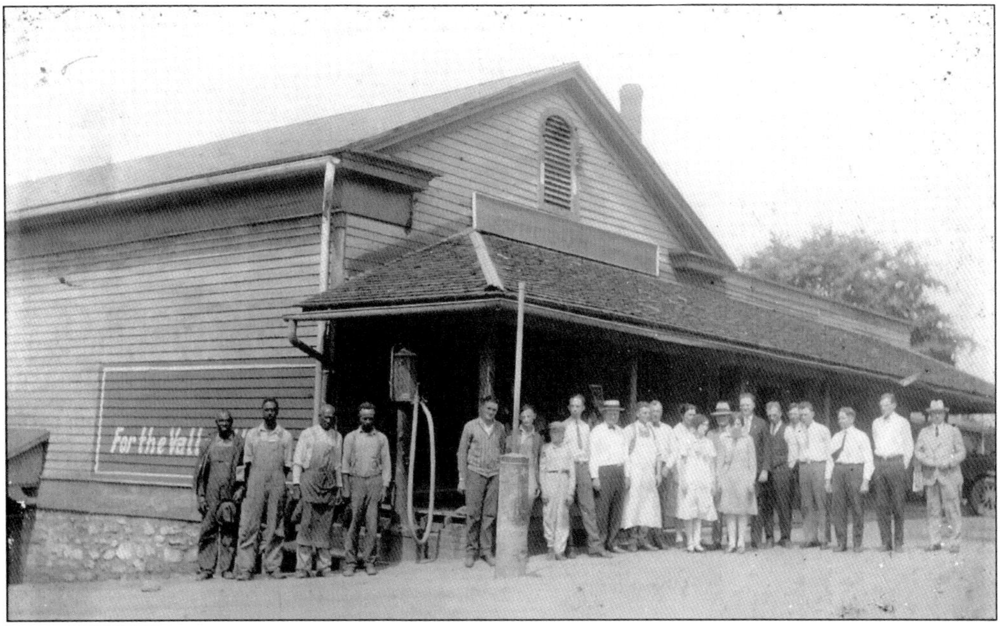

In 1916, John Will Johnson and his brother George bought their uncle's interest in a mercantile business and renamed it Johnson and Company. By the 1930s, grocery orders could be called in to the store and then delivered to the home on credit. The Johnson brothers also operated a funeral parlor, and the first Langdale post office was located in the rear of this building. (Courtesy of CMA.)

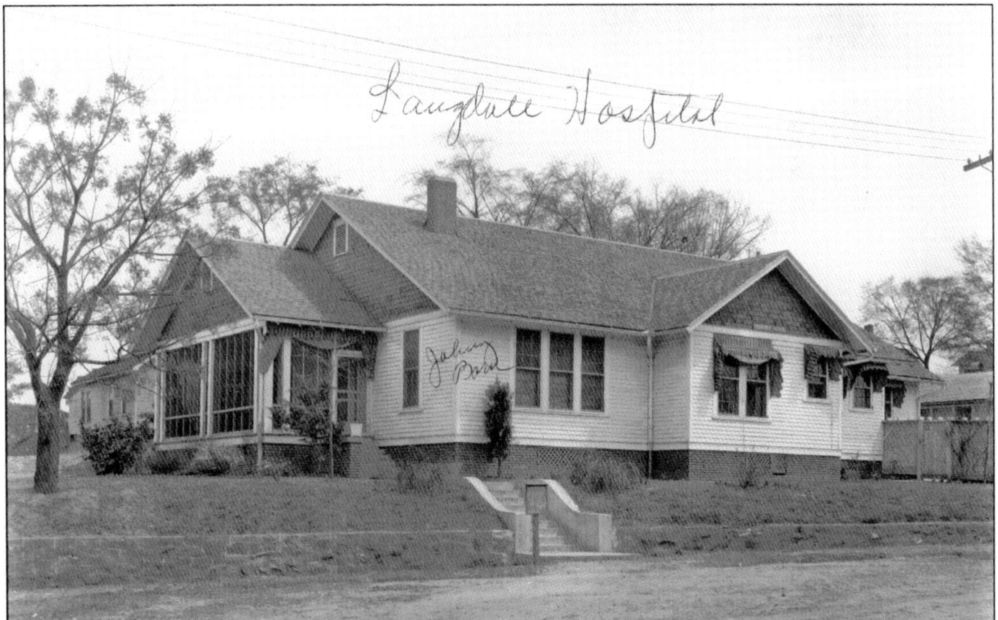

The West Point Manufacturing Company built the Langdale Emergency Hospital prior to 1924 in Johnson's curve on US Highway 29. The facility had the external appearance of a large arts and crafts bungalow. This emergency hospital provided medical services to the mill communities until the Lanier Memorial Hospital was constructed in 1947. (Courtesy of CMA.)

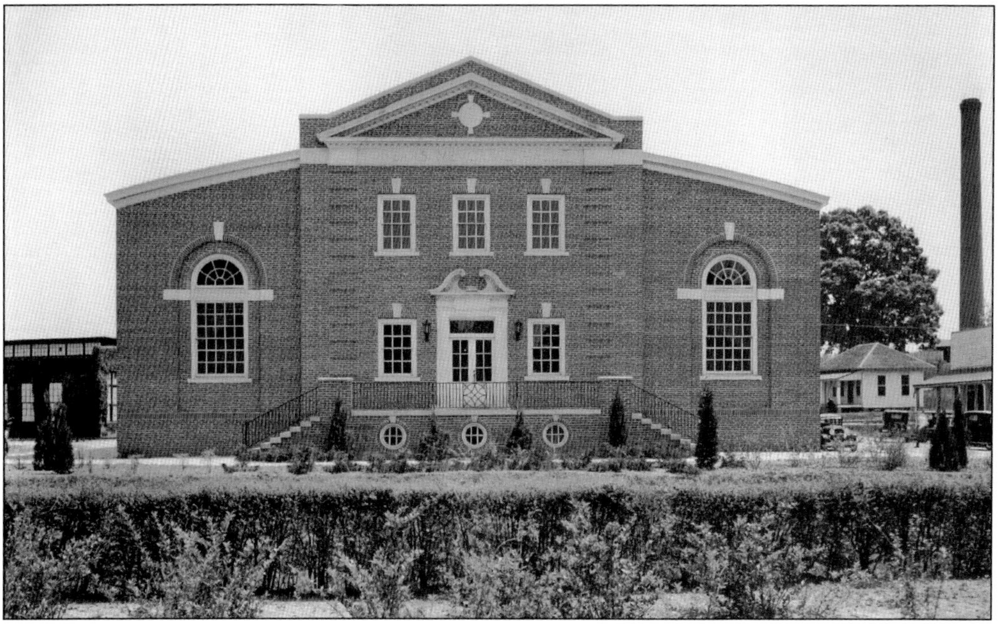

Sears Memorial Hall in Langdale was built about 1935 by the West Point Manufacturing Company for indoor athletic activities. Many residents remember the annual Christmas tree that reached to the rafters in the middle of the basketball court, where each child in a mill family would be presented with Christmas candy and an appropriate gift. (Courtesy of CMA.)

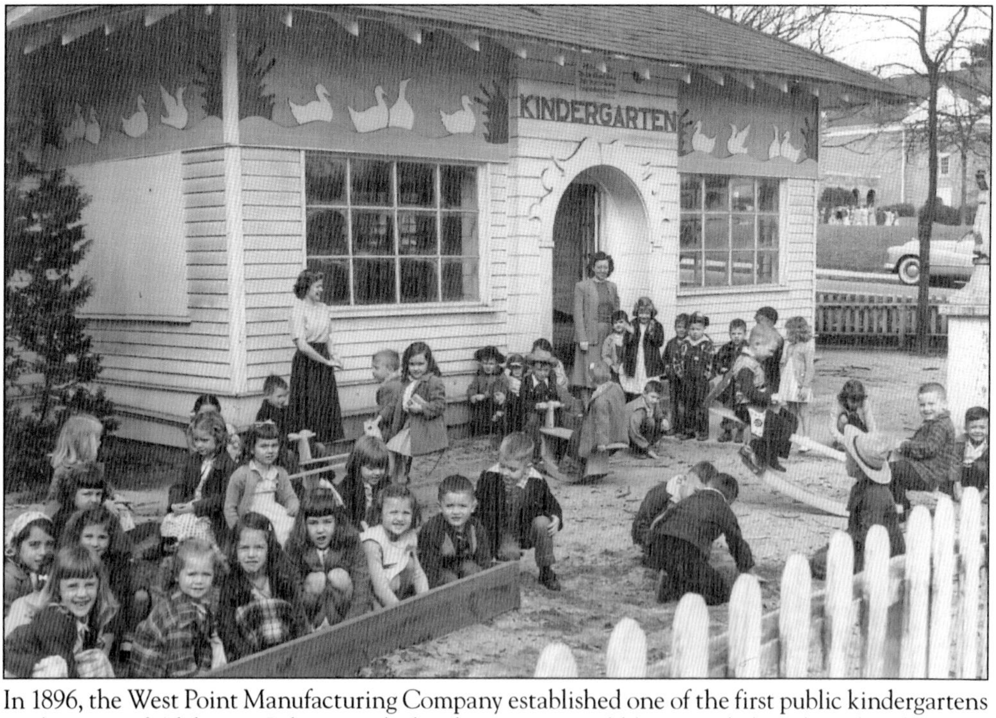

In 1896, the West Point Manufacturing Company established one of the first public kindergartens in the state of Alabama. Subsequently, kindergartens would be provided in the other four mill villages. The photograph shows teachers Bobbie Terry Wingo (left) and Madge Kennedy with the children in front of the kindergarten in the 1950s. (Courtesy of CMA.)

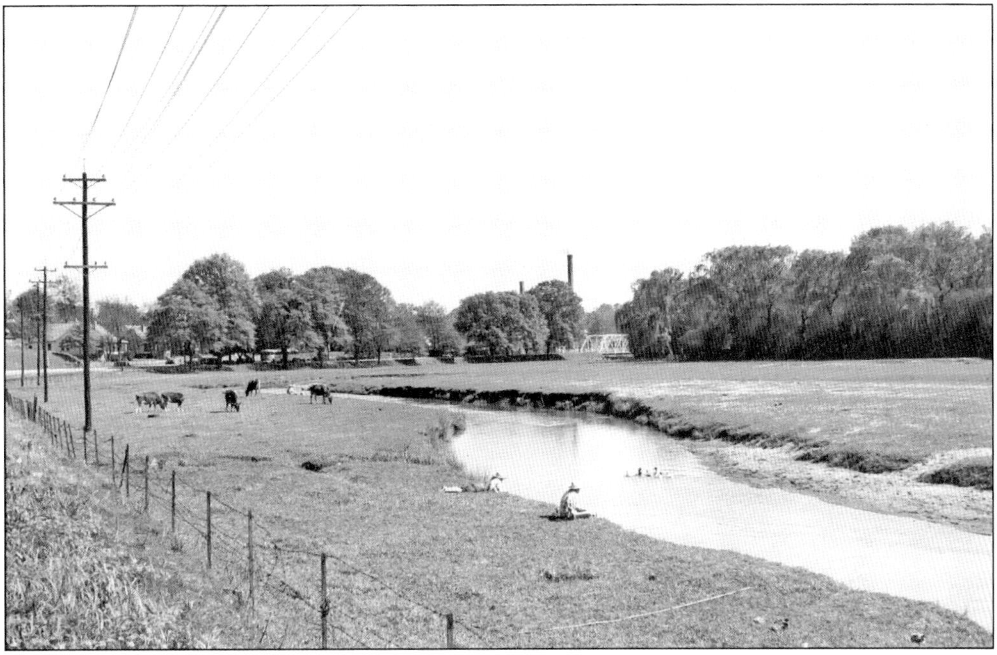

The photograph of Langdale meadow and Moore's Creek was taken about 1945. For many years, the meadow was provided by the company as a common pasture for the milk cows of the mill workers. Moore's Creek provided fishing and recreation for hundreds of little boys and girls over many decades. (Courtesy of CMA.)

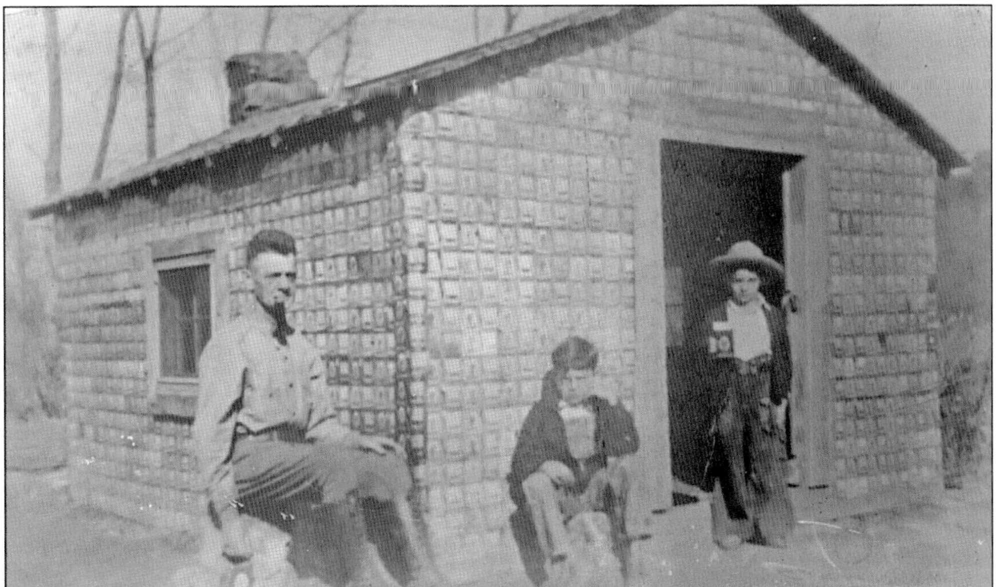

The West Point Manufacturing Company allowed its employees to use islands in the Chattahoochee River for gardening and fishing. In the 1935 photograph, Calvin H. Roberson, an employee of Langdale Mill, sits beside his island cabin, which is covered with tin from Prince Albert tobacco cans. Grandson Handley Davis stands in the doorway of the Prince Albert cabin and grandson Batson Davis sits on a stump. (Courtesy of Handley Davis.)

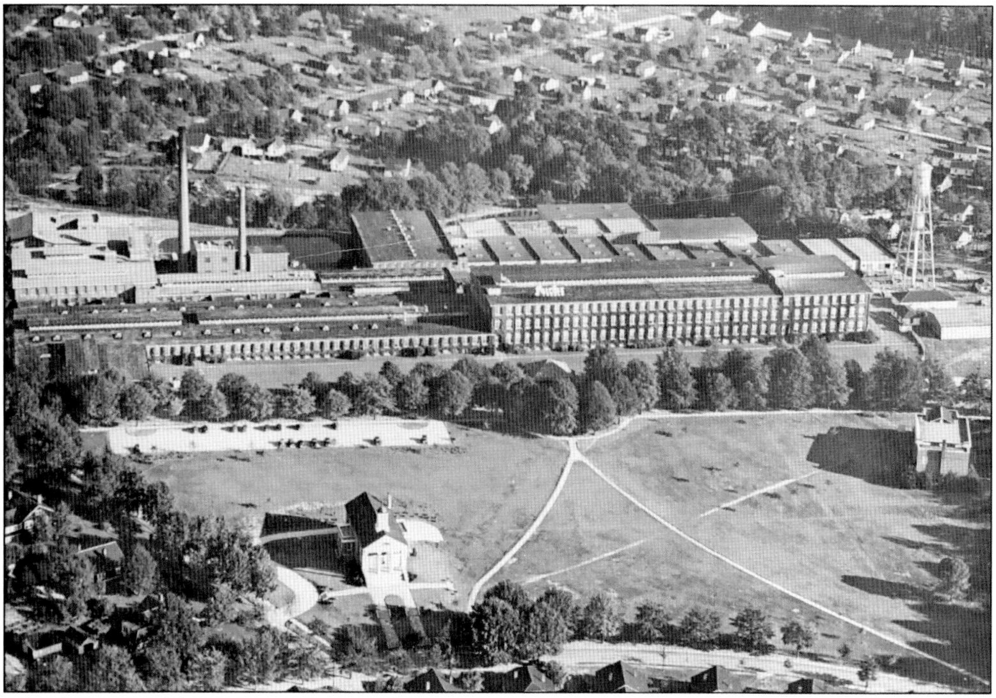

The directors of the West Point Manufacturing Company decided to manufacture a new product, terry cloth towels, requiring the construction of a new mill and its village. The Fairfax Mill began operation in 1916 but was required to produce heavy army duck for the military services in World War I. In 1936, the plant employed 1,100 workers and utilized 34,000 spindles and 1,200 looms. (Courtesy of CMA.)

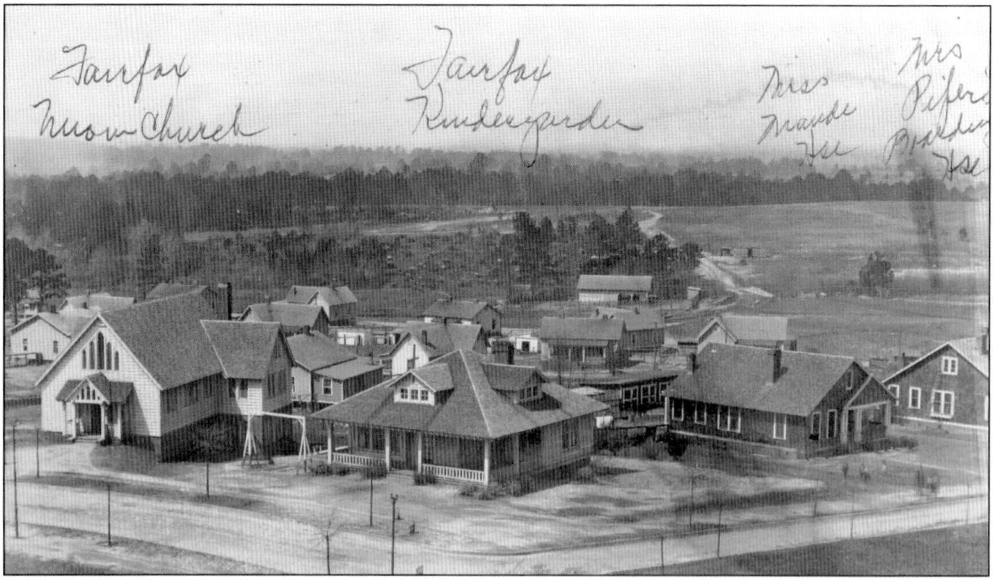

The Fairfax mill village was still under construction in 1917 when this photograph was taken from the roof of the mill. The mill was located on a low hill west of the Chattahoochee Valley Railroad Line. Although a planned village, the streets were not laid out in rigid geometric form, such as in Shawmut, but coiled around the hill on three sides of the mill. (Courtesy of CMA.)

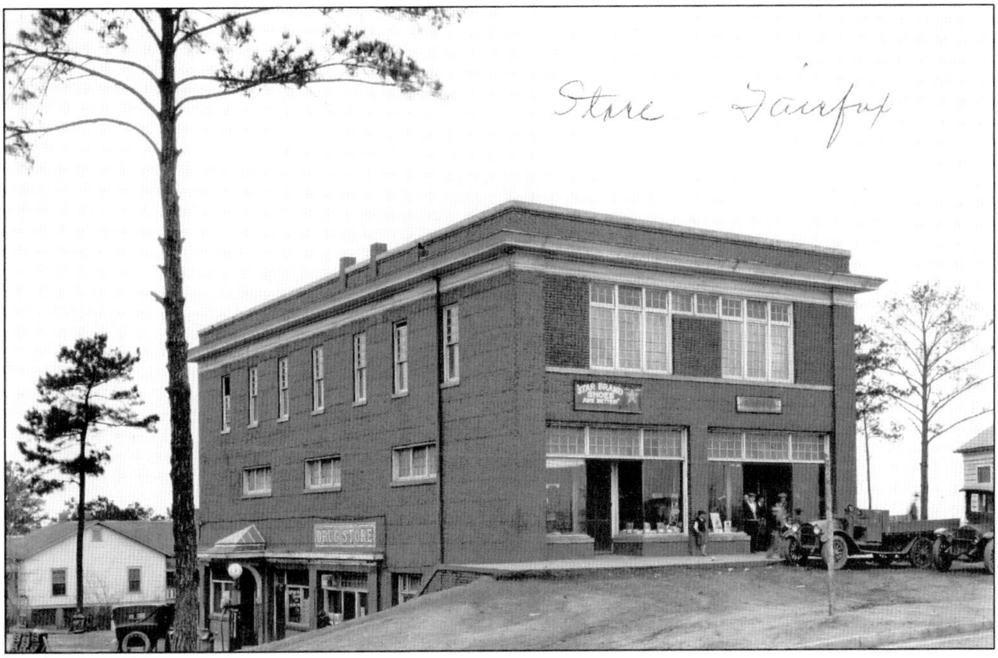

This three-story store building built in 1918 on the boulevard in Fairfax provided commercial space for many businesses over the years. On the first floor are two businesses, including a drugstore with a gravity gasoline pump. On the second floor was space for two businesses, and the third floor was reserved for community activities. (Courtesy of CMA.)

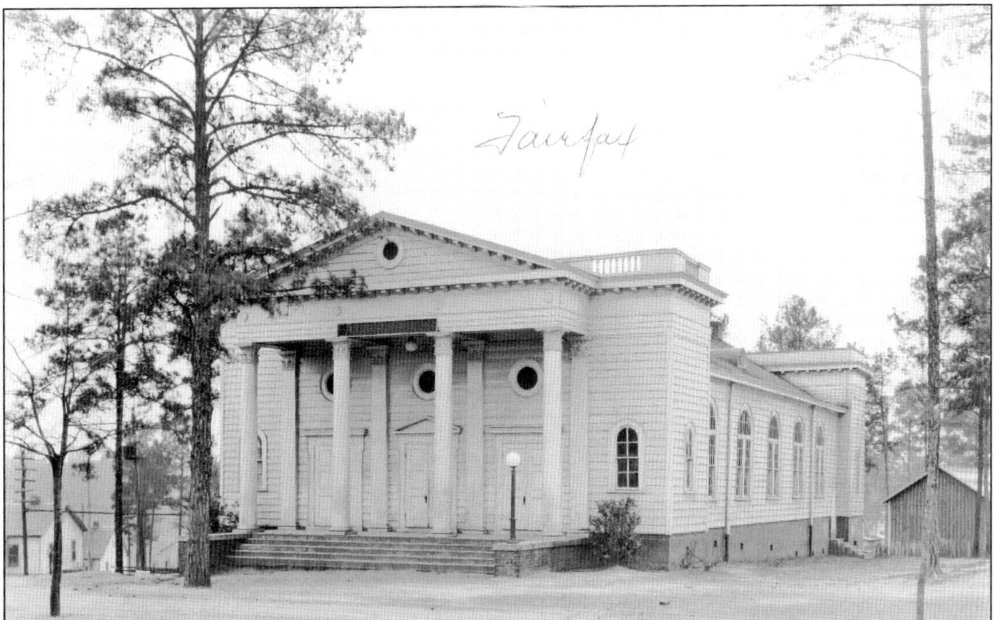

The first Fairfax Theater, with its Greek Revival facade, was a white wooden building built about 1916. The auditorium would function as a theater for motion pictures, plays, and commercial entertainment, as well as an auditorium for school functions. This building was replaced in the 1920s by a larger brick theater built by West Point Manufacturing Company. (Courtesy of CMA.)

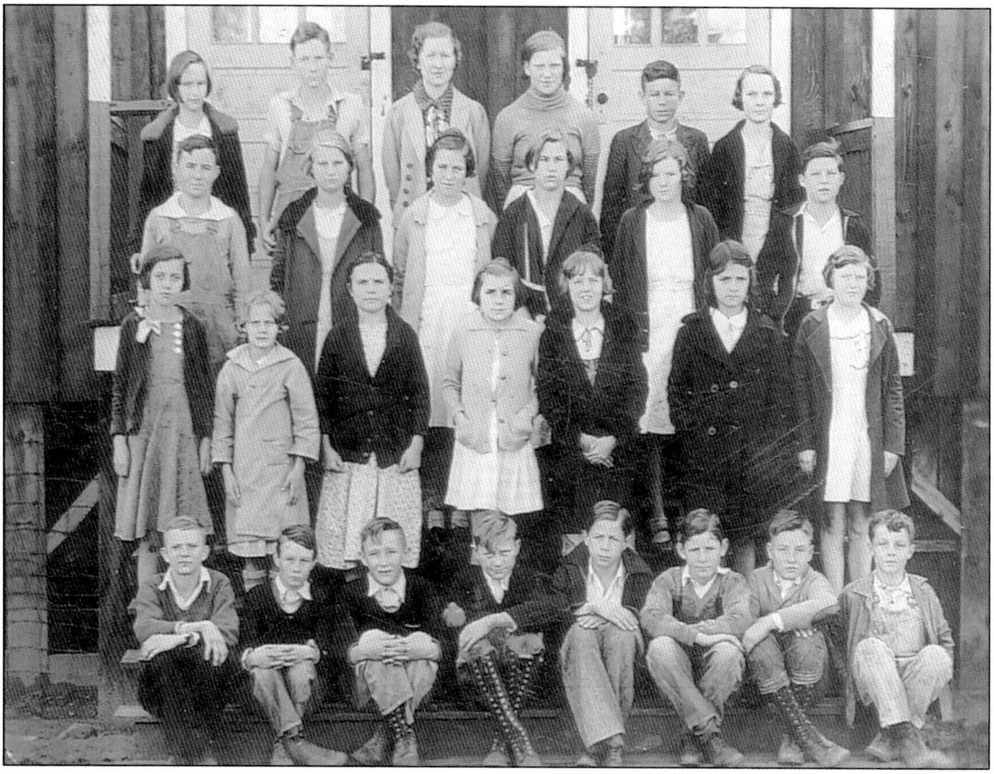

In this Fairfax School photograph from the early 1920s, the little girl in the third row, second from right, is Rosa Land. In 1917, her father had been a member of the Georgia National Guard detachment activated during the period of organized mob violence against Gov. John M. Slaton and Leo Frank, who was unjustly convicted of the murder of Mary Phagan and subsequently lynched. (Courtesy of Ronald David Williams Jr.)

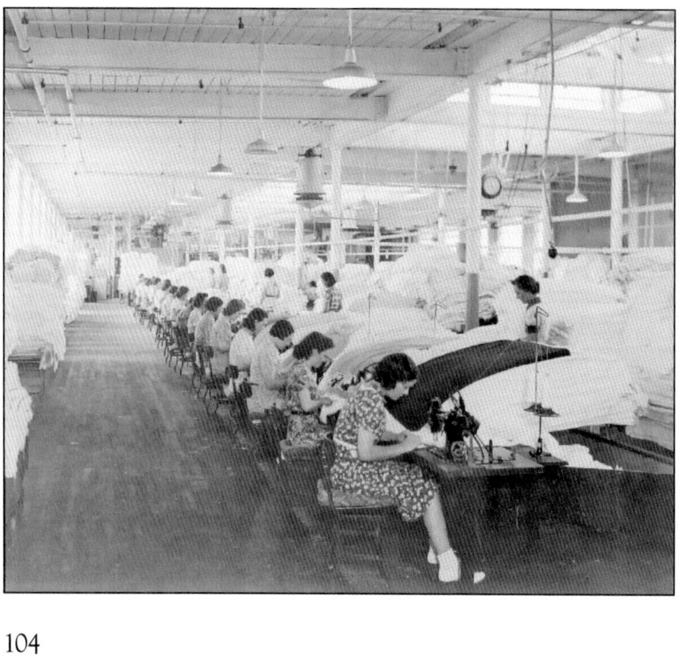

For many decades, Fairfax was known as the "towel city." In 1932, the West Point Manufacturing Company purchased the Margarson Textile Company and its well-known towel product name, Martex. The high-quality Martex towels contained delicately woven designs and were marketed to expensive hotels, resorts, and department stores across the United States. The photograph shows employees hemming these towels. (Courtesy of CMA.)

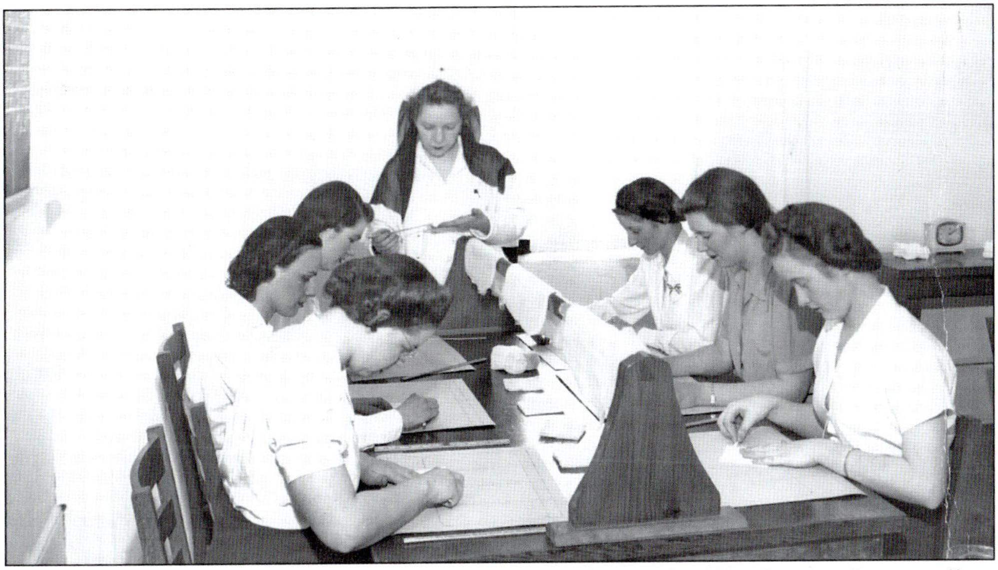

This February 18, 1943, photograph shows women in the Fairfax War Service Center rolling bandages for wounded soldiers. War Service secretary Marielle Branch is standing, and seated to her left is Virginia Landers Addison. After the war, Marielle married William Hunter Smith, an employee of the Fairfax Mill and a highly respected Disciples of Christ minister. (Courtesy of CMA.)

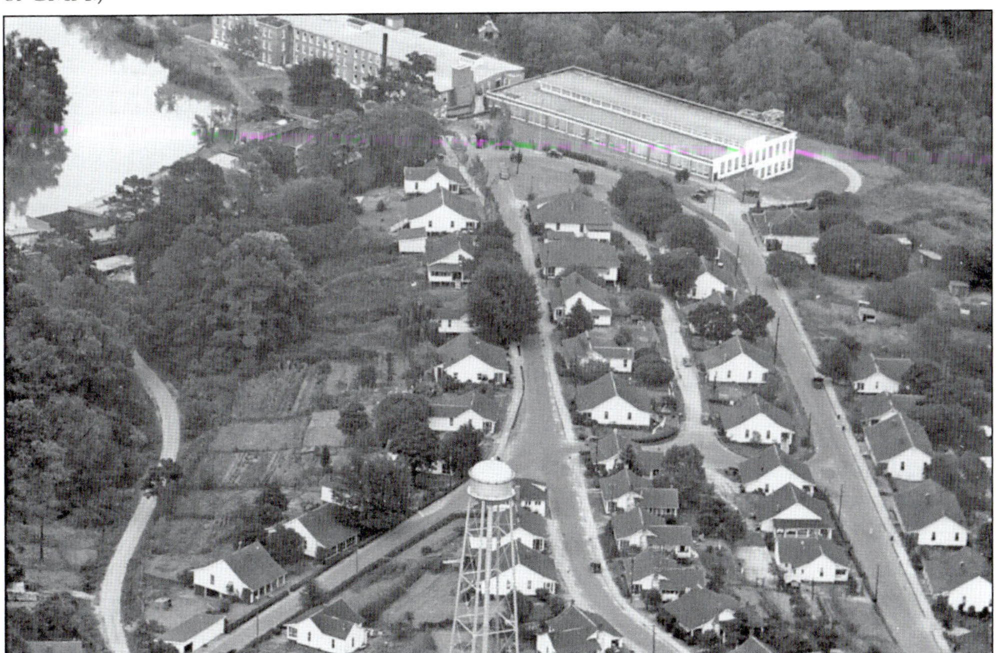

The 1940 photograph shows the Riverdale Mill and its Riverview mill village. Prior to the Civil War, a gristmill operated at this location. In 1866, George Huguley, planter and large landowner, organized the first Chattahoochee Valley cotton mill, which would later become part of the West Point Manufacturing Company. At the time of this photograph, the mill operated more than 1,500 spindles and 400 looms. (Courtesy of CMA.)

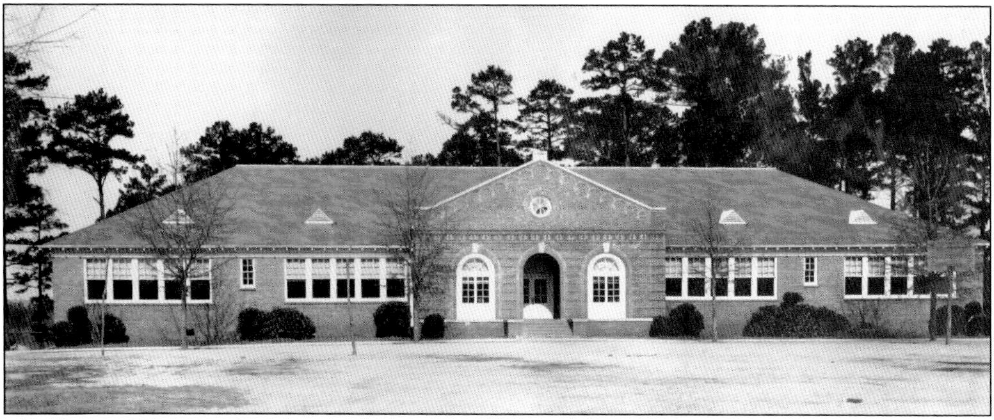

The first public school in Riverview opened in a blacksmith shop in 1867. Later, a one-room, plank-sided building with a fireplace was built midway between Riverview and Langdale. The Riverview School, shown in this photograph, was built by the West Point Manufacturing Company in 1910. When this photograph was taken in 1939, the school had seven teachers and 250 students. (Courtesy of CMA.)

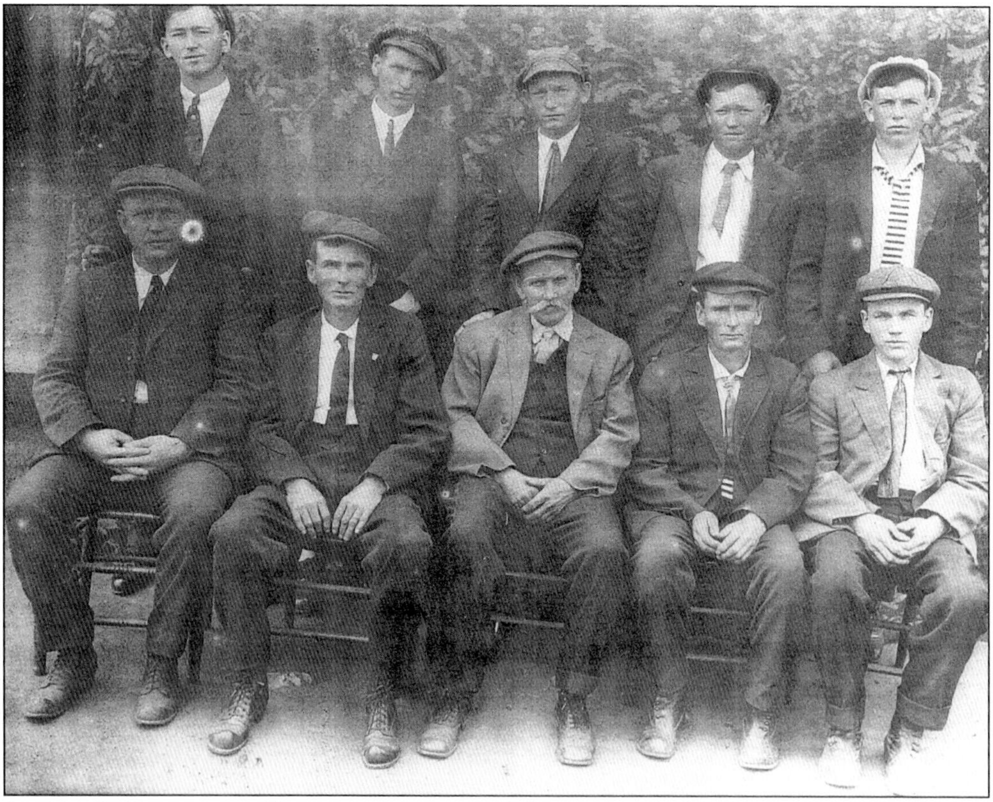

In 1914, the Riverview mill community organized the first baseball team established among the valley mills. The Milner family was outstanding in its contribution to the sport. At times, the father was the coach, and all the sons constituted a team. In this photograph are, from left to right, (first row) John, Henry, Richard B., Joe Brown, and Holt Milner; (second row) Glenn, Ben, Dan, Bonner, and Charlie Milner. (Courtesy of Ronald David Williams Jr.)

Five

PEOPLE WITH A STORY

Each life story illustrates how a person shapes his progress through time and how societal conditions and circumstance may shape the person. These images present people who demonstrated leadership in politics, vision in economic development, frustration in failed agricultural endeavor, craftsmanship in stone and wood, contentment as agriculturalists, misfortune as a manufacturing worker, joy as musicians, integrity as educators, love through spiritual leadership, and other qualities that define the richness of human life. Some of the persons in the photographs created and gave work to many people. Other images present individuals who took work, through which they defined themselves and their families. The influence of over four generations of the textile Lanier family in shaping Chambers County and the lives of thousands of persons cannot be adequately presented in a few images. Not only did the textile industry absorb surplus rural population and increasing supplies of local cotton for a hundred years, but the second-generation George Lanier leadership created one of the most progressive village environments for textile mill employees in the nation. Each village had a kindergarten, school, library, theater, ballpark, playground, and planned recreation. The villages built in the 20th century were designed by landscape architects, reflecting progressive values of the City Beautiful movement. Industrial textile employment was laborious and sometimes dangerous, but in the 20th century, the operatives increasingly enjoyed amenities that were not available in many rural areas.

These images of people document that the earth that nurtured the farmer and planter, would also produce an iconic African American athlete/boxer and an iconic American lawman. A genre of American literature began at the hand of a young newspaperman in LaFayette in the 1840s, and the hymns of America were enriched by the work of a minister in rural Chambers County. Just as the image of Heflin on the cotton bale in the first chapter symbolizes cotton as the foundation of the economic and social institutions of the county, the final image in this chapter again stresses the importance of this plant fiber from the 1830s until the disappearance of the cotton culture in the 1950s.

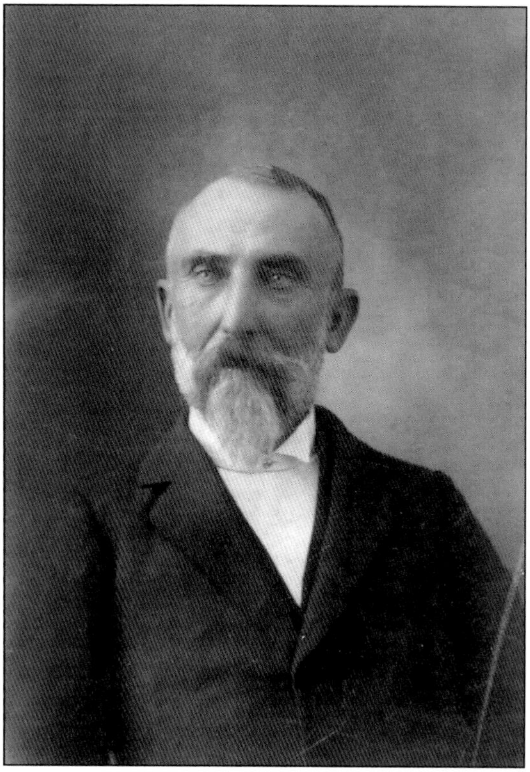

James Jefferson Robinson Sr. served for 10 years as probate judge, beginning in 1882. He graduated from the University of Georgia in 1861 and the following year enlisted with the West Point Guards into the Confederate army. In 1863, he lost his right arm in the Battle of Chancellorsville. Judge Robinson also served in the State Senate and House of Representatives. (Courtesy of Louise Chambers Smith.)

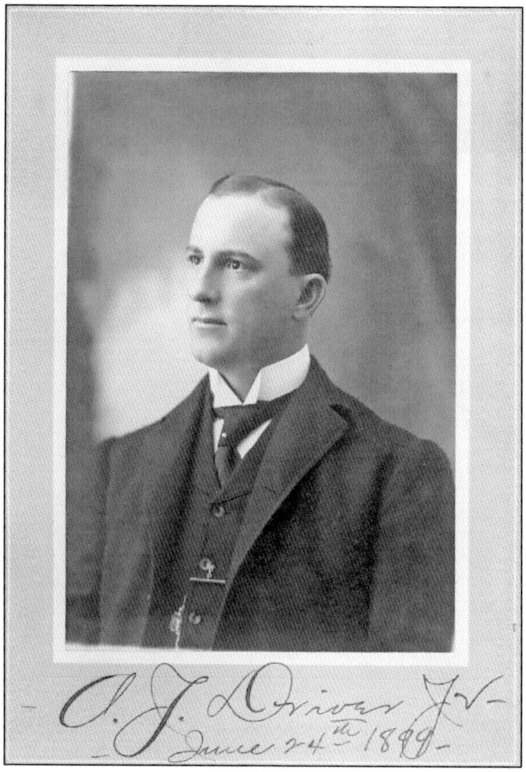

Allen J. Driver served as Chambers County probate judge for 14 years. Under his administration, the 1899 Chambers County Courthouse was constructed. He was one of the first probate judges of the state to begin the construction of highways. After his retirement from politics, he sold road machinery and equipment for the construction of highways throughout the state and was connected with the State Highway Department. (Courtesy of CMA.)

Col. Charles S. Moon, a native of Clay County, came to LaFayette to practice law. He was a well-recognized figure around the courthouse in the first half of the 20th century. His fondness for watermelon is remembered in this photograph. He enjoyed eating and sharing watermelon with friends on the courthouse steps. (Courtesy of Horace McLean Holderfield from the Alice Smith Carroll Collection.)

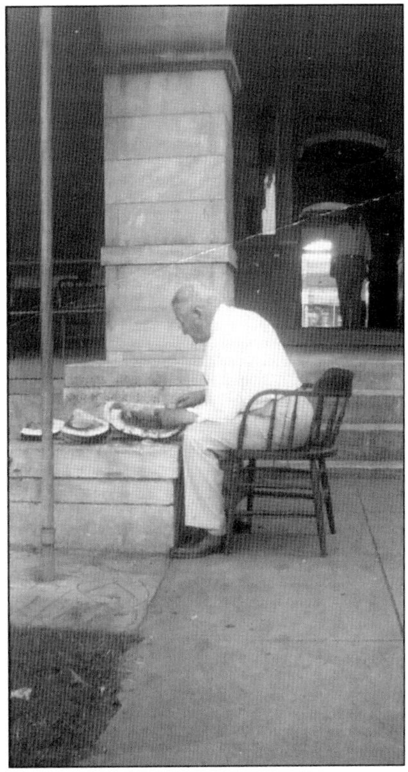

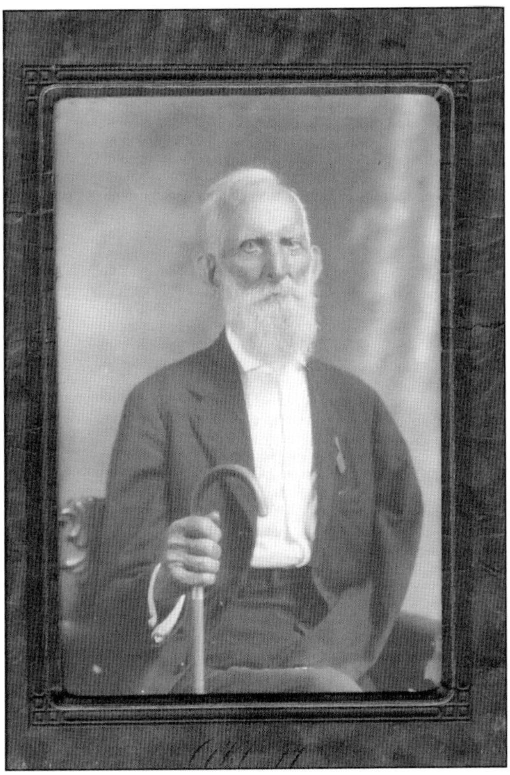

David Hugh Boyd Abernathy was born in DeKalb County, Georgia, and came to Chambers County with his parents in 1848. During the Civil War, he served as sergeant in the 47th Alabama Infantry Regiment, where he lost his left arm at the Battle of the Wilderness. After the war, he raised a large family and served four terms as Chambers County tax assessor. (Courtesy of Sara A. Yancey.)

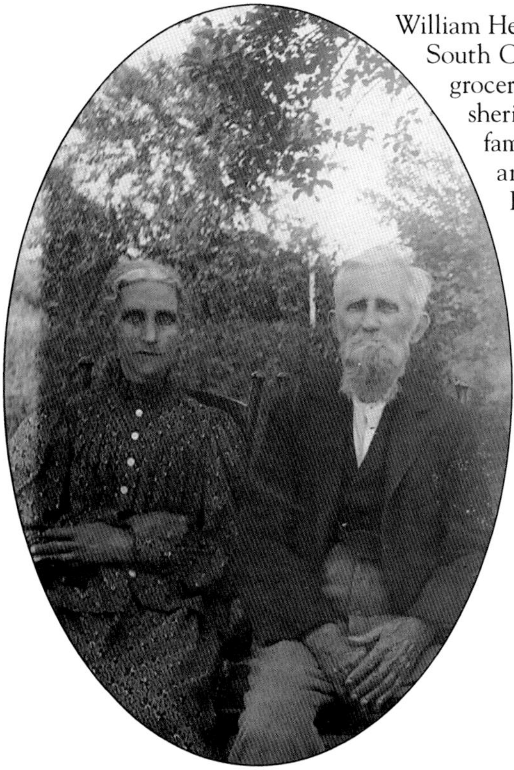

William Henry Harrison Hunter came to LaFayette from South Carolina in 1836. He worked as a blacksmith, grocer, and miller and was elected tax assessor and sheriff. In 1859, he moved his wife, Margaret, and family to Buffalo, where he was the first postmaster and depot station agent. For 100 years, the Hunters were prominent in the local affairs of their community. (Courtesy of Drusilla Lamb Abernathy.)

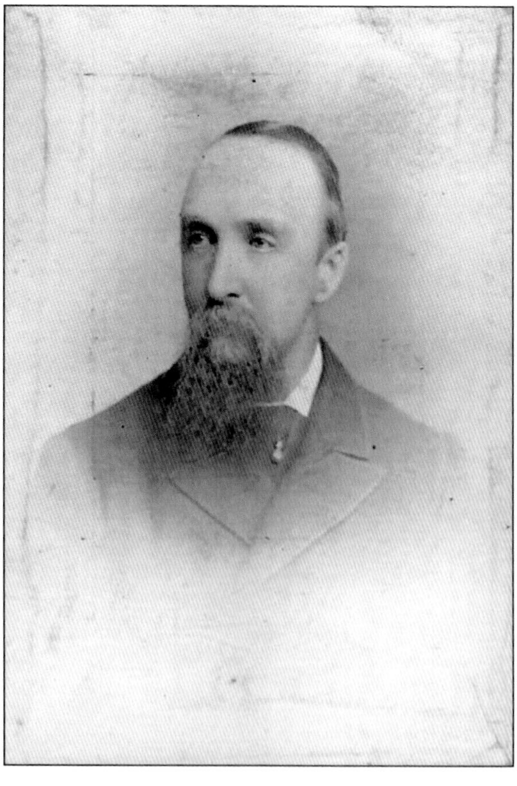

In 1867, John Howard Parnell purchased 1,482 acres from George W. Huguley to establish a peach farm. This plantation south of West Point eventually contained 700 acres of planted peach trees and became one of the largest orchards in America. The Sunny South Peach Farm shipped fruit to cities in the northeast. Experiencing a crop failure in 1883, Parnell sold his plantation and later returned to Ireland. (Courtesy of CMA.)

William Rufus "Rock" Jackson was born in Mecklenburg County, Virginia. By 1836, he and his first wife, Martha Foster Jackson, were in Chambers County. His primary occupation was the manufacture of tombstones from a native rock he advertised as blue marble. A grandson remembered his grandfather, also an inventor, designing and building a prototype of a "horseless carriage" many years before such an idea was considered feasible. For the convenience of his family, he situated the well that furnished water for his family inside the kitchen instead of outdoors. An 1874 advertisement from the *LaFayette Clipper* lists the products of his craft. His bluish-green headboards and box tombs can be found in practically every cemetery in east Alabama and west Georgia. (Both, courtesy of Bobby Jackson.)

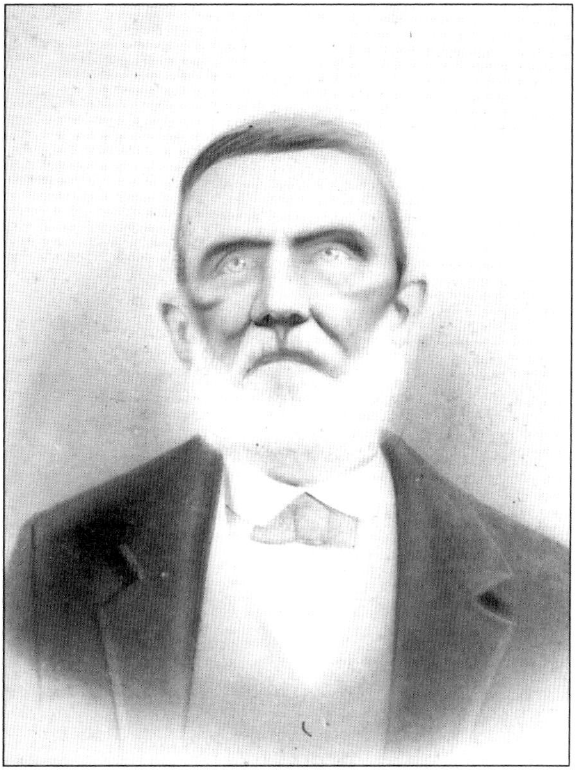

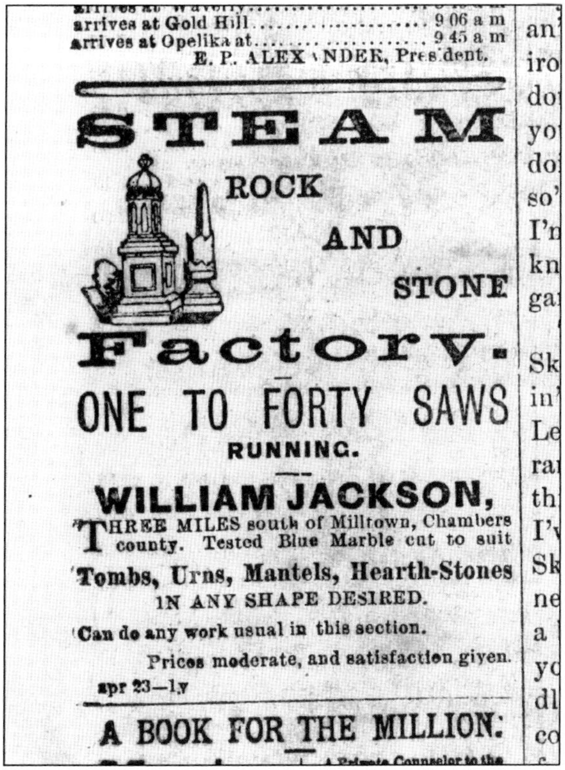
arrives at Gold Hill.................... 9 06 a m
arrives at Opelika at.................... 9 45 a m
E. P. ALEXANDER, President.

STEAM ROCK AND STONE Factory.

ONE TO FORTY SAWS RUNNING.

WILLIAM JACKSON,

THREE MILES south of Milltown, Chambers county. Tested Blue Marble cut to suit

Tombs, Urns, Mantels, Hearth-Stones IN ANY SHAPE DESIRED.

Can do any work usual in this section.

Prices moderate, and satisfaction given.

apr 23—1y

A BOOK FOR THE MILLION:

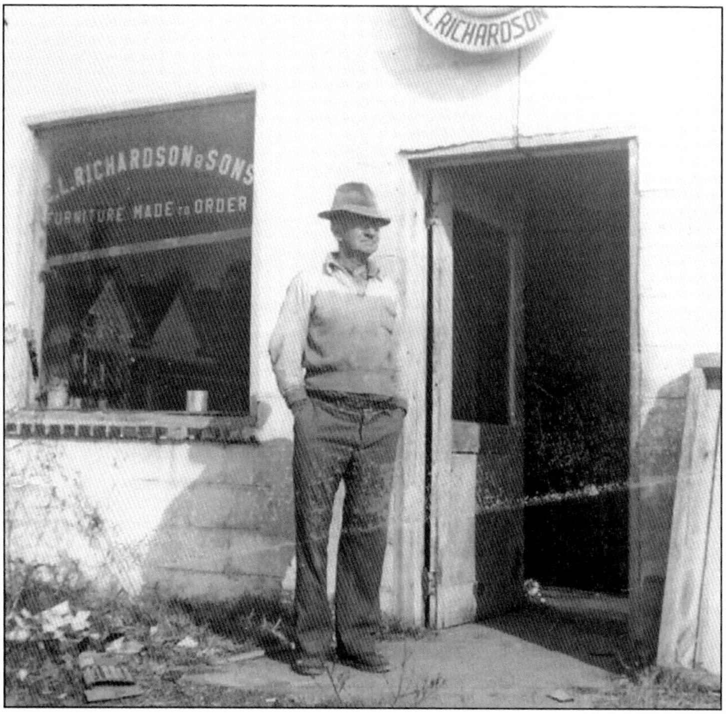

C. L. "Charlie" Richardson of the Marcoot community was well known throughout east Alabama and west Georgia for his craftsmanship in the manufacture of custom furniture. He and his sons were capable of supplying any type of furniture. Cedar bedroom suites, chests, and picture frames were his specialties. His furniture may be found throughout the county and is highly prized by its owners. (Courtesy of Paul Richardson.)

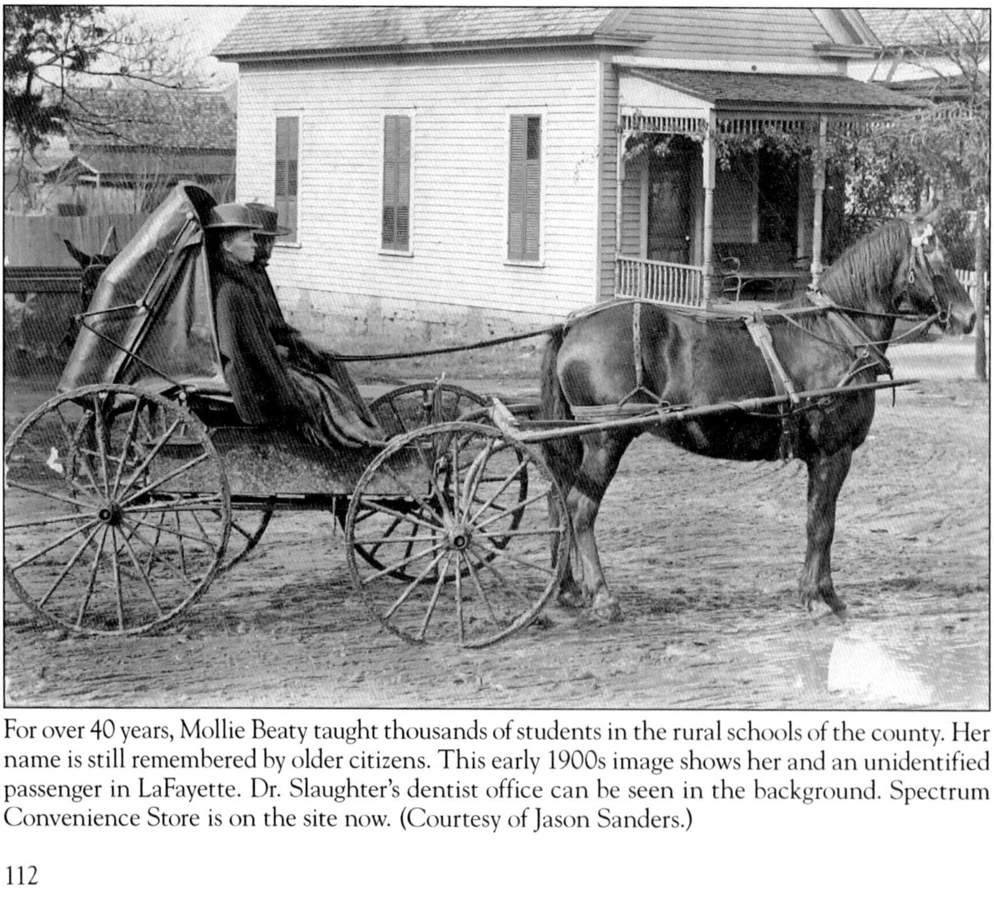

For over 40 years, Mollie Beaty taught thousands of students in the rural schools of the county. Her name is still remembered by older citizens. This early 1900s image shows her and an unidentified passenger in LaFayette. Dr. Slaughter's dentist office can be seen in the background. Spectrum Convenience Store is on the site now. (Courtesy of Jason Sanders.)

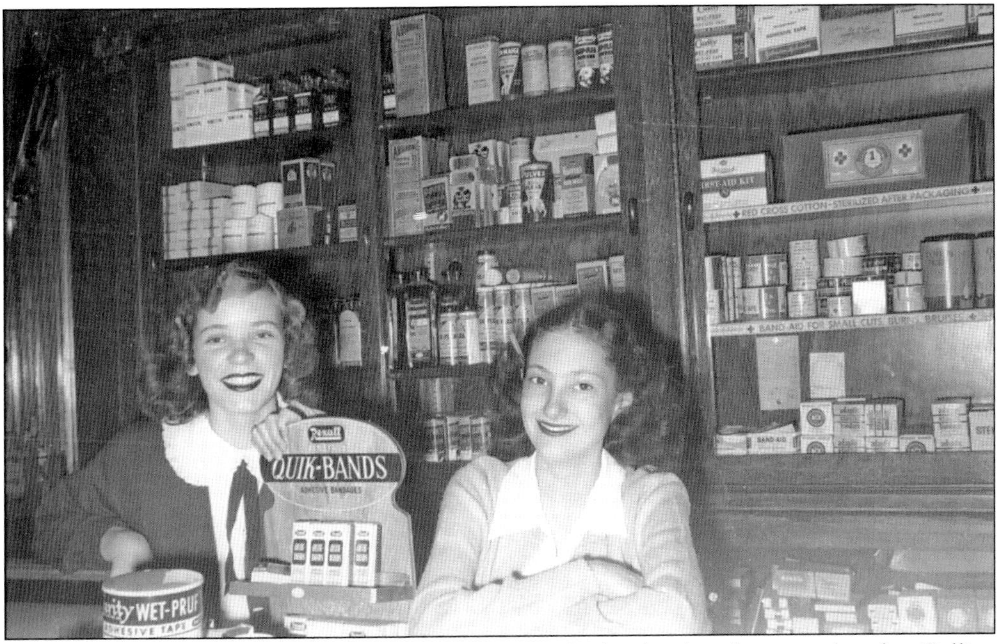

Faye Davis (left) and Sara Abernathy were two young high school students employed at Collins Drug Store in LaFayette. They greeted customers with smiling faces after school on weekdays and on weekends. Some items stocked on the shelves include Globe Flea and Lice Powder, Glover's Canker Medicine, Ace Bandages, and Absorbine Veterinary Liniment. (Courtesy of Sara Abernathy Yancey.)

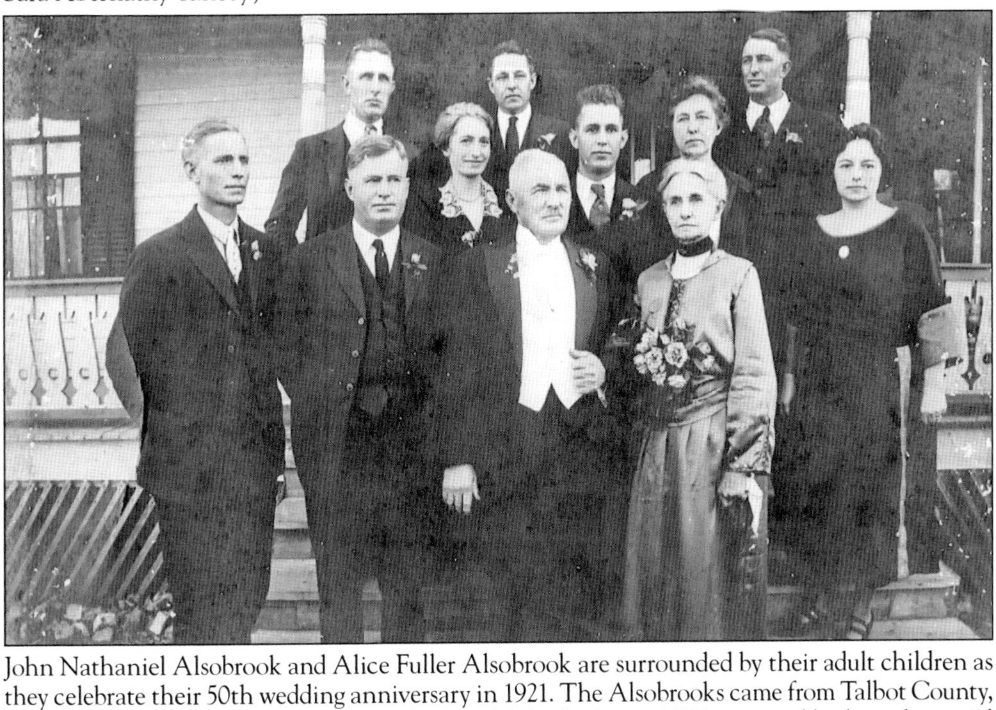

John Nathaniel Alsobrook and Alice Fuller Alsobrook are surrounded by their adult children as they celebrate their 50th wedding anniversary in 1921. The Alsobrooks came from Talbot County, Georgia, to Five Points in 1877. There they established a farm of 275 acres and built a substantial two-story house. (Courtesy of Mary Reeves Alsobrook.)

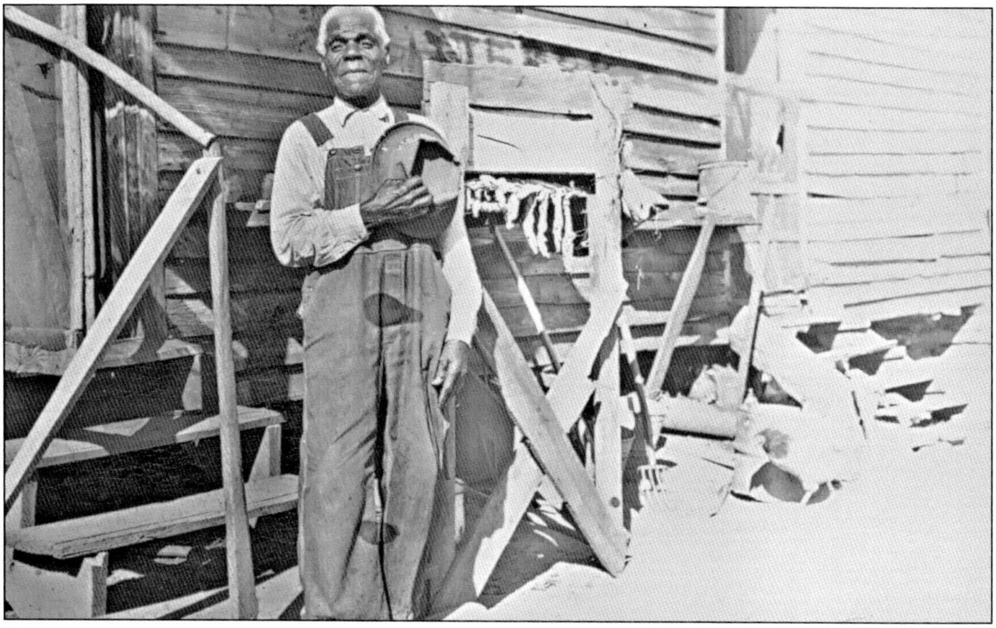

Jerry West Copeland Hill was born June 23, 1835, and in the days of slavery belonged to Alpheus F. Copeland. His father's name is unknown, but he was believed to have been a slave on the plantation of John Hill at Long Cane, Troup County, Georgia. Known to all as "Uncle Jerry," he was photographed on his 107th birthday. (Courtesy of CCM.)

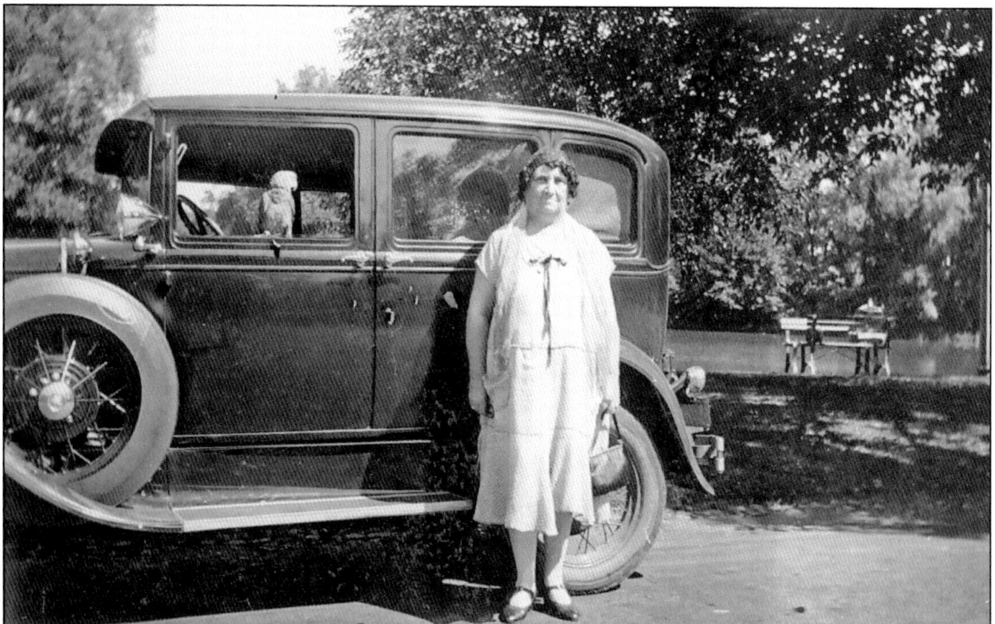

By 1896, Jane Alice Estella Abernathy Newman had experienced the death of her husband, Obediah Newman, and son Albert. After she married Dr. Russell D. Stallings of Atlanta, she made frequent trips home to LaFayette. She was devoted to her parrot, Mack, seen perched in the window of her 1920s automobile. After her death, Mack's golden years were spent with her niece Kate Talley Sharman. (Courtesy of Sara A. Yancey.)

Elder John T. Satterwhite, born in 1856 in Harris County, Georgia, moved to Chambers County as a young man. In 1882, he was ordained a minister at Mount Pisgah Primitive Baptist Church at Stroud, where he served as pastor for 42 years. He also served as pastor to other churches in east Alabama and west Georgia over a half century. (Courtesy of Mount Pisgah Primitive Baptist Church.)

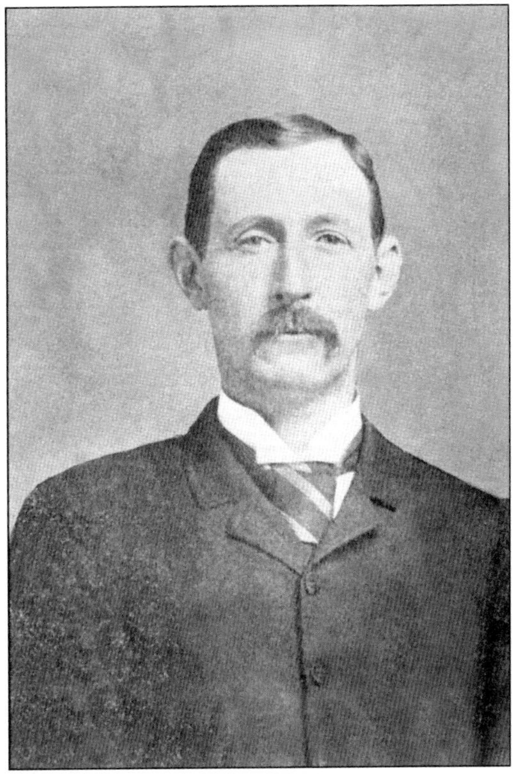

On April 2, 1887, William Commodore Lowe and Ella Clifford Whatley were married by elder John T. Satterwhite. Their golden wedding anniversary was celebrated 50 years later at their home near Penton. In this image, they are surrounded by their surviving children, from left to right, Mildred Henry, Francis Marion, Annie Laura Hodges, John Thomas, Mary Elizabeth Luke, Marvin Clifford, Ella Lorena Ruple, James Henry, Kathryn Finley, Herbert Mitchell, and Sue Emma Freel. (Courtesy of Bob Lowe.)

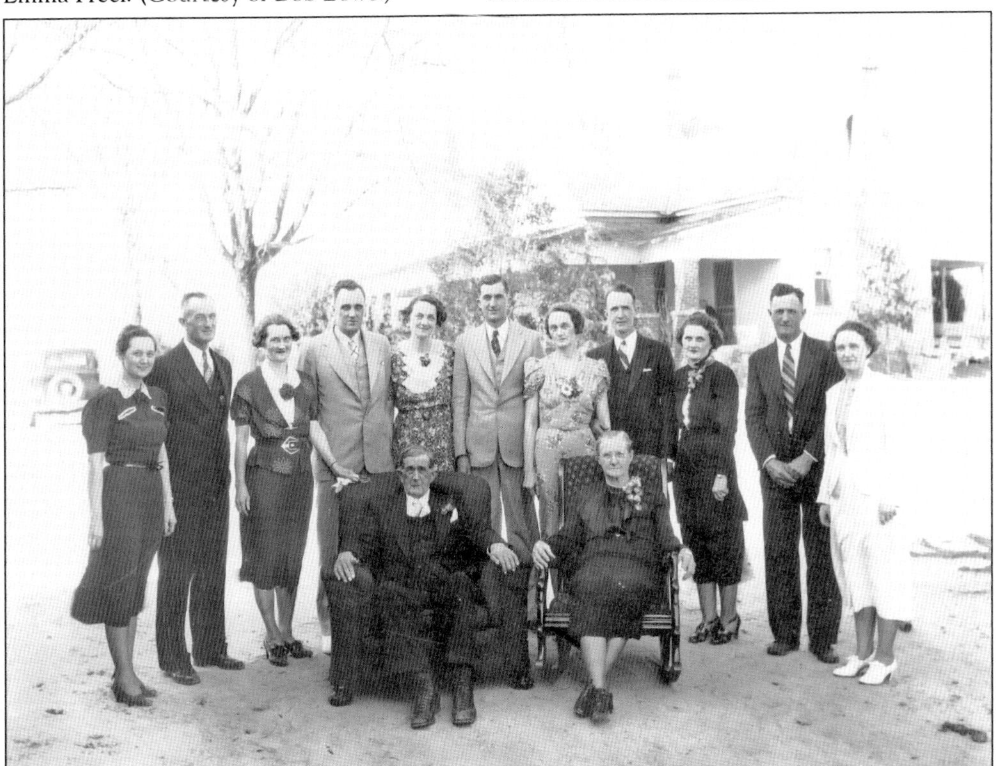

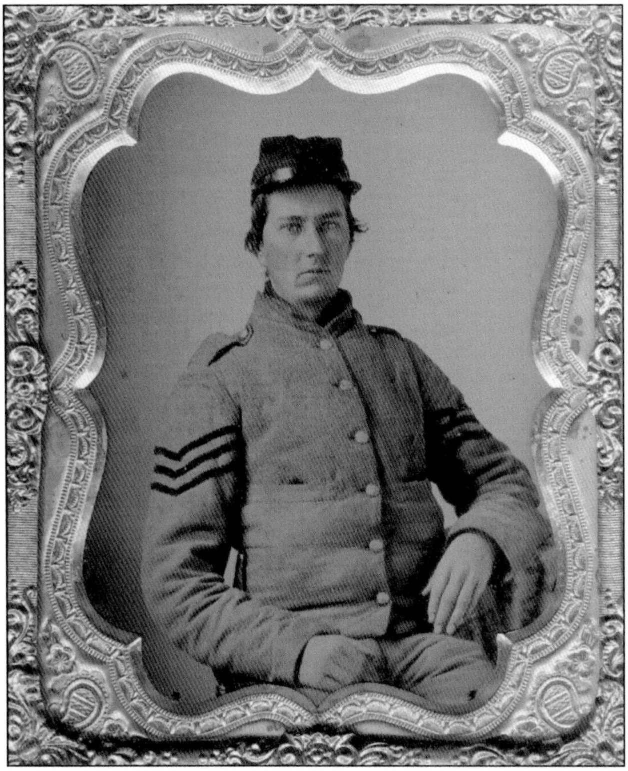

Sgt. George Washington Newman enlisted in the Confederate army as 4th sergeant of the 14th Alabama Infantry and was paroled at Appomattox in 1865. He was a prominent farmer in the Rock Spring community, a Mason, and a justice of the peace. He represented Chambers County in the 1896–1897 session of the Alabama Legislature. (Courtesy of Helen Andrews Sheppard.)

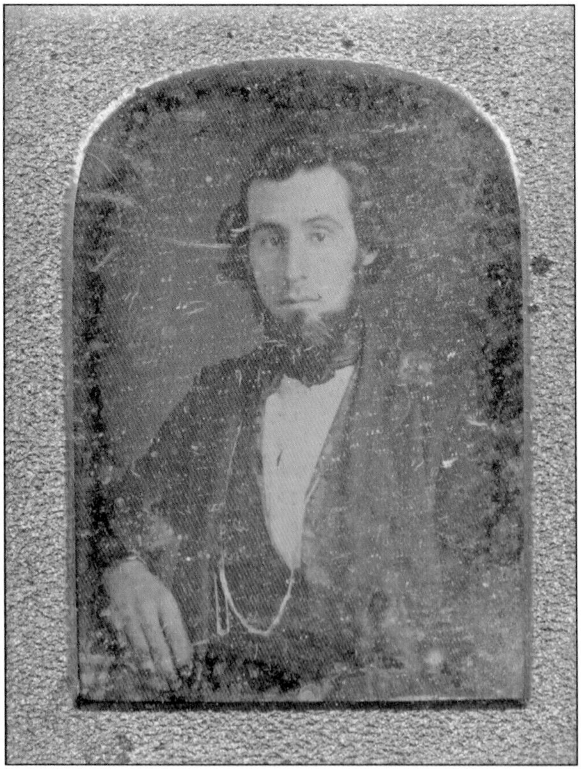

Dr. Frederick Woodhull Buckelew was born in 1812 in Newark, New Jersey, and was licensed by the New Jersey Medical Society in 1833. Dr. Buckelew later lived in Coweta County, Georgia, before migrating to northern Chambers County near Bloomingdale around 1843. He practiced medicine and managed a prosperous plantation. The daguerreotype image is from the mid-1840s. (Courtesy of Don Clark.)

Farr Harris Trammell Jr. (1825–1895) is buried in the Fredonia United Methodist Cemetery. This photograph, made from an 1850s ambrotype, shows the clothing of the well-to-do antebellum planter. His father owned 21 slaves, and he owned 6 in 1860. By 1860, the slave population of Chambers County was almost equal to the white population. (Courtesy of Cobb Archives.)

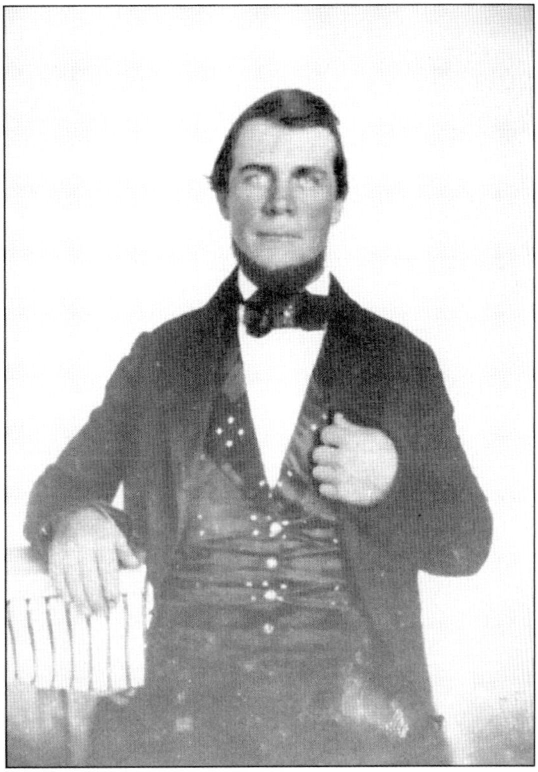

The Fuller family sat for this photograph on the steps of the Tatum house in LaFayette. From left to right are (first row) Joseph Franklin Newman Jr. and Anne Elizabeth Newman; (second row) Sarah Tatum, Mary Newman, Susan Fuller, and Jesse James Newman; (third row) Absalom Tatum, Elizabeth Fuller Tatum, Sally Fannie Fuller Newman, and Joseph Franklin Newman; (fourth row) Jesse Gunn Fuller, Confederate veteran, and Sally Kellam Fuller. (Courtesy of Margaret K. Newman.)

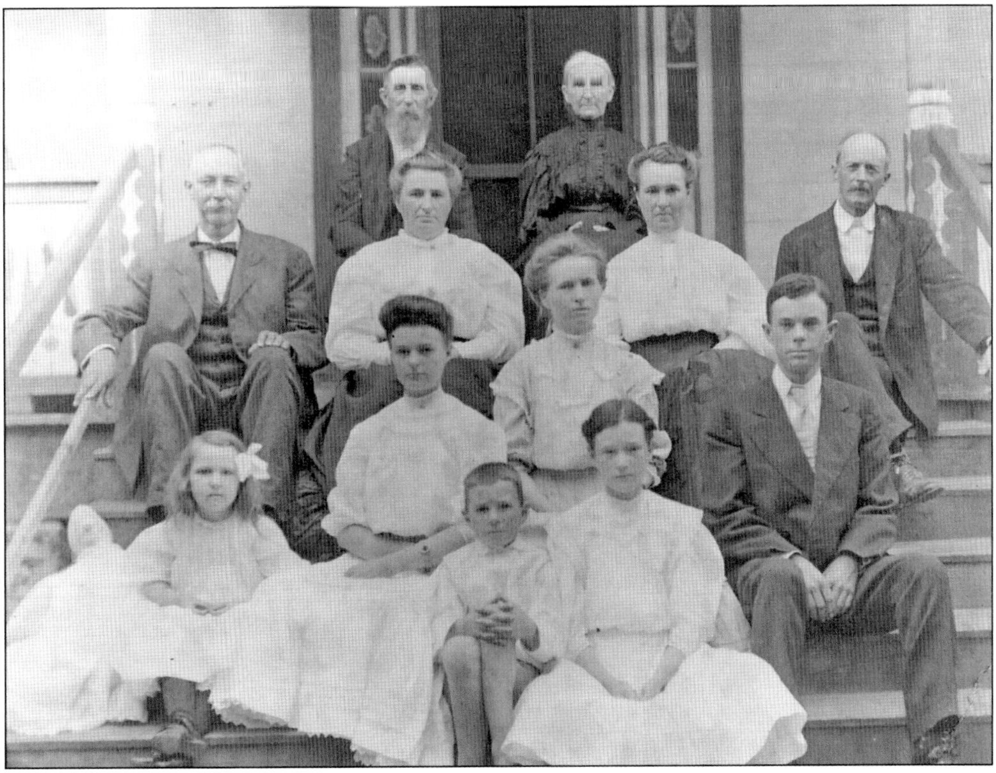

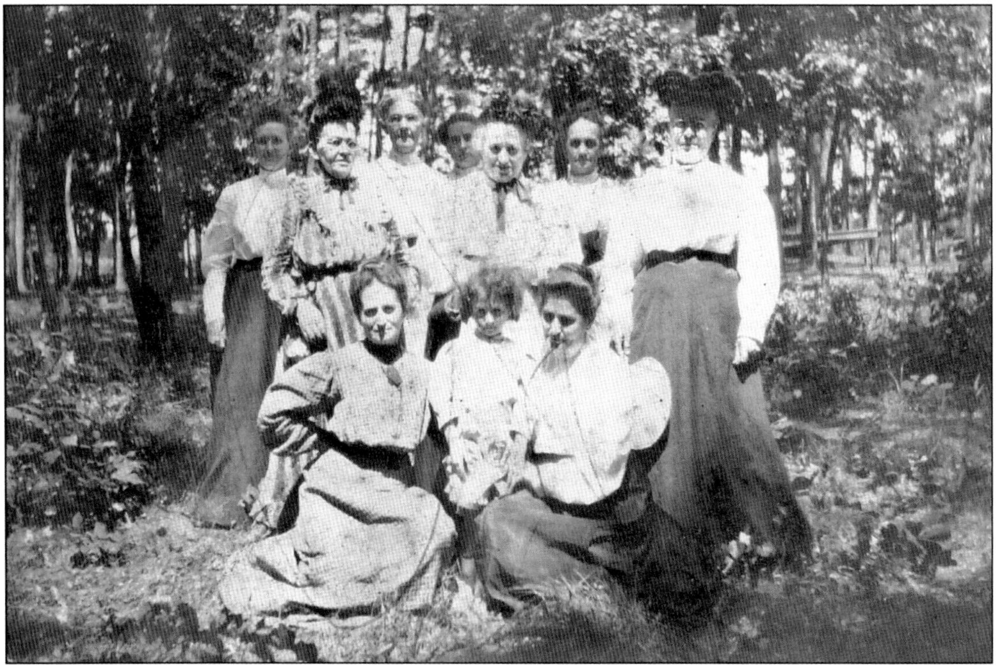

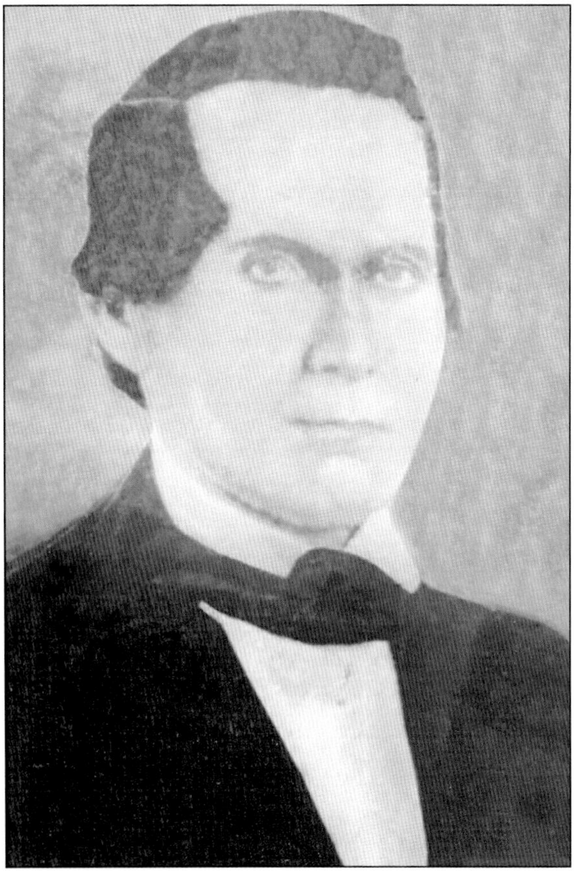

The ladies identified in this late-19th century photograph are (first row) Helen Heyman Herzberg, Ruth Hagedorn, and Jennie Heyman Hagedorn. The woman directly behind Ruth with the bonnet tied under her chin is Betty Merz Heyman, who in the 1850s married Herman Heyman in Cincinnati and later came to live in Bluffton. David and Louis Merz, who first located in West Point and Bluffton, were her brothers. (Courtesy CMA.)

Elder Benjamin Lloyd (1804–1860) was a pioneer Baptist minister and land speculator who settled in the county in the early 1830s. He was instrumental in establishing many of the early Baptist churches and the Liberty and Beulah Associations. In 1841, he published a words-only hymnbook called *Lloyd's Primitive Hymns* that has the distinction of being the longest continually used hymnbook in America. (Courtesy of CCM.)

This image of Simon Suggs was created by Felix Octavius Darley for the frontispiece page in the 1845 publication of *Some Adventures of Captain Simon Suggs* by Johnson Jones Hooper. In the 1830s and 1840s, Hooper lived in LaFayette, where he edited the *East Alabamian* newspaper. Drawing upon his experiences with people on the Alabama frontier, he created a new type of writing called southwest humor, which inspired Samuel Clemens. (Courtesy of Ronald David Williams Jr.)

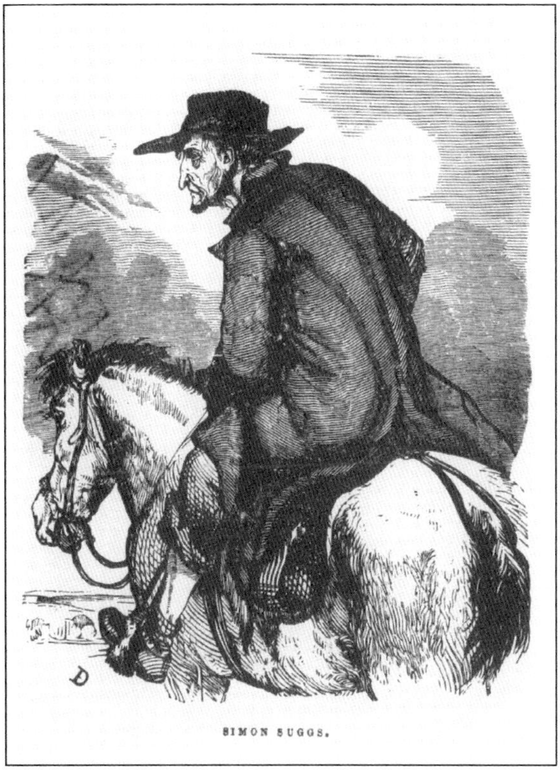

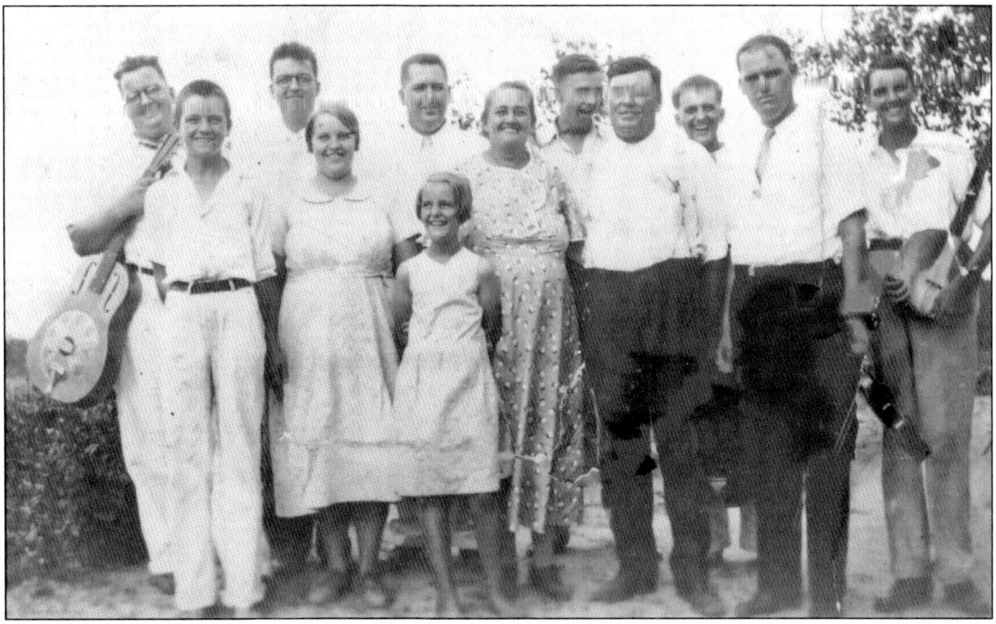

The Sorrell family was well known in White Plains for their musical talents. In the days of party-line telephones, by giving the Sorrell family a ring in the evening, neighbors could listen to a musical treat. In this early 1930s photograph are, from left to right, (first row) Jack, Ruby, LeMerle, mother Odecie, father Rufus, Rae, and Engman; (second row) Glenn, Curtis, Horald, Lewis, and O. D. Sorrell. (Courtesy of Vanessa Sorrell Burnside.)

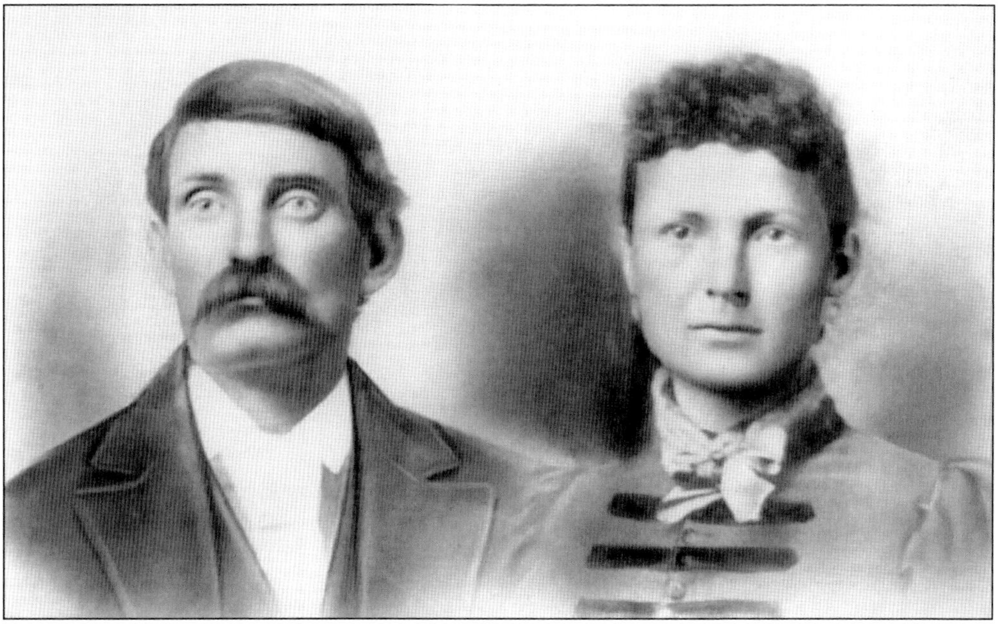

Born near Cusseta in 1850, Patrick Floyd Jarvis Garrett latter lived in Louisiana, Texas, and New Mexico. The photograph shows Garrett and his wife, Apolinaria Gutierrez Garrett, whom he married in 1880. As sheriff of Lincoln County, New Mexico, he killed the famous outlaw Billy the Kid in 1881. Garrett was killed over a land dispute in 1908 and buried in Las Cruces, New Mexico. (Courtesy of CCM.)

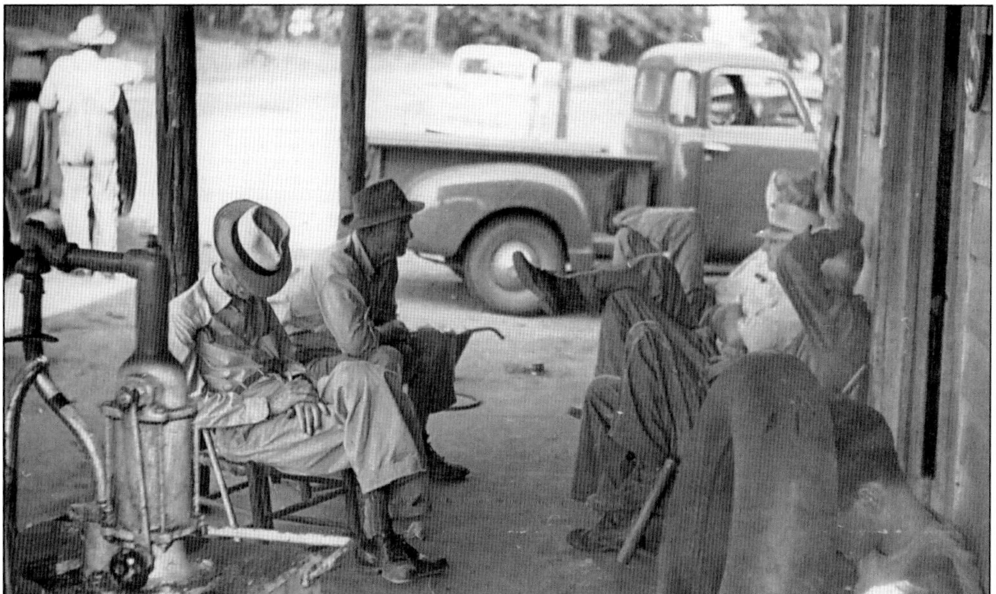

In the early 1950s, James Henry Baker is sitting, asleep, in his straight-backed chair on the porch of Baker Brothers General Store in Standing Rock. Ambrous M. Dodgen sits next to Henry, leaning forward in conversation with the men who have propped their chairs against the wall of the building. The porch of the country store was always a popular gathering place. (Courtesy of William Coughlin.)

Dr. Benjamin Franklin Frazer attended LaFayette schools, the University of Alabama, Tulane University, and the Army Medical School. During World War I, he served two years in France in the Medical Corps. After the war, he practiced in different locations and returned to LaFayette in 1933. He was very interested in and knowledgeable about Chambers County history. (Courtesy of Bill Bowling.)

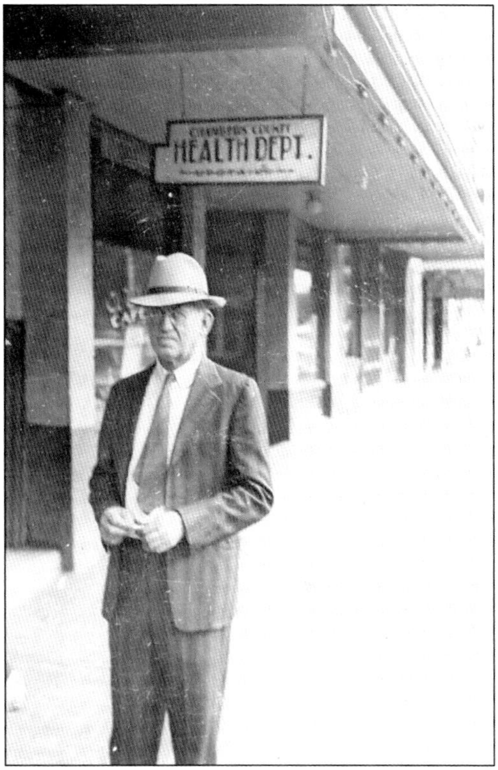

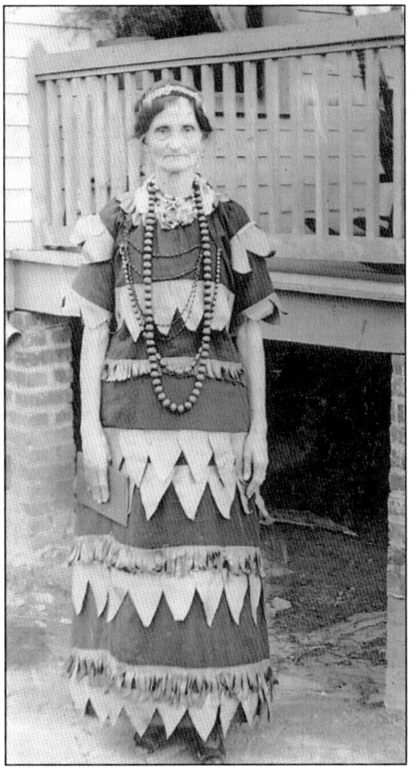

Catherine Anne "Kate" Hanson Crowder, a charter member of the Order of Pocahontas, was photographed about 1920 dressed in her sorority costume. Her husband, Asbury N. Crowder, was permanently disabled by machinery in Riverdale Mill and died in 1915. George Lanier and other mill officials provided Kate with free use of a mill house, free utilities, and a $5 per week pension for her lifetime. (Courtesy of CMA.)

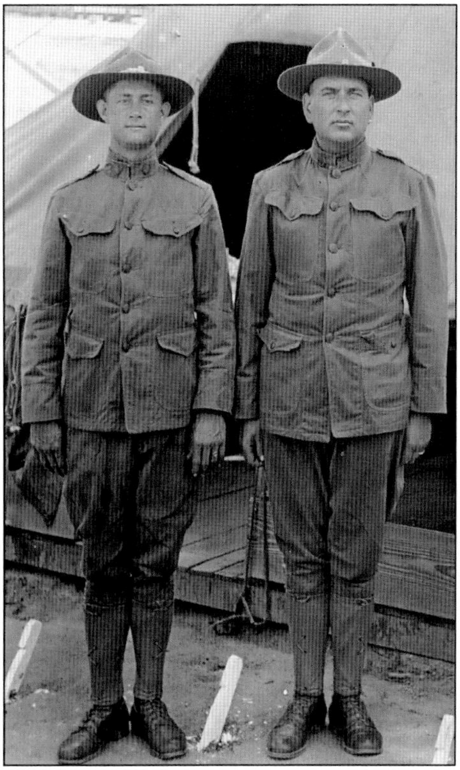

Lem Winston Slaughter (left) and Pierce D. Lee, farm boys from the Doublehead and Welch communities, belonged to the 167th Regiment of the 42nd (Rainbow) Division in France during World War I. Both young men experienced combat. Lee was a light machine gunner firing the French Chauchat and came home safely. Slaughter was killed on the morning of November 11, 1918, hours before the war ended. (Courtesy of Cathy Burnett Sellers.)

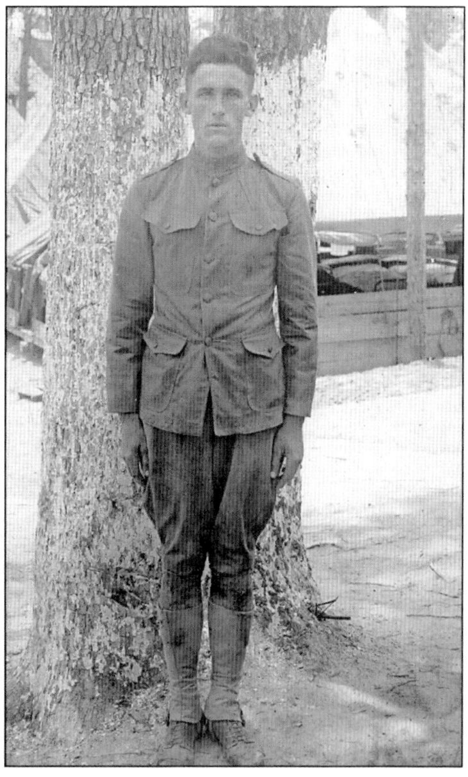

James Ulysees "Jake" Royston, from the Doublehead community, was a close friend of Slaughter and Lee. They were together throughout the war. Royston was with Slaughter when he was killed. After the 11th hour, as Allied and German soldiers met celebrating the armistice, Royston slugged the first German soldier he saw. He regretted this act, realizing Germans also lost dear friends needlessly that morning. (Courtesy of Mary Helen Benford.)

In the 1930s to 1950s, every community had a Home Demonstration Club under the auspices of the extension service. This 1940 photograph of a retreat at Pine Mountain, Georgia, contains two generations of rural women, the oldest of whom are Lucille Patterson Howell, Verna Anglin Smith, Ruby Grady, Anne Holderfield Newell, Lena Lee Holderfield, Phelan Ophelia Holderfield, and Ava Widner Holderfield. (Courtesy of Carol Cumbee Holderfield Shelnutt.)

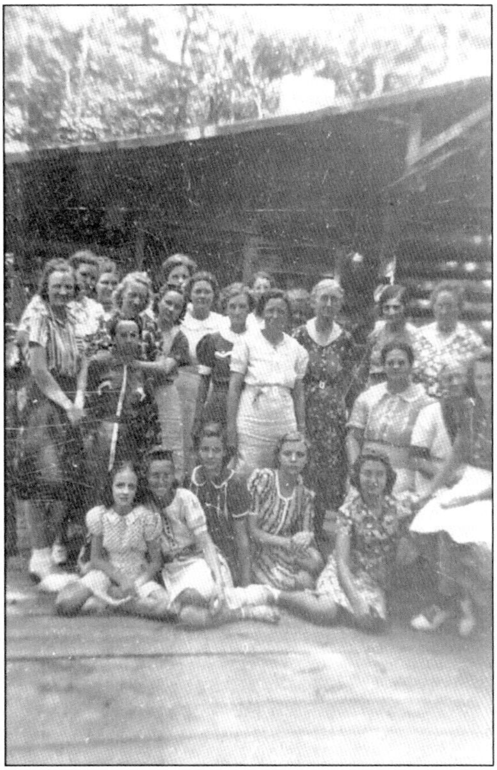

This 1951 photograph shows H. Grady Bradshaw with Boy Scouts on a round-trip train ride on the Chattahoochee Valley Railroad from West Point to Bleeker. Bradshaw was an executive with the George H. Lanier Council of the Boy Scouts of America for more than 25 years. During his tenure, the local Boy Scout council grew from 12 to 98 units and from 227 to 1,662 registered Boy Scouts. (Courtesy of CMA.)

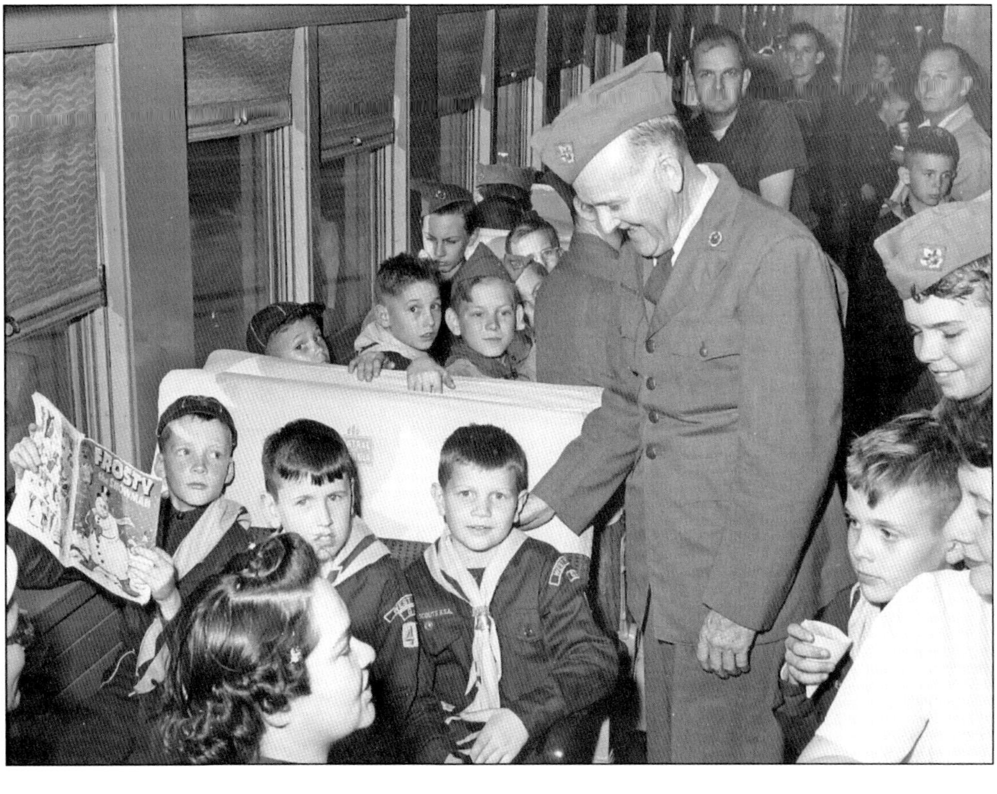

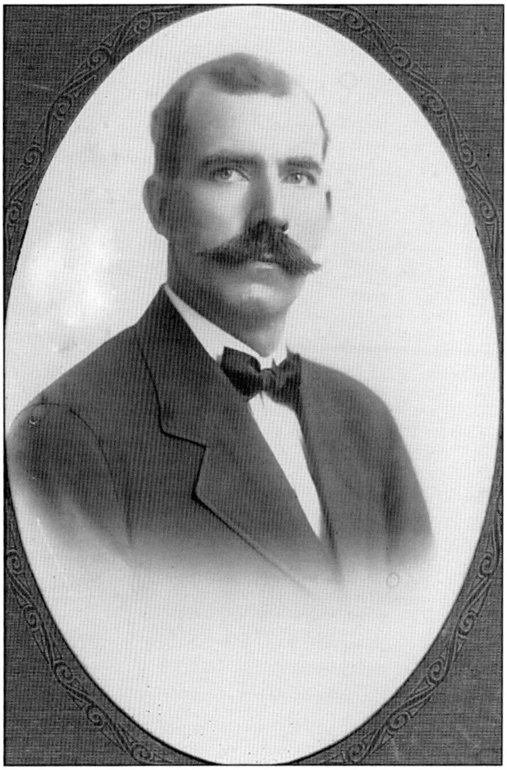

In 1880, a 10-year-old James Whitehead came with his family from the coalfields of Yorkshire, England, to live in the coalfields of Birmingham, Alabama. James worked, saved his money, and moved to the Shawmut area to open a store before World War I. Later he moved his dry goods and grocery store into the brick commercial building on Shawmut Circle. (Courtesy of Jeanne Whitehead.)

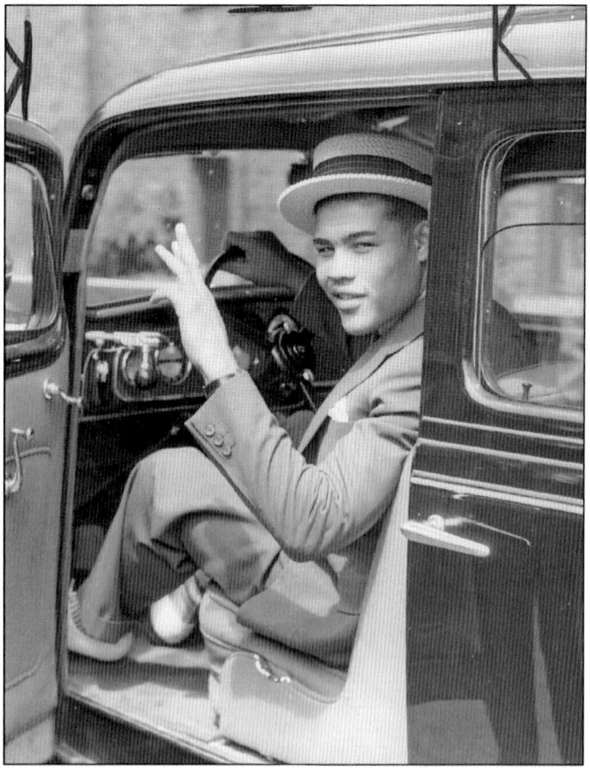

Joseph Louis Barrow was born in rural Chambers County in 1914. In 1926, Joe Louis moved to Detroit with his family, where he became interested in boxing. His professional career began in 1934. He won the heavyweight championship in 1937, defended the title 25 times, and retired in 1949. This photograph was taken in 1935 by the *Detroit News* following his defeat of Max Baer. (Courtesy of Horace McLean Holderfield.)

In 1948, Rev. B. B. McGinty presents the man of the year award to James O. Turnipseed. Both men were loved and respected by generations of Valley residents. Rev. McGinty, employed by West Point Manufacturing Company, was a Baptist minister who pastored churches across the county over many decades. The performances of Turnipseed's choral and drama students at Valley High School are remembered for their excellence. (Courtesy of CMA.)

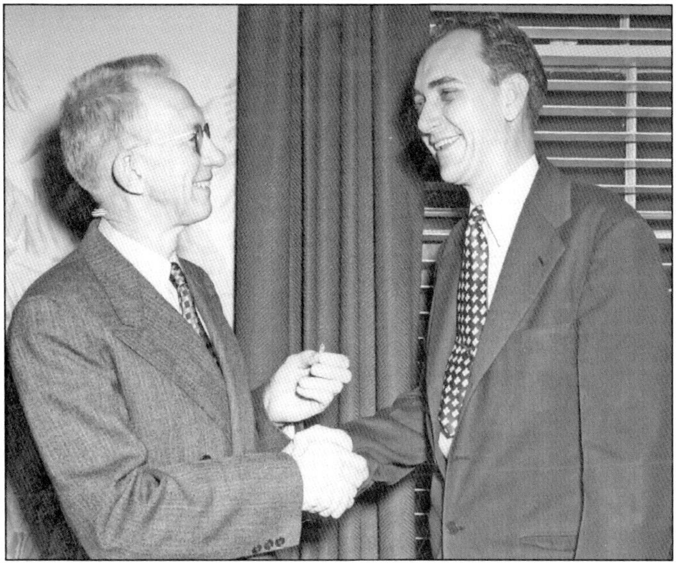

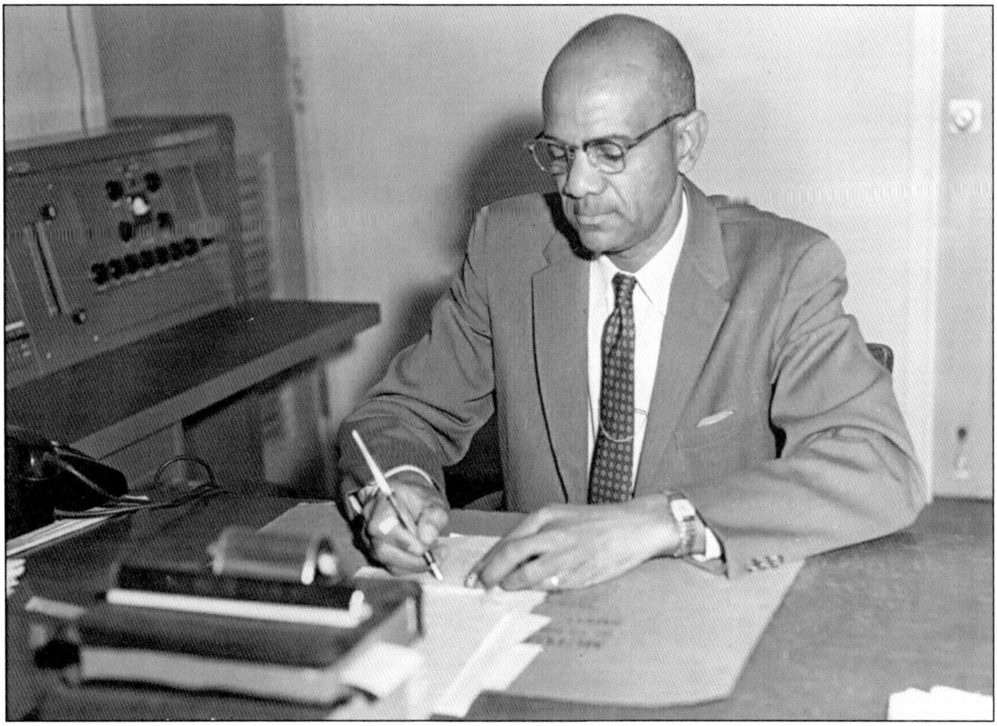

In the early 1950s, L. B. Sykes became the principal of Lanier High School in Lanett. During his administration, James Hardy, the athletic director, organized the L Club to build community support for the school and Joe Brooks started the school band. All students were brought into a single facility when the original building was expanded in 1958. Sykes retired in 1974. (Courtesy of Florine L. Griggs.)

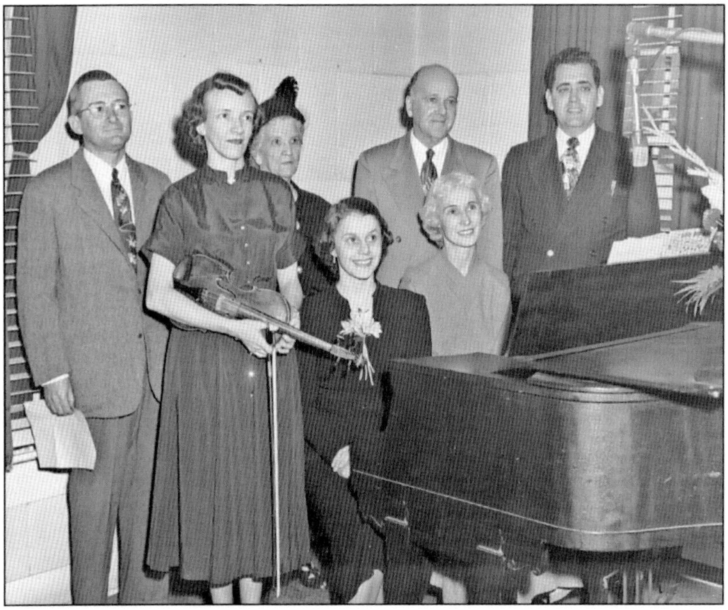

In the 1950s, the West Point Manufacturing Company sponsored the local *Friendly Half Hour* radio program in the studios of WRLD-AM. Musical programs were frequently presented. In this photograph, seated at the piano are Ann Powell (left) and Margaret Hall; standing from left to right are Scott Avary, two unidentified women, Grady Bradshaw, and Woodrow Hill. (Courtesy of CMA.)

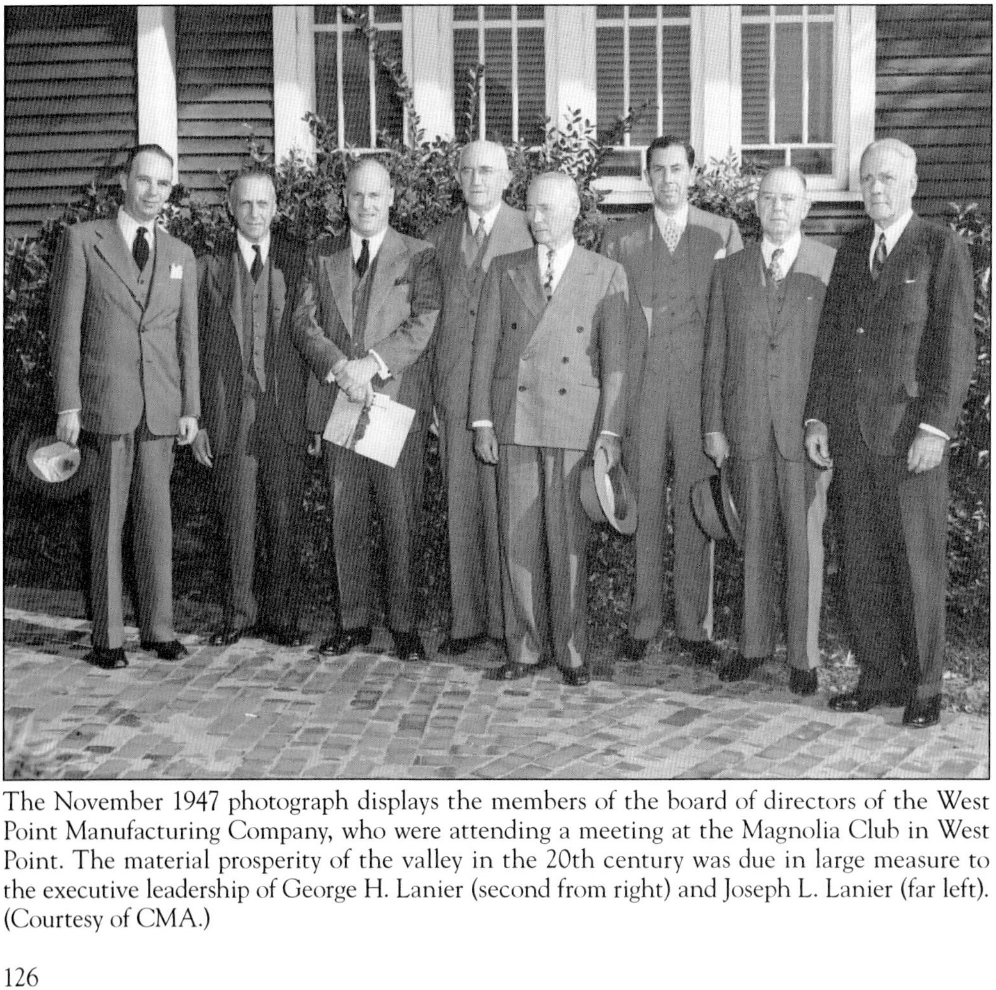

The November 1947 photograph displays the members of the board of directors of the West Point Manufacturing Company, who were attending a meeting at the Magnolia Club in West Point. The material prosperity of the valley in the 20th century was due in large measure to the executive leadership of George H. Lanier (second from right) and Joseph L. Lanier (far left). (Courtesy of CMA.)

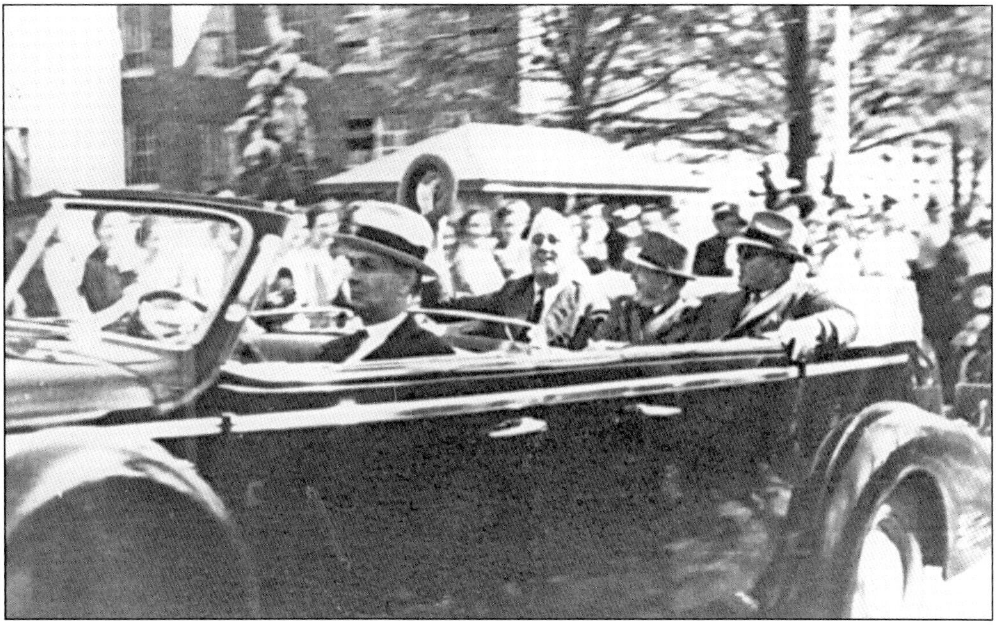

The photograph of Pres. Franklin Delano Roosevelt and J. Smith Lanier was taken in front of the Lanett Mill in 1939. Lanier invited the president, who had been his friend for many years, to visit and review the flood control work completed through a $560,000 federal project. Lanier personally lobbied federal officials for 12 years seeking flood control assistance. This project provided work for 500 unemployed men. (Courtesy of CMA.)

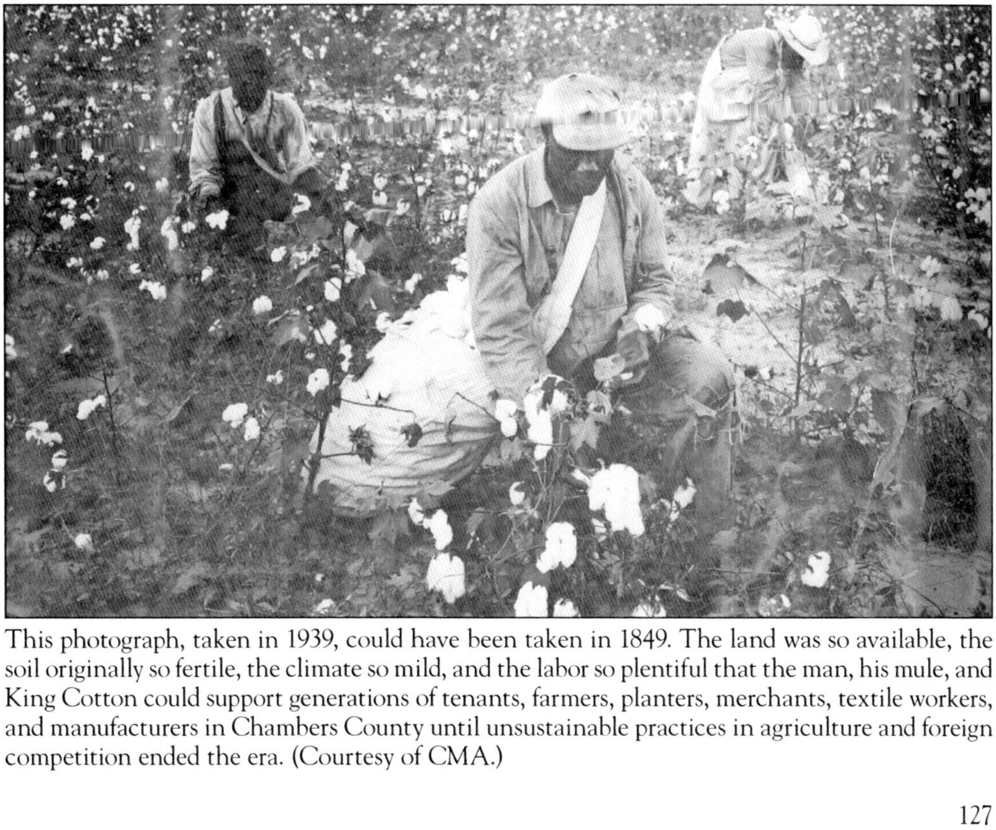

This photograph, taken in 1939, could have been taken in 1849. The land was so available, the soil originally so fertile, the climate so mild, and the labor so plentiful that the man, his mule, and King Cotton could support generations of tenants, farmers, planters, merchants, textile workers, and manufacturers in Chambers County until unsustainable practices in agriculture and foreign competition ended the era. (Courtesy of CMA.)